SHADOWS ON THE

KOYUKUK

An Alaskan Native's Life
Along the River

SIDNEY HUNTINGTON

AS TOLD TO JIM REARDEN

ALASKA NORTHWEST BOOKS™

Anchorage • Seattle • Portland

Fifth printing 1999

Library of Congress Cataloging-in-Publication Data
Huntington, Sidney, 1915–
    Shadows on the Koyukuk : an Alaskan native's life along the river / by Sidney Huntington as told to Jim Rearden.
        p. cm.
    Includes biographical references (p. 225) and index.
    ISBN 0–88240–427–x
    1. Huntington, Sidney, 1915–   . 2. Koyukon Indians—Biography.
3. Koyukon Indians—History—20th century. 4. Koyukon Indians—Social life and customs. 5. Koyukon River Valley (Alaska)—History—20th century. 6. Koyukon River Valley (Alaska)—Social life and customs.   I. Rearden, Jim.
II. Title.
E99.K79H864   1993
979.8'6—dc20
[B]   92–38360
                                                                                          CIP

Edited by Ellen Harkins Wheat
Cover and book design by Bergh Jensen, Seattle
Map by Vikki Leib

Cover Painting: *Twilight* by Sydney Laurence, c. 1919. Oil on canvas over board, 15 3/8 x 11 5/8 inches. Reproduced courtesy of the Masonic Grand Lodge of Washington. Photograph by Paul Macapia.

ALASKA NORTHWEST BOOKS™
An imprint of Graphic Arts Center Publishing Company
P.O. Box 10306, Portland, OR 97296-0306
    503-226-2402

Printed in the United States of America

CONTENTS

✦

PREFACE

❂

I met Sidney Huntington in 1972, when he was appointed to the Alaska Board of Fish and Game on which I served. At our meetings, which often lasted weeks, the twelve members decided all fish and game policies and regulations for the state of Alaska. And the depth of Sidney's knowledge of wildlife soon became evident. To make a point, he'd often tell the board wonderful stories of his life in the Koyukuk River country in northern Alaska, and I was fascinated by his experiences.

In 1975 Alaska's legislature split the Board of Fish and Game into two bodies, each with seven members. Sidney and I, now friends, found ourselves serving on the Board of Game.

At a Fairbanks meeting I saw another side to Sidney when we encountered a young Indian from Galena, Sidney's current Yukon River home. "I thought you were at school," Sidney said.

"No more money, Sidney. I'm going home to earn more so I can go back," the young man answered.

"How much you need?" Sidney asked.

"Eight hundred dollars."

Sidney opened his wallet and handed the young man eight $100 bills.

"You go back to school," he said.

The young man stared at the money in his hand as if he couldn't believe his eyes, then he said softly, "Thank you, Sidney. Maybe I pay you back one day." He walked off with a spring in his step.

I asked Sidney if he thought he'd ever get the money back, and he said, "I don't care if I don't. That boy belongs in school."

I learned later that Sidney has financed schooling for many young people from the Koyukuk.

I left the game board in 1982, but Sidney remained, apparently impervious to political winds which, with each change in governor, produced a virtually new board. He finally resigned in 1992, after twenty years of unpaid service to the state.

In 1988, recalling his wonderful stories, I proposed writing a book with him about his adventurous life. When he agreed, I flew to Galena with a tape recorder. I discovered that he had spent the weeks before my arrival writing down many details of his life. *Shadows on the Koyukuk* was assembled from those written accounts and my tape-recorded interviews with him.

About that $800: while I was at Galena, I asked Sidney if the young man he had given the money to in Fairbanks had ever repaid him. "He paid me back after he got an education," Sidney replied. "He now has a family, a home, and a job. He's doing well."

The Koyukuk valley, where Sidney Huntington was born and where his family ties extend into the dim past, covers about 33,000 square miles of wildland drained by Alaska's Koyukuk River. This gin-clear stream, Alaska's third-largest river, arises in the arctic Central Brooks Range and meanders southwest for 554 miles before it pours into the Lower Yukon. Immense forests of birch, aspen, and tall spruce thrive on its banks. In the uplands, the northern taiga gives way to treeless tundra, with tree line at 2,000 to 3,000 feet. Moose, caribou, wolf, grizzly, and black bear populate the region, and in season, the area teems with birds.

Koyukuk country is a land of extremes. At winter solstice, the sun appears at Bettles for only an hour and forty minutes. But between June 2 and July 10, the sun circles endlessly, never dropping below the horizon. Winter temperatures commonly skid to 60 degrees below 0 Fahrenheit or colder, and summer temperatures can reach the 90s. Most of the soil is rock-hard permafrost—permanently frozen ground— which traps surface water, and so lakes, ponds, and marshes abound. Precipitation is only ten to twenty inches annually, which may include up to six feet of fluffy snow.

Most Americans might think of Koyukuk country as unpopulated wilderness. Even in the last decade of the twentieth century, fewer than 600 men, women, and children live along the wild Koyukuk River. These predominantly Koyukon Athapaskan Indian residents (named for the Koyukuk and Yukon rivers where they live) reside primarily in four riverbank villages: Allakaket, Bettles, Hughes, and Huslia. Villages situated along the Yukon River and occupied by another 2,500 Koyukon Indians are Stevens Village, Rampart, Tanana, Ruby, Galena, Koyukuk, Nulato, and Kaltag.

The Athapaskans are a large and diverse family of Indians who live throughout much of central Alaska and across a vast region of western Canada. In Alaska, there are eleven cultural groups, including the Koyukons, who live along major river drainages, in the uplands, and on the Pacific coast.

———

Shortly after 1900, Klondike gold rusher James S. Huntington wandered down the Yukon River, where he met and married Anna, a Koyukon daughter of the land. Their son Sidney has now lived for three-quarters of a century in the Koyukuk country where he was born. His life's story is a fascinating slice of Alaskan history.

Sidney grew up in a subarctic wildland of birchbark canoes, dog teams, trappers, gold miners, and Koyukon Indians. He continues to live in essentially the same culture, now modernized with snow machines, bush planes, and satellite TV. He is a product of the land, who thoroughly knows his region, the animals, and the people who live there. The memories he shares in this book bring alive a way of life that is gone forever, for as a teenager and young man he lived primarily off the land; his interest in traditional Koyukon tales provides an intriguing peek into Koyukon Indian prehistory.

In addition to leading an incredibly adventurous life, Sidney Huntington is a special kind of person. His is a bootstraps-up, inspirational success story of survival. Despite this, Sidney has always found time to help others—a trait that in recent years has brought him statewide respect and an honorary doctorate from the University of Alaska. Long before he received that degree, I regarded Sidney as holding a doctorate in life, for he is self-educated, with knowledge that extends far beyond the horizons of Alaska's Koyukuk country.

In telling Sidney's story, I have made every effort to retain his straightforward, honest, laconic style, because I want the reader to hear it as he told it to me. I hope I have succeeded, for Sidney Huntington has left a clear, straight trail that is worth following.

Jim Rearden   Homer, Alaska
Sprucewood   September 1992

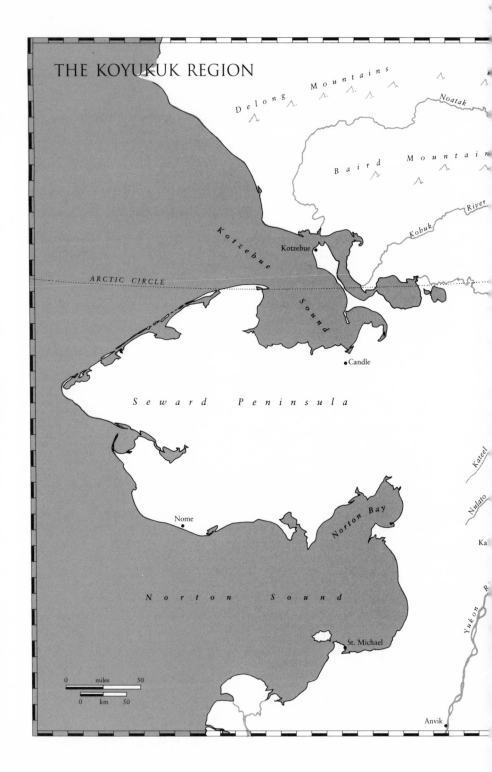

THE KOYUKUK REGION

Delong Mountains

Noatak

Baird Mountains

Kobuk River

Kotzebue

Kotzebue

ARCTIC CIRCLE

Sound

Candle

Seward Peninsula

Kateel

Nulato

Ka

Norton Bay

Nome

Norton Sound

Yukon River

St. Michael

0   miles   50

0   km   50

Anvik

OKS RANGE

Endicott Mountains

River

Heart Mountain

Koyukuk River Middle Fork

Wiseman

Bettles

Kobuk

Sun Mountain

Hog R.

Alatna

Clear Ck.

Allakaket

Pah R.

Zane Hills

Hog R.

Bear Ck.

Koyukuk River

Yukon River

ountains

Dakli R.

Batza R.

Hughes

Tozitna River

Rampart

Cutoff

Huslia

River

Fort Gibbon

Tanana

kuk River

Dulbi River

Melozitna River

Yukon River

Tanana River

Coffee Can L.

hips Island

Nenana

land

Galena

Ruby

KUSKOKWIM RANGE

Nenana R.

DENALI NATIONAL PARK

ALASKA RANGE

ALASKA RAILROAD

Broad Pass

Denali

U.S. USA

ALASKA

CANADA

Fairbanks

Anchorage

PACIFIC OCEAN

1

ANNA

✲

It was the Koyukon "month of the hawk." The long days of March had arrived, when migratory hawks return to the Koyukuk River valley. Schilikuk, a coastal Eskimo trader, had come to visit and trade with my Athapaskan mother. He was a big man, perhaps six feet tall and 190 pounds. On his face, instead of tattoos carried by some Eskimos, he had tribal cuts through his cheeks on each side. He amazed me, a four-year-old, by putting his crooked stem pipe through the slit on one cheek and blowing smoke out the other cheek. This was one of my earliest memories.

My mother's family lived at Hogatzakaket (*kaket* is "river" in the Athapaskan tongue), which on maps is simply called Hogatza. We call it Hog River. It is a tributary to the big Koyukuk River, which in turn flows into the Lower Yukon River.

My grandmother—I've always called her "Old Mama"—had fifteen children. Eight of them, five daughters and three sons, survived to adulthood. Of these, my mother, Anna, was the oldest. She was born sometime in the late 1870s.

Her father—my grandfather—was a Koyukon Indian who traded, not only with his own people of the Koyukuk Valley, but also with Schilikuk, although the Eskimos were traditional enemies of the Athapaskans. Peaceful contacts between these peoples were few, but my grandfather's unusual relationship with Schilikuk was approved by both Eskimo and Indian leaders because each side needed goods that the other had. By the time I met Schilikuk, in 1920, the enmity between our peoples was mostly forgotten.

My mother told me how each year my grandfather and Schilikuk enacted an age-old drama—that of two dissimilar peoples trading goods. Grandfather would load a dogsled with birchbark baskets, furs of wolverine, beaver, marten, fox, and lynx, and chunks of soft red rock found along the Koyukuk River. When crushed and mixed with water, the rocks made a colorful dye used to paint snowshoe frames, ceremonial wood masks, and porcupine quills for decorating garments and other objects.

Each March, Grandfather traveled from the Koyukuk River up the Dakli River into the Zane Hills, where he camped on the Dakli side of a low pass. This was as far as it was safe for him to venture. The mountainous land that lay before him, between Eskimo and Athapaskan country, was then known as "No Man's Land."

Meanwhile, Schilikuk would make his way up the Selawik River on the other side of the pass, his dogsled full of coastal products—sealskins, fawn caribou hides, mukluks (both waterproof and warm winter types), seal oil, salt, and walrus ivory. He would camp on the Selawik side, for he dared go no farther.

My grandfather would walk, alone and unarmed, to the pass, carrying a long pole. If he saw no sign of Schilikuk, he thrust his pole into the deep snow and returned to camp. Every day he snowshoed to the pass to see whether a second pole was planted in the snow beside his—the signal that Schilikuk had arrived and trading could begin.

When there were two poles in the snow, Grandfather took his loaded sled to the pass to meet Schilikuk. Each would lay everything out for the other's inspection. The Eskimo especially wanted fine wolverine furs, prized for use as a face liner in wolf-fur ruffs in the hoods of parkas. Although any long-haired fur can be used for this purpose, wolverine is the best because the hairs do not easily break or pull out when built-up frost from the wearer's breath is pulled off.

My grandfather was eager to get caribou fawn skins, which are easily made into soft winter undergarments and socks. Also in demand in the Koyukuk valley were seal oil, which is a high-energy food, walrus ivory tusks from which useful items could be carved, sealskins for winter outer garments, and tough-as-iron ropes made from walrus skin.

Each trader always went through the motions of being offended at the offers of the other. My grandfather, for example, would act insulted at an offer of three caribou fawn skins for one wolverine skin. He would pick out of the Eskimo's pile two or three more fawn skins and add them to the stack, insisting that this particular wolverine skin was worth at least five, maybe six fawn skins. Sometimes it would take hours for a single transaction. Time wasn't important. They might haggle for days.

When my mother was old enough, in the late 1880s and early 1890s, she accompanied her father on these annual trading trips to the Dakli. From Schilikuk she learned to speak some Eskimo.

———

In 1900 or 1901, my mother married Victor Bifelt, a Finn who, like about a thousand other gold rushers, had left the Klondike to prospect and trap in the Koyukuk country, where gold had been found several years earlier. "Marriage" in the Koyukuk in those days consisted of choosing a partner and living together. If the relationship was good, it lasted; if not, it dissolved. At that time, whites lived with Koyukon women and there were no bad feelings; only the missionaries resented the practice. Although rough-spoken, Bifelt treated my mother well, and the couple had two children, Fred and Edith.

They settled in Hogatza country, where they built a log cabin two miles below where Hog River runs into the Koyukuk, and Victor began trapping. He enjoyed living off the land, but he wanted the whole country to himself and didn't respect the claims of others.

Their nearest neighbors were at Hog River, where Ned Regan, another white, lived with my mother's mother, Old Mama. These two had a daughter, Eliza, whose son, George Attla, would one day become one of Alaska's most famous sled dog racers. Ned trapped from his Hog River cabin.

Victor and Ned soon began quarreling over trapline rights. Koyukon Indians often spend a winter, or even years, in close vicinity of friends or family without conflict, but these two hard-headed white men were different. Since they both sold firewood to steamboats plying the Koyukuk River and were trapping in the same region, they regarded each other as competitors and their dispute became a bitter feud.

Bifelt accused Regan of trying to take over his trapline and ordered him off, but Regan refused to leave. "I'm going to kill Regan," Victor told my mother one day, after the two men had clashed. Frightened, the next day while Victor was away, my mother hurried to Hog River to warn Old Mama. "Get out of here, Mama," she warned. "I think Victor is going to shoot Regan." Old Mama, capable of living from the land as were all Athapaskan women of her generation, fled and set up camp some distance away.

She also told Regan about Victor's threat. "I'll take care of myself," Regan said, and my mother ran home.

The murder must have taken place a short time later. Regan saw

Bifelt coming, and when Bifelt walked through the door of his cabin, Regan blasted him at point-blank range with a double-barreled shotgun.

Details have dimmed with time, but I believe that Regan buried Bifelt before he went to the Yukon River village of Nulato to turn himself in. The local marshal took Regan to Nome, the center of legal matters in those gold rush days.

The following summer, two deputies arrived to take Anna to Nome as a witness at the trial set for February of the next year. They had to leave quickly before the winter freeze closed their watery route. Anna was distraught at having to leave her children with Old Mama for the many months that she would be gone. Also, she dreaded going into forbidden Eskimo territory. All her life she had heard of the savagery of the Eskimos, who always killed Athapaskans who ventured into their country, with the truce between her father and Schilikuk being one of few exceptions.

My mother was a small woman (about ninety pounds) but she was strong and courageous. With the deputies, she traveled by river steamer down the Koyukuk and Yukon rivers to St. Michael, near the mouth of the Yukon. From there they crossed Norton Sound on the last steamboat of the year, arriving at Nome in September 1904. Theirs was a trip of about 1,000 miles, although the distance was only 320 miles as the raven flies.

Nome was then a chaotic boomtown filled with gold rushers. Tents stretched along the beach in a solid row for five miles. The air was filled with sounds of hammering and sawing, as residents prepared for the coming subarctic winter. To Anna, who had spent her life in the wilderness, twenty-five people was a crowd; Nome, with its 15,000-plus people was a nightmare. The court found a couple to feed and house Anna until the trial. Throughout the five-month wait, she was homesick and lonely.

At the trial, she was the only witness. She knew little English and the court could find no one to translate her Athapaskan. Regan, who pleaded self-defense, was found innocent and released.

After the trial, Anna insisted on returning home to her children immediately. The judge explained that the court would pay her way back by the same river route she had come, but that she would have to wait until breakup in the spring. Until then, the way was locked in ice and snow, and boats were useless.

So a determined Anna decided to walk overland. The distance was at least 400 miles, the midwinter weather was severe, she didn't know the way, and she'd be crossing Eskimo country.

There was no stopping her, so the judge gave her a document explaining that she was a responsibility of the court and was going by foot from Nome to her home on the Koyukuk River. It warned that anyone who harmed her would be punished by the United States government, and concluded, "The court will appreciate any help or guidance this woman receives."

"Show this to people. They will help," the judge promised.

Although Anna didn't know the route across the windswept, mostly treeless coastal land, she knew that Schilikuk lived on the Kobuk River, which she had learned was somewhere beyond Candle, on the north side of the Seward Peninsula. So she set out to walk to Candle.

The well-traveled, snowy trails between Nome and Candle were packed, so Anna did not need snowshoes. When she became confused, she waited until someone came along and showed them her note. Each time she received directions.

She walked from sunup until dark. Each night she wrapped herself in a blanket and burrowed into a snowbank for the insulation it provided, or shivered near a small fire. She stopped at roadhouses along the way for food and rest. Invariably, when the owners read her note, they refused the gold coins she offered in payment. Usually they tried to dissuade her from continuing her long, dangerous journey, but when they sensed her determination they gave her food, matches, and other supplies. Soon word spread along the trail about the tiny Indian woman who was returning to her family in the distant Interior.

Anna's moccasins were worn out when she reached Candle near the end of March. A miner and his wife took her into their home, and she made several new pairs of moccasins while regaining her strength. In late April, the Koyukon "month of the spring crust," she set out again, now on snowshoes, with a small pack on her back, walking north and east into country with no human trails.

In May, the Koyukon "month boats are put in the water," near the Arctic Circle light floods the land around the clock although snow still lingers. Anna traveled mostly at night when it was cool and the snow was crisp and frozen and easy to walk on, and she rested during the warm days when the snow became too mushy to support her. Rivers were still frozen, so she had no difficulty crossing them.

Using the sun as her guide, she traveled toward where people had said the Kobuk River lay. Spring storms delayed her, but she pressed on, some days traveling only a few miles. A lone prospector she encountered gave her several ptarmigan and some matches. He was the last person she saw for weeks. Days passed in a blur.

Breakup came in June, and the ice in the Kobuk River went out. This is a major turning point in the North, for without ice on the rivers, travelers must build rafts to cross deep rivers. Bogs, frozen and level in winter, become impassable, and travelers must detour around them. Anna walked upstream, following a bank of the deep and swift Kobuk as the easiest and most direct route into the mountains that separate the coast from the Interior. For food she snared rabbits, ate roots, and found berries of the previous year that became exposed when the snow melted. In this Koyukon "month when everything grows," swarms of mosquitoes hatched, adding to her hardship.

One July morning she awoke to see an Eskimo boy staring at her from a few feet away. In a moment he was gone. With a sinking heart, she remembered his look of elation. Weary and weak from hunger, she was sure that he would return with other Eskimos to kill her.

Soon a small band of Eskimos called to her from a distance. Anna thought that her end had come. She didn't try to escape, for she knew it was hopeless. When the Eskimos neared, her heart leaped, for with the boy she had seen, and several other Eskimos, was Schilikuk, the trader friend of her father.

His words warmed her heart. "I saw your father two months ago. He had word you were walking home and asked me to watch for you. My son has been waiting for you along the river every day."

Anna rested, regaining her strength in the home of the hospitable Eskimo. "You had better stay with me until March, when your father and I trade again," Schilikuk told her one day. "You can go with me to the trading place."

"No. I must get back to my children. I've been gone nearly a year now. I won't wait until March," she declared.

Schilikuk, seeing her determination, persuaded her to stay at least until snow came again and the rivers froze so she could travel more easily. Each winter he trapped at the head of the 100-mile-distant Pah River. Anna agreed to wait and go with him to the Pah. From there she faced a ten-day walk across the mountains to the Hogatza River and her father's home.

Fall came, and finally, snow fell and the rivers froze. The Eskimo family loaded sleds, harnessed dogs, and started the journey to the headwaters of the Pah. Several times they stopped for a few days to hunt caribou. They reached the trapping grounds in November.

A few days later the old Eskimo walked with Anna to the top of the low divide that separates the coast from the Koyukuk drainage of

Interior Alaska. He pointed across No Man's Land toward the distant Hogatza River, saying, "There is your home. You'll have to go alone from here. I don't dare take you any farther."

She was dressed in warm furs. Her pack held caribou meat and dried fish, warm blankets, matches, and an axe. On her small feet she wore moccasins she had made for herself and snowshoes made by Schilikuk. After thanking him, she set out alone down the slope, bravely heading for the spruce forests of Koyukuk country.

Now she was in the kind of land she knew. Timber was abundant, so firewood and shelter were easy to find. She spent the nights next to the trunks of big spruce trees, sheltered by thick green branches and warmed by fires she built of dead lower limbs. Green spruce branches, piled deep, insulated her from the snow and provided her with a comfortable bed.

After ten days of solitude, Anna came upon snowshoe tracks. She followed them for a day until, suddenly, she recognized the place: she was only five miles from her father's winter cabin. She stopped and forced herself to eat, because she wanted to walk to her father with her head up, strong and proud, not tottering as if exhausted from her long trek.

As Anna approached the cabin, chained sled dogs set up a clamor. The door was flung open, and a man stepped out, rifle in hand.

"Who comes?" he called in the Koyukon Athapaskan.

"It is me, Anna," she replied in the same tongue.

The man was Hog River Johnny, her brother. Their reunion was joyous, for the two were close. When she told of her long solo trek home, he could scarcely believe it.

"Tell me again," he asked, wanting to hear repeatedly about various adventures she had experienced.

The reunion was tinged with sadness, for her father had died the previous summer. But her children were well. News of Anna's overland journey from Nome spread swiftly by moccasin telegraph. No Koyukon hunter, much less a slip of an unarmed woman, had ever dared to traverse the forbidden Eskimo land to the west. Not only had she braved the fierce Eskimos, she had traveled on foot for hundreds of miles, much of it alone, during parts of two winters. She was regarded with awe by the close-knit Koyukon people for years.

My uncle Weaselheart, another of my mother's brothers, once told me that the family was convinced that my mother would never return. When they learned that she had started her long trek, they thought she would be seized by some Eskimo wanting a woman. Such an act would have been much easier than the raids that Eskimos once made into Koyukuk country to steal women. Many tales of such raids were told and retold among the Koyukon people, and, of course, those raids perpetuated the traditional war.

Weaselheart also told me that for the help Schilikuk gave Anna, our family rewarded him with many gifts, including a large pile of wolverine furs of the finest quality.

Ned Regan returned to the Koyukuk, wanting to take up with Old Mama where he had left off, but she would have nothing to do with him. The Indians of the Koyukuk felt that his killing of Victor Bifelt had been too cold-blooded, and it made them uneasy around him. He left the Koyukuk never to return.

During my three-quarters of a century, I have watched with pleasure as the ancient hostility between the Koyukon Athapaskans and the Eskimos has gradually disappeared. Today there is only friendly rivalry between our peoples. And the legend of the long overland journey made by my mother from Nome to the Koyukuk is still recounted by the Koyukon people.

2

KALLYHOCUSES

✶

Nine years after my mother's great trek, I was born at Hughes, Alaska, on May 10, 1915. Hughes is still a cluster of log cabins, a tiny Koyukon village on the south bank of the Koyukuk River. My English-Scot father, James S. Huntington, was born in 1867 in Buffalo, New York. He was one of the thousands of gold rushers who, in 1897, stampeded to the frontier mining camp of Dawson, Yukon Territory.

He often talked of the excitement of Dawson—the saloons, dance halls, banks, tent stores, mud streets, and the milling mob. Under the watchful eyes of the redcoats (Canadian mounted police), each of the thousands of stampeders was seeking his or her fortune.

In Alaska, my father prospected, mined, trapped, freighted with horse-drawn river scows, hauled mail and passengers by dog team, and owned his own trading posts. Around 1904 he hauled mail by sled dog over the ninety-mile route from Tanana and Fort Gibbon to Louse Point on the Yukon River. Fort Gibbon was on the outskirts of the Koyukon village of Tanana at the junction of the Yukon and Tanana rivers. With the gold rush to Alaska, the army had established military camps, pretentiously calling them "forts," along the prospectors' routes of travel. There was Fort Davis at Nome, Fort Gibbon at Tanana, Fort Egbert at Eagle, and several others. Telegraphic communication was established between the forts and with the states (Alaska was a territory).

Dad liked being a mail-team driver. All sleds were required by law to give right-of-way to mail teams, and the mail driver was given preferential treatment at roadhouses, receiving the best bunk, the best seat at the table, and the first hotcakes at breakfast.

Dad became friends with many of the Indians, and eventually he became very protective of them. It was illegal to sell liquor to Indians, and he frequently fought the Army authorities at Gibbon, and others, who conveniently forgot the ban on Indian use of alcohol.

Trapping of marten, which had become scarce, was illegal. Asking Indians not to trap was like asking fish not to swim. Indian trappers continued to accumulate contraband marten furs, and several of Dad's Indian friends asked him if he would market the furs for them. Unfortunately, a fur warden caught him with the illegal furs and he was jailed at Tanana. In those days you remained in jail until trial.

Dad's trial was to be held at Rampart, sixty-one miles northeast of Tanana on the south bank of the Yukon, a three-day walk. During the early 1900s, 1,500 people lived there, and it was the location of the main court for the region.

Monkey John, an Indian friend who lived near Tanana, visited Dad in jail. Dad had left most of his money in Monkey John's keeping, and frequently stayed with him.

"You want to get away?" asked Monkey John.

"Sure, but there's no safe place to go."

"You can go to the headwaters of the Tanana and then to the Copper River country," said Monkey John. "A long time ago people traveled that way."

"That's a long way to go alone and afoot," said Dad.

"They can't catch you once you get away. We'll help. I'll talk to Chief Thomas," promised Monkey John. Chief Thomas, of Nenana, was the powerful leader of the Athapaskan Indians of Interior Alaska, and was widely known and respected.

After meeting with Chief Thomas, Monkey John returned to the jail. "When they take you to Rampart, we'll have everything ready. At the first camp, there's a cabin. That's where you go over the hill."

"What good will it be for me to go over the hill?" Dad asked.

"We'll wait for you on top of the hill. It will be night. Be sure to wear mittens and a good parka. When you get to the cabin and it gets dark, tell them you're going to the outhouse. Those fellows won't bother to go out with you in the dark. As soon as you get out of the cabin, run. You'll find a pair of snowshoes along the trail. They'll be rigged backwards. Put them on and come up that hill. We'll be waiting for you there."

"Snowshoes, rigged backwards?" Dad asked.

"Yes. The tail will be in front. That'll fool them. They won't know which direction you've walked," Monkey John grinned.

"All right," Dad agreed.

In a few days, a U.S. marshal and a guard escorted Dad from Tanana on the trail to Rampart. At the first rest cabin, before going to bed, Dad told the marshal he had to go to the outhouse.

"Go ahead," he said.

"He can't go far in this weather," the marshal told the guard. "Don't worry about him."

Dad headed downriver on a dead run. In a mile he came to a pair of snowshoes standing upright in the snow. The shoes hadn't been there when they had passed earlier.

As promised, the harness on the snowshoes was rigged backwards. He put the crazy things on, wondering whether he could walk with them. But he found that walking was easy; his friends had made sure they were balanced. And anyone seeing his tracks would assume they were made by a man coming down the hill rather than one going up.

On the hilltop, Dad found Monkey John and two other Indians. I don't know the exact route Dad followed in his escape, but various Indians passed him from area to area, providing him with dogs, a sled, food, and other necessities. Chief Thomas's name was the key to help all the way. Monkey John had returned Dad's savings, so he was well financed. He arrived at Valdez, caught a ship to Seattle, and traveled east to New York to see his mother.

After running away from home as a kid, he now arrived home triumphantly, with enough money to buy and furnish a new home for his mother.

After a year and a half in New York, Alaska beckoned, and Dad returned to Nulato. Soon he encountered the former marshal he had escaped from, who had lost his job for allowing a prisoner to escape.

"How in hell did you get away? We patrolled for miles up and down the river looking for you. We found snowshoe tracks coming down the hills into the river, but none leaving. How did you do it?"

Dad grinned. "I flew!"

For some reason, the charges against Dad had been dropped.

My mother had married James Huntington in September 1908. One of my first memories is of the spring flood at Hughes in 1918 when I turned three. As the water rose, Dad drilled holes with an auger through planks of our cabin porch deck. He then tied the porch to a tree to keep it from floating away. I learned then that I couldn't walk on water when I stepped off the porch and promptly sank. My father fished me out and turned me upside down to drain the water out.

Another memory is of a pair of tiny snowshoes that my uncle Little William made for me—a Christmas gift following my second birthday. I was tremendously proud of them. One day at Hughes I was walking on the snow with these shoes when two gigantic horses came down the trail toward me. I started to scamper out of their way, and fell headfirst into the deep snow. I hollered my little head off.

The horses, in tandem, were pulling two bobsleds. Phil Main, who, like most miners of the day had a huge beard, rode the lead horse. He used the horses to freight supplies from Hughes to his gold-mining camp at nearby Indian Creek. He leaped off, scooped me up snowshoes and all, and put me on one of those big horses. Thrilled but terrified, I quit crying. I vividly remember the warmth, smell, and movement of that horse under my short legs.

That spring and summer, I developed a habit of wandering off into the bushes. I watched jacksnipe flitting high in the sky as they made their unique, wing-whistling, twittering mating sounds and then landed out of my sight. I'd trot into the bushes trying to find these little long-beaked brown birds. Since a three-year-old doesn't have much business going out in the bush where he could easily get lost, fall into the river, or meet a hungry bear, my parents scolded, gently at first.

Finally, in exasperation, my father warned, "Better not go back there! There are kallyhocuses out there!"

"What's a kallyhocus?" I asked.

"A kallyhocus has a great big, long beak, and one big eye in the middle of his head, and if you get close to one it'll raise hell with you."

His warning stopped my wandering for a time, and I feared kallyhocuses for many years.

The following spring, Dad planted a garden at Hughes. He cut seed potatoes so that each chunk had an eye which would sprout into a plant. I talked him out of two pieces so I could plant my own garden. Eagerly, I watched the first green sprouts come out of the soil, then the leaves. Fascinated, I regarded each plant as my own and from that experience came a lifelong love of gardening.

That same year a new gold strike attracted a rush of prospectors to Hog River. The Hog flows into the spruce-lined Koyukuk River forty miles south of the Arctic Circle. The mines near Hughes were playing out, so my father decided to move his trading post to Hog River.

The "hog" name comes from an interesting coincidence of geography and history. Pronunciation of the Athapaskan name *Hogatzakaket* was difficult for early miners, and they shortened it to Hogatza, now the official name. About 1907 a prospector struck gold on Clear Creek, a tributary to the Hogatza, and this started a stampede of miners there. One man took horses and pigs to Clear Creek. He planned to fatten the pigs and butcher them for food. When the first snow arrived, his horses starved, but the hogs survived for some time on the salmon that he caught.

Eventually *Hogatzakaket* became "Hog" River. Some people call it "Hog" because of the hogs that were once there, others call it "Hog" as a short version of *Hogatzakaket* or Hogatza. Today Clear Creek is important mainly as a salmon spawning stream.

For the early summer move to Hogatza, Dad dismantled our log store and home and made them into a raft. On it he loaded everything we owned—sled dogs, trading goods, household items. To me, the raft was as big as an island. We drifted down the winding Koyukuk River with two Koyukon Indians, Little Sammy and George Attla, Senior, who manned twelve-foot sweeps, or long oars, to keep the raft in midstream. Little Sammy was married to one of my aunts, Sophy Sam.

We drifted several days through rolling hills and spruce forests. A mile below the mouth of Hog River, Dad picked high ground as the site for our new home, and we lived in a tent while he worked at reassembling our trading post and cabin from the raft logs.

Even before the trading post was rebuilt, trappers, miners, and rivermen arrived, eager to buy or barter for supplies—coffee, flour, salt, shovels, webbing for dog harness, ammunition for hunting, clothing. At the time, steamboats plied the Koyukuk River, and from time to time Dad replenished his supplies from them. Woodcutters who lived on the river constantly sawed firewood from the riverbank forest for the greedy boilers of the steamers.

During the summer I began to worry about the potato garden we had planted at Hughes. I pestered my father until he agreed to take me with him on his potato digging trip to Hughes in early September after the first frost. My dad, my uncle Weaselheart, and I made the upriver trip in Dad's small riverboat powered by a three-horsepower Evinrude single-cylinder outboard motor, one of the first produced. It weighed more than 100 pounds. To start it, Dad grasped a spool-like wooden handle bolted to the flywheel and spun for all he was worth. He had to be cautious, for once the engine started, that spinning handle was hazardous to hands and arms.

Because the Evinrude didn't run very well on that trip, I had my first lesson in cussing when Dad used a few words I had never heard before. At Hughes I dug a satisfying two-gallon bucket full of potatoes out of the hill I had planted, and Dad's potato hills produced several bushels. We loaded the harvest into the riverboat, covered them with a tarpaulin, and kept a lighted kerosene lantern under the tarp to keep them from freezing as we returned downriver.

That winter, when I was four, my mother told me I could accompany her trapping if I learned how to set a trap. I spent hours practicing with a No. o Newhouse single-spring trap, and then my mother took me with her on her short traplines. She taught me how to keep my hands, face, ears, and feet warm on the trail, and how to avoid getting overheated and then chilled. Too, she taught me patience. She often left me with the sled and dogs while she set traps. Once she hurried off chasing a porcupine, calling "I'll be back soon." She was gone for hours, but I stayed with the sled, waiting patiently.

I caught one marten and some squirrels in my traps. My mother taught me how to skin the little furbearers, and, though I cut some of the skins, my skills improved with time.

In February, Dad decided to travel by dog team the twenty miles to the mine at Bear Creek to take orders for supplies, and he took me with him. On the trail he became ill, and we had to stop. He was afflicted with a chronic internal inflammation that persisted most of his adult life. When it flared up, he suffered terribly. We camped in the open, although the temperature was well below zero. Before lying down that night, Dad cut a large pile of firewood, enough to last the night. He must have remained awake most of the night while I slept. Before daylight, which arrives around ten o'clock in February, he knew that he had to have help. "I can't cut any more firewood, Sidney," he said. "I'm too sick."

I was too small to cut wood for the fire he needed to keep warm.

"Can you go get help?" he asked.

"Sure, Dad," I replied, full of confidence. I had become accustomed to being alone in the woods and had no fears.

Wrapped in a wolfskin robe, Dad lay within arm's reach of the fast-diminishing pile of firewood. At daylight I set out in the direction of the mining camp, an experienced "man" of four. As I left, I saw tears running down Dad's pale pain-wracked face. He worried about me, and he felt guilty having to send me for help, but there was no other way.

I walked for hours through tall, snow-burdened spruces. My little snowshoes creaked, barely breaking the silence that always seems deeper during deep-snow time. Occasional red squirrels scampered near, launching sudden avalanches of snow from overloaded spruce branches. Sometimes the little creatures scolded as I passed. Chickadees flitted about, chirping cheerfully.

As the sun dropped below nearby ridges, I was still walking. I had eaten only a few bites of dried salmon for breakfast, and I was hungry. I wanted to stop and rest, but I was afraid my dad might die. Near dark I came to a fresh dogsled trail in the deep snow. Gratefully, I followed it for perhaps half an hour before coming to a Y. Confused about which way to turn, I started to yell. Soon I heard the warning bark of dogs that heard my cries.

I headed toward the sounds of the dogs. My tired legs could barely lift my snowshoes as I forced myself forward. The dogs continued to make a ruckus. Then all was silent. Darkness descended. I yelled again and again.

At last I heard a man call, "Where are you?"

I yelled again and moved toward the voice. I came to a deep prospect hole that yawned in the earth, abandoned by miners. Its sides were frighteningly steep. Cautiously, I walked around it, continuing in the direction of the man's voice.

Then a man called out from sixty feet behind me. It was Dominic Vernetti, a miner we knew. I ran to him as fast as I could move my little snowshoes. He swooped me up and held me tightly, and I pressed my face into the warm fur of his parka hood.

"Where's your dad?" he asked.

"He's sick on the trail. I've come for help."

"You're alone?" he asked, astonished.

"I been alone all day."

My words brought tears to his eyes. He carried me to his sled and then drove me to the mining camp. On the way he told me his dogs had alerted him by barking, and then he had heard my distressed voice, so he'd harnessed the dogs to search for me.

I told my story again to the other miners, and several left immediately to rescue my dad. Joe Notti fed me and covered me up on a bunk, and I passed out.

The miners nursed Dad for many days before he could take to the trail again. When he could travel, he was busy selling trading goods to miners, arranging for shipments, watching the flow of people to and from the mine to determine the best areas of commerce. The Hog River gold strike had fizzled, and he planned to move the trading post again. My mother hated to leave.

At April's end, while Dad stayed with my younger brother, Jimmy, and baby sister, Marion, my mother took me on a spring muskrat trapping trip. We left Hog River with a five-dog team early in the morning and traveled on the frozen Koyukuk River for seven miles to a point across the river from Sam Dubin's store, operated for him by Jack Sackett. There, we left the river and followed a portage for several miles.

Muskrats were scarce, so we spent two days cutting into the top of a beaver house—the old Koyukon method of harvesting beaver in winter—and caught several beaver. I also caught a few muskrats. After we'd been out ten days, we decided we'd better head home. Most of the snow had melted, leaving much bare ground, and there was up to a foot of water covering the ice on lakes. The heavy sled pulled hard on the bare ground, so we meandered, hitting all the ice and snow patches we could find. I had to walk most of the time to lighten the sled. About a mile from the Koyukuk River as we traveled through a portage, we met Jack Sackett, who'd grown worried because we'd been gone so long.

Sackett was a U.S. marshal at Nome during the gold rush there. He also lived at Candle, and on the Kobuk River during that time. He had been there when my mother had made her journey from Nome to the Koyukuk. About 1918 Jack arrived in Koyukuk country, and stayed for the rest of his life. He loved to yarn about his early years; one of his favorite stories was about my mother's long trek.

We accompanied Jack to Dubin's store, where he fed us. Ice on the Koyukuk River was still solid, although the water was rising. We were only seven miles from home. Even pulling our light load, our heavy-coated sled dogs were exhausted by the time we had covered five miles—it was too warm for them. We cached the sled and all our gear on the riverbank. A couple of feet of water flowed atop the river ice near the shoreline. Breakup was near.

Mom stuffed our essentials and the muskrat and beaver skins we had collected into two dog packs and a pack for herself. After cutting some short logs and tying them together into a raft, she poled us and the five dogs out to the solid midstream ice. Then she fastened packs on the two oldest dogs and put leashes on them, "So they won't get into trouble," she explained.

Off we headed, walking on the solid ice, dodging water puddles. Our speed was limited by how fast my short legs could move. I was tired, and the day had been long.

Dad spotted us coming as we rounded the point a mile below the cabin. To bring us off the midriver ice, he launched a small log raft he had made. Marion and Jimmy rode with him. Seeing them come down the river gave me new life. As they neared, I took off running, still clutching a pack dog's leash.

"Don't let the dog go," Mom yelled in warning, still holding the leash of the other pack dog.

She was too late, for I turned loose of the leash. The other loose dogs caught him, and the four animals tangled in a big fight. By the time Mom had waded in and broken up the fight, the pack was torn, precious muskrat and beaver skins were scattered, and a couple of the dogs looked satisfied as they licked their chops. Eating had been skimpy for the dogs for several days. There had been food in that pack.

While we were away Dad had worked on his small riverboat, caulking and painting it, and tuning up the three-horsepower Evinrude motor. Because my mother missed her three oldest daughters so much, he had promised to go downriver to the mission schools at Anvik and Holy Cross on the Lower Yukon to bring them home.

There were no schools or missions on the Koyukuk River and if parents wanted their children to be educated, they had to send them great distances to the nearest teachers. Edith, my half sister, was at the Catholic mission at Holy Cross, 540 river miles from our Hog River cabin, because her father, Victor Bifelt, had been a Catholic. She had been away for three years. My half brother, Fred, in his teens, now lived with Old Mama at Hughes. Dad was Episcopalian, and Elsie and Ada, my older sisters, were at the Episcopal mission at Anvik, also on the Yukon River, thirty-five miles from Holy Cross. They had been away a full year. It was difficult and expensive to travel that great distance for visits, or for the girls to come home.

"I'll never see those girls again," Mom had mourned during the previous winter. So intensely had she longed to see her daughters that in March she had considered making a dog team trip to the Lower Yukon. But Old Mama and Dad talked her out of the long, hazardous trip. At the time the Koyukuk and Lower Yukon Indians weren't on the best of terms.

"I'll take the boat down and get the girls right after breakup," Dad promised.

Spring came early in that year of 1920. Geese flew over by the thousands in flock after flock of unbroken formations that extended clear to the horizon. Millions of ducks blackened the sky. On my fifth birthday, May 10, I received my first gun, a single-shot Savage bolt-action .22 rifle. I spent hours learning to shoot it, supervised by my mother or dad.

Dad waited three days after the last ice of breakup had drifted down the Koyukuk River past our cabin. Then early one morning, he loaded his boat with gasoline, camping equipment, and food. "I'll be back in a couple of weeks," he promised, pushing off. Starting the motor, he waved and soon disappeared around a bend, leaving Mom, Jimmy, Marion, and me alone at our Hog River cabin.

While he was away, my world turned upside down.

THREE BABES ALONE

✹

Dad was scarcely on his way downriver when my mother put the three of us into our little boat and rowed us about a mile upstream. The water was high, and we could float through a portage to several lakes, following the route of the winter trail. We hunted with a .2 2 rifle, and bagged two muskrats. We set a fishnet and caught several pike and one big whitefish.

It was June, and we enjoyed the long hours of warm sunshine and had a wonderful time. I was five, Jimmy was three, and Marion was a year and a half. That night, we camped by one of the lakes.

After returning the next morning, Mother pulled our boat up on the bank broadside to the beach, for the river was still rising. We played in the sunshine most of the rest of the day, while Mom worked at tanning the beaver skins that she and I had taken in April.

Supper that night was rice and fish we had caught the day before. Whitefish have a hard gristly part in their gut that looks as if it has tentacles all over it, which is a favored delicacy of Koyukon Indians. Mom fried and ate this part.

That whitefish gut killed my mother.

June in the Koyukuk country is light twenty-four hours of the day, and that evening we kids played outside until late. Mom called us into the cabin and told us she wasn't feeling well. "Go upstairs and go to bed," she said. She was sitting on the floor at the back of the house, with her feet and legs across the threshold outside the door. She had a smudge burning, because there were many mosquitoes.

When I awoke the sun was low, so it was probably some time after midnight. Jimmy and Marion were also awake. "Sidney, mosquitoes are biting us," complained Jimmy. The whine of the pests was incessant, as they swarmed in our bedroom. Mom hadn't come upstairs to change Marion's soaked diaper.

"I better go get Mom," I said. Jimmy started to go downstairs with me, but Marion screamed, not wanting to be left alone. Finally, between us we managed to change her diaper, then we all went downstairs. The stairs were too steep for Marion, so Jimmy and I held her as she sat and slid down one step at a time.

We found our mother lying at the bottom of the stairs, half out the door, as she had been when we had gone to bed. Her eyes were closed. Most of her tongue protruded from her mouth, and it was bitten almost in two.

"Wake up, Mom," I pleaded, frightened, as I shook her shoulder. Her skin felt cold. I couldn't wake her.

Marion was hungry and yowling. I began to realize that Mom was dead and that I, as the oldest, was now responsible for my little brother and sister.

I managed to put kindling and wood in the woodstove and light a fire to heat milk which I poured into Marion's bottle as I had seen Mother do many times. Marion lay on a couch and stopped crying as she sucked on her bottle. For our breakfast I cooked some oatmeal, but I made it too thick and it burned. It tasted awful, but we were hungry, so we all ate some.

Outside, our five sled dogs, tied to their houses, howled a lonely, sad sound. Jimmy and I fed them some dried salmon and gave them water, but they continued to howl in a low, forlorn way, almost constantly that day. I believe they sensed my mother's death.

We spent hours trying to awaken Mom. She wouldn't wake up, so we decided to try to move her inside. The house was full of mosquitoes and they almost ate us alive. Poor Marion's little face and arms were swollen from the bites.

"Pull harder, Jimmy," I shouted in frustration, as the two of us tried to move Mom.

"I'm pulling as hard as I can," he said, half crying.

After tugging for a long time, we managed to work Mom's body back into the house and we shut the door. Mosquitoes continued to pester us, and finally I angrily said, "I'll fix those mosquitoes."

I lit a smudge—some bracket fungus that grows on birch trees, an old Athapaskan remedy. The fungus, gathered and dried early in the year, smolders when lit, and the pungent smoke repels mosquitoes. Sometimes, to repel mosquitoes when traveling, the fungus is burned in a can fitted with a long handle.

I had the right idea, but I lit two pieces instead of one, and my smudge made too much smoke, driving us out of the house, and we couldn't return until the house was cleared of smoke. It was a warm, sunny day, and our mother's body had started to decompose. Ugly blue blowflies laid eggs on her. Frightened and horrified, we covered her body with blankets, trying to contain the terrible smell and keep the flies away.

Earlier that spring Mom had stretched a tarpaulin over a pole on the riverbank where she cleaned fish, tanned hides, and did other chores. Under the tarp, she had put a mattress on the ground, creating a workplace where she could comfortably sit to do her tasks. We had taken the tarp with us in the boat when we had gone on our overnight picnic. I decided to make a shelter with it, so Jimmy and I pulled it from the boat and with difficulty wrestled it back over the pole and tied the four corners. How we tied the knots, I don't know, but they held.

We went back into the house to get our mosquito net and bedding, holding our breath as we hurried past our mom's body. We hung the netting underneath the tarpaulin, which took Jimmy and me a long time, and after spreading the bedding inside the mosquito net, the three of us crawled in and went to sleep. The makeshift shelter became our home. We went into the house only when we really needed something.

Earlier in the day we had fed Marion thick, sweet Eagle Brand condensed milk. We probably didn't add enough water to it, for not long after we crawled into our blankets, she vomited. We all started to feel sick because we hadn't eaten well and were hungry. But as soon as I opened the door to the house, that awful smell met us. I closed the door right away, and we decided to not go into the house at all.

We had been told never to go into the store unless adults were present, but we had no food. Poor Marion was constantly crying, and Jimmy's bravado was wearing thin. I was growing weak from not eating. We decided we had to disobey and go into the store, at least to find some milk for Marion.

Inside the store we found a can that looked like the condensed milk cans Mom had used in the house, but then I had the problem of opening it. I used my boy's axe, and of course spilled some of the rich creamy liquid. I poured the milk into Marion's dirty bottle, a ketchup bottle topped with a stretchy rubber nipple, and to dilute the milk we added river water.

After drinking a couple of these haphazard mixtures, Marion seemed to feel better. Jimmy and I tried some of the Eagle Brand without diluting it. It tasted good, so we drank two cans, and ate some hardtack, cookies, and candy. Then, sleepy again, we all crawled inside our shelter and dozed off.

All three of us woke up sick and vomiting. To add to our problems, Marion had developed diarrhea. We had run out of clean diapers, so we rinsed the dirty ones in the river and hung them on a pole to dry. Despite our efforts, Marion's skin became raw from diaper rash.

Feeling sick, we slept fitfully. Into what was probably the second day after our mother's death, I was awakened suddenly by Marion's screams; a black bear had its teeth clamped on her diaper and was dragging her from under our shelter. I grabbed Marion's arms and pulled her back, and the bear ran over to her two big cubs nearby still carrying the dirty diaper.

The bears must have located us by smell. We were surrounded by our vomit, and that must have attracted them. Surprisingly, they didn't return. I have always felt that the mother bear sensed that something was amiss. She could easily have killed and eaten all three of us. Since then I have experienced more instances in which bears and other wild animals have respected the helpless young of other species.

Days passed. Every so often one of the dogs, and sometimes all of them, cried with that long low wail—a sound almost like sad singing. We continued to feed Marion Eagle Brand milk and tried to keep clean diapers on her. Although we slept under the mosquito netting, all three of us were badly bitten, for early June is the peak of the mosquito season in the Koyukuk. We had accepted the death of our mother. Our ideas of Dad were vague; we knew he was gone, but we really didn't know when or whether he would return.

"We have to get someone to help us, Jimmy," I finally said. "Dominic will help. He helped me last winter." I thought I could find Dominic Vernetti by traveling overland to the Bear Creek mine. Dominic had helped me just four months earlier, and I was sure he would help again.

We took a can of milk and a few crackers and set out through the portage, which I knew quite well. Two big lakes lay behind the house, with grass along the edges and deep water out in the lake. A mile from home, at the edge of the lake, we came upon the mother black bear and her two big cubs. Standing tall on hind legs, they studied us for a long time. As we moved, they shuffled about uneasily. Then they walked out into the water, away from us.

Each time we started to pass, the mother bear would lumber closer to us. Frightened, we would back up, and she would wade back into the lake. Again we'd head along the trail, and again she'd come toward us.

In the deep grass, the mosquitoes were fierce. The bears kept blocking us, and we were tired. I finally said, "We've got to go home." Jimmy and Marion were subdued and left the decision to me. When we turned around and left, the bears didn't follow us.

Our only other avenue to get help was by boat. But the river had dropped, leaving the boat high and dry on the steep bank. I had seen my dad and my mom push a pole under the ends of the boat to pry it into the water. I found a pole, put it under the back end, and moved the boat a little. I kept working on that end, but the other end didn't move. Then it dawned on me; the far end was tied, and the rope was stretched tight. I tried to untie the knot, but my five-year-old fingers weren't up to the job, so I decided to cut the stake the boat was tied to. Swinging my axe, I missed the stake and cut the rope instead. I then went back to the pry pole at the stern, and bit by bit I moved the boat. Finally the front of the boat hit the water with a bang. It was floating, and I tied it to a stake. Then, to our disappointment, the boat sank. The lumber had dried in the sun, and the seams had opened. We stood looking at it for some time, and then gave up on it for a time.

The dogs were still moaning and howling softly. Jimmy and I had watered and fed them daily, finding some comfort in their greetings, their wagging tails, their affection. After our failure with the boat, the dogs cheered us some. We crawled onto our soiled mattress and fell asleep.

The sun was high when we awoke. Night and day had become blurred as the sun circled, never setting. All three of us seemed to be OK. We hadn't gone in the house to see our mom's body for days, so I looked through the window. The sight I saw—a mass of squirming white maggots spread on the floor—has remained an ugly scar in my mind. Jimmy and Marion also wanted to look, but I wouldn't let them, and for that I have always been thankful. It has been bad enough for me to carry that image all of my life.

I decided then we had to make a move for sure. We went back to the boat, which was half full of water. Its seams had swollen shut enough for it to float. As the sun moved across the sky, I bailed with a can. I asked Jimmy to help me although he was really too young to do much, and by late in the day we'd gotten the boat almost emptied. We were weary, so we slept again. We must have slept quite a spell, for the sun was low when we awoke. We ate a few crackers, which had become our staple food, and drank some milk. Then we finished bailing the boat.

In the boat we loaded a blanket for Marion, more crackers, and one can of milk, and with my little brother and sister huddled on board, I shoved off into the swift, broad Koyukuk and leaped aboard myself. We had hardly left the beach when the five dogs again lifted their muzzles to the sky with their end-of-the-world howls.

Suddenly the wind came up, blowing straight across the river from the east. We drifted with the current, of course, for paddling the boat was beyond my strength, and the wind blew us around. We were caught in eddies, and then pushed onto the beach, fortunately on the same side as our cabin. We had spent hours in the boat, but traveled only about a mile downstream. Then a hard spring rainstorm struck and we quickly became soaked. Jimmy and Marion started to cry, upset because I had not brought the tarp. I decided to return home through the woods to get it.

"You and Marion stay in the boat," I instructed Jimmy. He was reluctant, but I insisted, and he finally agreed.

I started off by myself, walked about a hundred feet, and stopped, thinking. Would my mom have wanted me to leave my brother and sister alone in the boat? I knew the answer. I returned and got them. "We'll all go home," I said.

I knew the trail, for I had been on it in winter, snaring rabbits with my mother and hauling wood with my father. Just the same, on that day the woods frightened me; I had been warned to stay out of the trees because I might get lost.

We were sopping wet. Marion could scarcely walk on the rough trail; she kept falling. Finally, I carried her, but she was heavy for me. I piggybacked her for twenty or thirty steps at a time. We struggled for hours traveling that long mile back to the cabin. As we neared, the dogs again started howling.

Later, Jack Sackett said we were lucky the boat hadn't drifted downriver. He had no boat to retrieve us with, even if he had happened to see us go by. We might have drifted for days. Or if the boat had hung up on a beach, we might have gone ashore searching for help where no help existed.

When we finally arrived back at the cabin, the sun was high so it was probably near noon. Worn out, we sprawled in the sun and went to sleep. When I awoke, the sun was low. I looked at Jimmy and Marion, who were still sleeping. They had sores all over them from insect bites, and they were filthy. I began to cry, knowing they wouldn't see me. After a time, I brushed away my tears and woke them.

My eyes must have been red, or maybe he hadn't really been asleep, because Jimmy asked, "Have you been crying, Sidney?"

"No. A bug got in my eye," I answered lamely.

I didn't fool them. Both of them put their arms around me. My tears started again. For the first time I felt beaten. With tears still trickling down my cheeks, I decided we must go back to the boat and again try to go downriver. Mosquitoes swarmed around us while we fed the dogs and ate more crackers. Marion grew sleepy, as the sun dipped low in the sky, and we lay down to rest before walking to the mile-distant boat.

The sun was high in the sky when a strange sound awoke me. The dogs barked an alarm. Between the strange noise and the barking of the dogs I became frightened. It was the first time I had felt that kind of fear. I awoke Jimmy and Marion and urgently said, "We've got to run. Something is coming." I was afraid to run into the woods. Instead, we fled to the cellar of the store.

The unfamiliar noise I had heard was the steamer *Teddy H.*, owned by trader Sam Dubin. It almost passed our cabin, but then it slowed and reversed. People on board talked so loudly we could hear them even under the store.

"I don't see Anna," someone said.

"There's no boat," said another.

A third shouted, "I saw the kids run into the store."

People came ashore looking for us. I closed the hatch in the floor and locked it with a pole.

Then I heard, "The woman is dead and the kids are gone."

Another voice: "I *know* I saw the kids run into the store. The door was wide open."

"There's no one here. You must have been seeing things," was the answer. We heard footsteps on the floor overhead. We sat, petrified, looking upward.

"I'll bet a bear ate the kids. Didn't you see that bear on the hillside back there?"

About then Marion bumped against the wall and whimpered and someone yelled, "I hear something under the floor." They called and called, but we refused to answer. One of the men started pulling the floor apart with a pry bar. Soon a man's head came through a hole in the floor and he quickly spotted us.

They pulled me out first. I fought, and bit old Sam Dubin on the arm. Jimmy was frantic, and struggled like a wildcat. When the people tried to grab Jimmy or Marion, they clung to me for dear life. We had become terribly afraid and insecure during that terrible time. We felt that Mom and Dad had left us, and when the trust we had in them was violated, we lost our faith in all adults. This attitude would affect me for years.

Those wonderful people carried us to the boat, and with cake and other goodies bribed us into calming down. They gave us badly needed baths. Matthew Titus, one of the boat's crew, God bless him, rolled our mother's remains up in the tarp that had sheltered us kids, and helped make a coffin. The passengers and crew of the *Teddy H.* buried Mom near the house.

Then the steamer, with Jimmy, Marion, and me aboard, started downriver. Six miles downstream, we met Dad, Elsie, and Ada coming upriver in Dad's boat. I don't remember much about our meeting except that I sobbed and hugged Dad a lot. I remember saying, "Dad, we did something bad. We stole candy and cookies from the store." He hugged me and tears ran down his cheeks.

Sam Dubin had David Tobuk, the steamer captain, tow Dad's boat back to our cabin. Dubin and those aboard the steamer stayed for a few hours until Dad regained some composure. Then, with a mournful toot of her steam whistle, the *Teddy H.* chugged on her way, leaving us on the riverbank.

Word of our mother's death was carried downriver by those aboard the little steamer. In a few days, Old Mama, my uncles and aunts, and other relatives and friends arrived by canoe and poling boat. For days there was much singing of sad old Athapaskan songs and a great deal of crying—almost a continual wail in the old Indian way, as they held a memorial potlatch. There was much food, many words, and many tears.

Dad moved Mom's grave away from the house to a beautiful wild spot among the spruces and birches. He read from the Bible as everyone gathered around the crude coffin.

Seventy and more years have passed, but I still return frequently to that lonely grave. I am grateful for memories of my wonderful mother, and haunted by those two weeks when Jimmy, Marion, and I were three babes alone in the wilderness.

4

ANVIK

The loss of my mother was a blow from which our family never recovered. Never again did all of us live as a family under the same roof. When the relatives left after the funeral potlatch, Dad spent hours wandering up and down the riverbank, and he often sat quietly by Mom's grave.

He suddenly had the sole responsibility of caring for five children. Elsie, who was eight, and Ada, six and a half, now home from mission school, took care of Marion and Jimmy as best they could, but it was obvious that other arrangements had to be made.

Homemaking and child care on the Alaska frontier of 1920 was a rugged job for a woman. Life was difficult, although we thought nothing of it at the time. We carried our water from the river in buckets. For light we used candles or lamps fueled with kerosene or gasoline, which we hauled upriver with the rest of our supplies. We dug a pit for our outhouse toilet. We washed clothes by soaking them in a tub of boiling water on a wood-burning stove and scrubbing them by hand. We used those same big washtubs as bathtubs for a once-a-week bath. Women tanned furs and made them into winter parkas, mittens, and hats for every family member. Fish, a food staple for us and our sled dogs, had to be caught, then dried or smoked.

Usually, men caught the fish and women cut and dried them, although sometimes women did the catching. Even sawing and splitting the many cords of firewood for cooking and keeping a cabin warm through the long cold winter was a mammoth job in which women often participated.

Running the trading post was a full-time job for Dad. He barged in the goods and had to man the store. To drum up trade, he sometimes traveled to remote mining camps. It was clear that there was no way he could take care of us as a homemaker as well as earn a living.

Help for our family came from the Episcopal mission at Anvik. In late June, the *Pelican No. 1*, a 28-foot mission boat that annually traveled the Koyukuk and Yukon rivers, stopped at our place at Hog River. Above its inboard engine and large cabin flew an American flag. Missionaries on the boat served the scattered villages and isolated residents by holding religious services, performing marriages, baptizing children, and helping in whatever ways they could. Aboard the vessel that June was Episcopal bishop Peter Trimble Rowe, who had first come to Alaska in 1896 (and would serve as a missionary in Alaska for 46 years).

"Can you take my children?" Dad asked the bishop, after prayers for my mother and a long conversation.

"Of course," was the instant reply. "We'll be happy to have them."

Thus all five of us were loaded aboard the *Pelican No. 1* with our clothing and a few prized personal possessions for the trip to Anvik Mission, 500 miles down the Koyukuk and Yukon rivers.

The Episcopal mission at Anvik, an Indian village on the right bank of the Anvik River about a mile from its junction with the Yukon, was established in 1887. The Reverend John Chapman and his wife arrived that summer, and they would remain with the mission for sixty-one years. Their son, Henry, would become a priest and succeed his father at the mission.

I was impressed by the size of the mission when I got there, and, indeed, for the time and place it was a large establishment. The log church was about twenty-eight feet by forty feet. It had been built by two Russians, the story went, and that church building still stands today. The logs were hewed flat on four sides, and the corners were dovetailed. All other buildings were made of lumber sawed and planed by a small mill at the mission; sawdust was used as insulation. The girl's dormitory—a thirty-six-foot by eighty-foot single-story building—was the largest structure. It housed about twenty-five girls and the two women who watched over them, and included a kitchen and a dining room.

The smaller boys' dormitory housed up to twelve boys and included the quarters of The Reverend and Mrs. Bentley, who supervised the boys.

The Chapmans' two-story home also housed the occasional visitor to the mission.

The mission woodshed was big enough to hold at least thirty cords of stacked wood for the stoves. Water was hauled from the Yukon

River with a dog team during winter, and in summer was pulled up the bank with a small steam winch once a week. We also packed some water with buckets and a shoulder yoke.

The nearby Athapaskan Indian village of Anvik was made up of about 100 people who lived in small, mostly dirt-floored log cabins.

Early in this century missionaries fulfilled a need in Alaska when that need was great. It was a time of transition for the Natives from their original life of living off the land and migrating in search of food, to a partial dollar trade economy as permanent settlements became established around trading posts. At the time there were few federal or territorial public services on Alaska's frontier. For these reasons, missions and hospitals built by Bishop Rowe and others were the salvation of many, including orphaned Indian, Eskimo, and half-Native children. (As early as 1903 there were at least eighty-two missions and mission churches of eleven or more denominations in Alaska.) In some cases, white fathers left Alaska and didn't return, leaving Indian or Eskimo women alone with their offspring. Many of these children surely would have perished without the missions. The missions had an open door for all, including children sent by their parents to be educated, because there were few public schools for them.

Support for Anvik Mission came largely from donations from the eastern United States and overseas. The teachers, nurses, matrons in charge of the girls, and male attendants in charge of the boys received little or no salary for their dedication to the welfare of these young Alaskans.

Language was a major barrier in the early years. The Athapaskan language is complex and dialects vary widely from area to area. Yet some missionaries overcame that. Dr. Chapman, for example, learned to speak the Anvik dialect. I was amazed as a boy to hear him preach the gospel first in English, then in Koyukon Athapaskan. In 1922 at Nulato, I heard Father Rossi, a Catholic Jesuit, preach in three languages: English, Latin, and Athapaskan.

I was lonely at the mission at first, for I had been close to my mother. In addition to my loneliness, my distrust of almost everyone, especially adults, required years for me to overcome. Reading and studying finally helped me to understand the source of my distrust and to overcome the feeling.

The Reverend John Bentley—we called him "Mr. Bentley"—was one person I began to trust. He was a kind man and I became very attached to him. Before arriving at Anvik, he had been Captain

Bentley, a chaplain with the U.S. Army in France during World War I. He had left the service and, with his wife, had volunteered for missionary work. He seemed to understand me and my problems. On Sunday mornings he occasionally took me with him by dog team or in the mission boat to the Innoko River village of Shageluk where he held services. Occasionally he allowed me to accompany him on gas boat rides on the Yukon River.

Bishop Rowe, who traveled thousands of miles by dog team and boat, preaching, counseling, marrying, and burying, was respected by the gold rushers, for, two years before the great Klondike gold stampede, he mushed over treacherous Chilkoot Pass, one of the early routes from coastal Southeast Alaska to the headwaters of the Yukon River and Interior Alaska. On his first visit to Fairbanks in 1903–4, he saw that a hospital was needed because stampeders had no families and often no one to care for them when they became ill. Thousands died from diseases that came from dirty and crowded living. Rowe left money, telling the miners to build a hospital with it. The following spring he sent nurses, medicine, and furniture to the new hospital.

Bishop Rowe had a wonderful sense of humor and a large repertoire of stories. He often told how the famed "Blue Parka Bandit" had held him up, with a group of miners, instructing the party to line up and to lay their pokes of gold dust, watches, and money on the trail. Obediently Rowe placed his money on the heap. Then with a smile and gentle voice, he chided the highwayman for robbing a minister of the gospel.

"Are you really a minister?" the bandit asked.

"Yes. I am Bishop Rowe, of the Episcopal Church," he replied.

"Oh. Well, I'm pleased to meet you. Of course, I won't rob you; take your money off the heap, Bishop, and take that poke with the shoestring on it too. Why, damn it, Bishop, I'm a member of your church!"

Bishop Rowe traveled extensively. He spent little time at Anvik, and had been on one of his long trips into the bush when the *Pelican No. 1* happened to pass Hog River at the time of our need.

Shortly after I arrived at the mission, newly orphaned Athapaskan brothers Ezra and Homer Collins arrived. Like me, they were bruised emotionally. They were also dirt poor and badly clothed. I cried when I first saw their thin, sad faces. I knew from experience what it was to be left alone. Even after they had been fed, bathed, and dressed in new clothing, they looked sad. I did my best to be close to them, to give comfort. I bribed them with food or whatever I had, trying to gain their confidence. Ezra came around in a few days, but Homer took a while.

The boys' father had died, leaving the mother alone with the two boys. Following the custom of the Indians of the era, a memorial potlatch was held. Tradition demanded that all of the man's possessions—including everything owned by his woman—be given to relatives and friends. The woman had no say; everything she owned was given away, including her house, dog team, canoe, pots and pans, even the axe she used for cutting firewood.

A widow thus stripped of her property was dependent upon the generosity of friends and relatives to get started in life again. Ezra and Homer's mother had an additional problem: a local medicine man desired her, but she didn't want anything to do with him. Traditionally, such men wielded great power among the Natives and no one was willing to interfere. There were good medicine men and bad medicine men; this was a bad one.

The desperate widow solved her problem in the only way she knew how. Carrying a length of telegraph wire, she climbed a cottonwood tree, tied the wire around her neck, fastened the other end to a branch, and jumped. Her violent solution left the boys alone in the world, and Dr. Chapman welcomed the despondent brothers to the mission.

Jimmy and I became friends with Ezra and Homer, even though we didn't know each other's language; Jimmy and I spoke English, although we knew a few words of Athapaskan; they spoke only Athapaskan. Nevertheless we found ways to communicate.

Homer became my special ward. Where I went, Homer followed. He refused to eat at the table unless he could sit beside me. He was always my bed partner, for, in the crowded boys' dormitory, we knew no such luxury as having a bed to ourselves.

Homer fell sick in the spring of 1921. As he grew weaker and weaker, he wanted me by his side all the time, and I tried any way I could to help him feel better. One morning I awoke to find Homer unconscious in our bed. I ran for the nurse and she took him into her little hospital room. He died that day and was buried in the ravine below the mission. The loss of my friend was very painful.

During my leisure time I often watched an old Native known as Blind Andrew split wood. He lived by himself in a house built for him by the mission. Although he was blind, he held the block to be split with his right hand and swung a double-bitted axe with his left. Sometimes the blade struck close to his fingers, but I never saw him draw blood. Blind Andrew liked me, so I used to help him with his small chores. He earned $1.50 a day for splitting wood for the girls' dormitory.

Another village elder I knew was Old Harry, an Indian nicknamed "Sakeroni." Seeing that I was willing to help those in need, Dr. Chapman sent me to check on Sakeroni from time to time. He couldn't speak English, but we were able to understand each other. Sometimes if the old man was short of firewood, I would bring him wood split by Blind Andrew. I hauled the wood in a barrel-stave sled that Old Harry had made. Numerous whiskey and wine barrels were available, from which good four-foot-long oak runners could be obtained for such sleds, which were fairly common in villages along the Lower Yukon.

Harry Lawrence, an Irishman who owned a trading post at Anvik, often bestowed nicknames on the Indians. The Indians had their own Athapaskan names, of course, but when they were baptized, missionaries gave them Anglicized names. Lawrence claimed the Indians couldn't remember their church names, so he took it on himself to remedy that. He gave them names they could remember, and often his names stuck. Sakeroni was one. Others I remember are Jack Screw, Kentucky, and Sixmile John.

Lawrence was a colorful old-timer who had a contract to haul mail by dog team from Kaltag to Holy Cross, two Yukon River villages. The last run of that route, driven by Lawrence's son Herbert, was in 1920. I saw Herbert when he pulled into Anvik—the first time I had seen a team of twenty dogs. They were hooked up to two large mail sleds in one string.

One day before Christmas, Sakeroni wanted me to go with him across the Anvik River to pick up a big salmon he had buried there the previous summer. This traditional Athapaskan delicacy is still occasionally prepared. A fresh, whole ungutted salmon is wrapped with moss. Next comes two layers of birch bark to keep flies out. Carefully buried, the salmon decomposes throughout the summer and becomes cheeselike.

After I received permission from Dr. Chapman, we took off with the little barrel-stave sleigh and a small axe. The river was about a half mile wide; about halfway across, the old man said he was tired. He told me the salmon was behind a tree on the far bank, marked by a stick. I left Sakeroni on the river ice, moving back and forth to keep warm. His movements made me nervous, so I kept looking back, afraid he might leave.

I found the marker stick in the snow, and dug down, pulling out his package, which was about thirty inches long and ten inches in diameter. The package was frozen and very heavy for me, so rolling it onto the sled took some effort. I had to struggle through deep snow as I dragged it back to the river. Once on the river trail, pulling the sled was easier.

Before I reached the old man, he had started home. I followed as fast as I could, pulling the heavy sled. When I caught up with Sakeroni, Dr. Chapman was scolding him for keeping me out too long. Chapman had been keeping an eye on me from the mission. He sent me to get ready for supper while he helped the old man home.

The next day when I saw Dr. Chapman, I asked permission to go see Sakeroni. "Fine, but no more trips across the river," he warned.

When I knocked on the old man's cabin, he greeted me in Athapaskan. As I entered, a strong smell hit me. I could have cut the air with a knife. With a broad smile, he offered me some of his prized salmon, which was resting under the stove. He had already eaten a good-sized chunk of the fish.

I didn't have the nerve to eat any, because it smelled awful. He explained that the pink parts were really good, but, he warned, "Don't eat any of the gray."

To satisfy him, I used a stick to pick up a piece about the size of a blueberry and popped it into my mouth. It had no taste: perhaps the smell deadened my taste buds.

When I returned to the boys' dormitory everyone kept moving away from me because I smelled so bad from that fish. Shortly, Mrs. Bentley opened the door from her quarters and let out a "Wa-hoo, what's that awful smell?" In she charged, and I had to explain.

She tried everything she could think of to kill the smell coming from my mouth, without success. The only person who could stand being near me was Ezra Collins. "We used to eat that kind of fish all the time," he said. For this, poor old Sakeroni again caught hell from Dr. Chapman, and his cabin was off-limits to me for a time.

I remained at the mission until 1925, with a break of one year when I lived with my dad at Alatna. During the four years at Anvik I learned how to live with others. I learned discipline, for the rules were fairly rigid. I learned to respect my elders.

I learned to swim during my first summer at Anvik, when I was still five years old. I also learned not to leave my fingers in a doorjamb while it is being slammed: that intelligence cost me part of my index finger shortly after my arrival. I learned not to laugh at people because they were poor or in bad health. Perhaps the most important lesson I learned was the obligation all of us have to try to help those in need.

Until the late 1920s, the missions were the only source of medical treatment along the Lower Yukon. Every mission had a trained nurse, and I watched nurses and others at the mission give loving care to the sick. Often, with Bible in hand, they remained with the dying for hours and even days until the end.

For a time I was in a small singing group that went to the homes of sick villagers to sing while Dr. Chapman prayed. I saw many young people dying with no medicine to relieve the pain, aware that death was coming. Their homes were poor, seldom even having beds; generally they slept on the dirt floor on skin mattresses. Little could be done to help. I cried many times for kids my age or younger as I watched the nurse or Dr. Chapman try to give comfort.

The missions also distributed food to the needy and created small paying jobs such as cutting and splitting wood, a never-ending task on the Alaska frontier in those years, for wood was the primary heating fuel. Dr. Chapman recommended Indians for jobs on government steamboats. He protected the Natives from those who tried to take unfair advantage of their too-trusting nature. The missions provided both social services and welfare assistance.

During the last year or two at Anvik, I became intensely interested in the fish traps that the Native people made for catching salmon. Although I didn't realize it, this was to become an important part of my education as I watched these experts make these ingenious traps and fish with them. Using these wooden traps, it was possible then to catch from the Yukon River in one day the number of salmon a Koyukuk River fisherman might catch in an entire season.

To build one of these beautiful traps, a virtually perfect spruce log was required, and such logs are difficult to find. The grain had to be just right, because the log would be split into hundreds of strips. Each strip was about three-eighths of an inch square and up to twenty feet long. Hoops for the trap were made from spruce roots, and the strips were sewed to the hoops with threadlike spruce roots and willow bark.

A roughly twenty-foot-long fence diverted salmon into the trap. Each fence was built to fit the site, so that it sloped to fit the bottom of the river. The fence and trap both were moved in and out as the river level changed. When a lot of drift floated down the river, the trap and fence were taken from the water to keep them from being damaged. When the trap was in place and catching fish, a long slim log was tied to the beach and angled out to the end of the fence: this held the fence in place, and it diverted small amounts of downstream drift.

The trap was an elegantly designed, simple funnel. At the large end it was five or six feet deep and about four feet wide. Fished with the large end upstream, the opening was attached to the outer end of the fence. Migrating fish, following along the bank, encountered the fence and followed it out. The side of the funnel nearest the beach had a gap into which the fish could swim. The funnel had projecting pieces inside to discourage fish from swimming out once they were in it. The old-timers who made these traps were emphatic that they had to be made exactly right, with three sticks poking downstream so the fish wouldn't turn around and swim out.

The trap tapered down from the big funneled end to a straight or nontapered section that was twenty or twenty-four feet long, where the fish were held. The fish were removed at the very tail end, through a hatch covered with a lid hinged with spruce roots.

I watched many times as an Indian in a big birchbark canoe paddled to the end of a trap and opened the gate, using one hand. In the other hand the fisherman held a knife for killing the fish. The knife, usually made out of a bent flat file lashed to a wood or bone handle, resembled the crooked knife, a carving knife found through-out the North in the old days. The salmon-killing knife's blade was somewhat V-shaped, sharpened on one side. It was used to pierce the fish's head behind the eyes, instantly immobilizing it. The salmon was then tossed into the canoe. I've seen as many as 100 salmon lifted from a trap, killed, and loaded into a birchbark canoe in about twenty minutes.

As soon as one of these big canoes was loaded, the fisherman paddled to where the women waited to cut up the fish, for in the old days this was women's work. The women used a *tlaabaas*, a half-round knife made from the blade of a carpenter's saw. Eskimos call such a knife an *ulu*. The *tlaabaas* of an experienced woman cutting up salmon for drying (the main method of preservation) moves so fast it is a blur. First, the salmon is gutted and the head removed. Next, the fish is filleted, with the two slabs of meat on each side of the backbone left connected at the tail. Usually, but not always, the backbone is removed. Vertical cuts or scores are made on each of the fillets to aid in drying. Then the fish is hung over a pole to dry, with a fillet or slab on each side of the pole.

These traps must have taken centuries for the Athapaskans to develop and refine. Even as I was learning about these picturesque devices, the more efficient fish wheel (brought to Alaska from the

Columbia and Sacramento rivers by whites) and gillnets were replacing them, and while I was still a boy, the art of making the traps essentially disappeared.

In the spring of 1921 my dad arrived at Anvik for a visit. We five children were on the bank to meet the big sternwheeler he arrived on, when suddenly I panicked. I simply could not run and hug him like my sisters and brother did. I took off on a dead run for the woods where I hid all night and the next day. My sister Ada found me and talked me into returning to the mission. The Reverend Bentley seemed to understand, and talked it over with my dad. It was clear that I still had trouble trusting anyone, and in my mind my dad had abandoned the three of us when my mother had died.

Dad, Mr. Bentley, and Dr. Chapman decided that I should spend time with my dad to develop a stronger relationship. After he visited Anvik for a couple of weeks, I agreed to go with him to spend a year at his new trading post at Alatna. Jimmy and my sisters remained at Anvik.

Dad and I boarded the steamer *Jacobs* at Anvik and rode to Nulato. We then went to Koyukuk Station in a small gasoline-powered boat to prepare for the trip to Alatna, far up the Koyukuk River.

5

ALATNA

❇

Alatna is a small Koyukuk River village 350 miles northeast of Anvik as the raven flies and twice that distance by river. It was early August when Dad and I left Koyukuk Station and headed up the Koyukuk River on his annual trip with twenty-five tons of food, hardware, clothing, coal oil (kerosene), and white gasoline (new at the time for lamps and lanterns) for the trading post that Dad and John Evans jointly owned at Alatna. Charlie Evans, John's son, was pilot and captain of the forty-foot, eight-foot-wide *Koyukuk* that pushed the barge. An impressive (for 1921) twenty-eight-horsepower Redwing gasoline engine swinging a twenty-two-inch-diameter propeller with a twenty-four-inch pitch powered the boat, which belonged to John Evans. There was a cabin with bunks and a place to cook. Charlie was to gain fame in 1925 as one of the dog team drivers who took a turn at rushing diphtheria serum from Fairbanks to Nome in what was to become known as the historic Serum Run.

During that trip I saw millions of birds along the clear Koyukuk River—ducks, geese, songbirds, and shorebirds in numbers that were to dwindle slowly as I grew older.

We made frequent stops, for in those days riverboats always stopped at every camp and for every person seen along the bank. At each stop Dad sold supplies, breaking into the load of freight to accommodate. Most people wanted such things as ammunition, beans, clothing, tools, kerosene, traps, or axes.

Since it was still light all night, we traveled twenty-four hours a day. Another reason we kept traveling were the clouds of biting gnats common in some places along the Koyukuk River in August. The movement of the boat created enough breeze to help us escape these pests. The river's current was relatively slow, and we progressed at about four and a half miles an hour until we reached the Dulbi River, about a third of the way to Alatna.

Beyond the Dulbi, the water became swifter and progress was slower. When we reached Hog River, about 300 miles from the Yukon, Dad and I went to Mom's grave and said a prayer. A few miners were still at Hog River, and for them Dad unloaded potatoes, prospectors' supplies, and hardware that they had ordered. Then we continued up the Koyukuk. Upstream from Hog River the water became ever swifter, and in some stretches Charlie had to use full throttle to make progress.

I hadn't seen my grandmother, Old Mama, in more than a year. She had moved to Hughes, the pleasant Koyukon Athapaskan village along the river where I was born. My half-brother Fred, then a young man, still lived with her. When we arrived, she couldn't wait to wrap her arms around me, and she cried until she was exhausted.

"Sidney, you will be like your grandfather. He was a fine, strong man," she said, in the presence of all the friends and family who had gathered. Her words embarrassed me, but made me proud too. My mother had told me so many stories of my grandfather, the trader, that he seemed bigger than life to me.

Many fast riffles made travel difficult along the seventy-five-mile river route from Hughes to Alatna. Before leaving Hughes, Charlie Evans took aboard eight more Koyukon men to help pull the boat over the riffles in swift places. In the Koyukuk region, when someone needed help, others always pitched in. Sometimes when they helped with the trade goods barge, they were paid in cash or in trade goods. Sometimes all they received was thanks, a meal, and a promise for help when they needed it.

When we reached a riffle, every man got set on a heavy rope strung far upstream from the bow. When they were ready, Charlie goosed the Redwing engine with all the throttle she would take, pointing the nose of the boat into the deepest water. The men pulled, and slowly we struggled up and across the riffle and again reached deep water.

Three or four miles below Alatna, we were stopped by a swift, shallow riffle, which even the Redwing and the men's strength couldn't conquer. Downriver a few miles at a place we call the Canyon, we had picked up Johnny Oldman, a respected Athapaskan elder. Johnny told one of the younger Indians to pole a birchbark canoe to Alatna to get more help.

Native-built birchbark canoes were fairly common along the Koyukuk in 1921, although building them would later become a lost art. An expert could construct a birchbark canoe surprisingly quickly. A dry sandy spot on the river was selected. Posts were driven into the sand in the outline of the canoe frame. Birch ribs were shaped with knife and axe and tied to the posts with long, tough spruce roots. Then longitudinal strips of clear split spruce were tied to the ribs, making a framework for the birchbark covering.

Sheets of birchbark were stripped from the living tree as the sap was rising in the spring, and they were cut to fit the frame, allowing overlaps for sewing. The bark sheets were then sewn together with spruce root threads, using a bone awl to open the way for insertion. Bow and stern posts were carved. A piece of bark was cut and fitted over the bow, and the upper parts of the skin were trimmed and supported by an inner and outer gunwale. The whole length of the gunwale was then corded with long, flexible spruce rootlets.

Melted spruce pitch was then poured and rubbed into cracks and small holes. Many Koyukon builders painted the framework red, using the red powdery rocks found in the Koyukuk to make the "paint." I've seen birchbark canoes designed for freighting that were nearly twenty feet long. But most were ten or twelve feet long, and suitable for two paddlers.

The art of poling a canoe would also become lost, although it was a wonderful way to travel. Two poles were used, each about four feet long and less than three-fourths inch in diameter. While sitting on his legs, the canoeist traveled in the shallows close to the beach, one pole in each hand, by swinging the poles forward, and then pushing down and back. One could easily travel five miles an hour in this quiet manner. Hunters liked to use poles, for they made less noise than paddles. Whenever the canoe reached deep water, a paddle was used.

In a few hours the young Indian returned with about twenty men who had come downstream in canoes. Wading up to their waists, with two ropes they manhandled the Evans boat over the stubborn riffle that had stopped us. They continued to help at other riffles as we progressed to Alatna. Because of the swift water and frequent riffles, it required six days for us to travel the seventy miles from Hughes to Alatna.

Episcopal missionary Hudson Stuck had chosen Alatna as a mission site in 1906. On the upper Koyukuk, the settlement was on the route being used increasingly by Eskimos from the Kobuk River country who came to trade with the Indians. In addition to being a crossroad, Alatna was only twelve miles upstream from Moses Village (also briefly called Arctic City, after a trader arrived there), a Koyukon village. Stuck believed that a new start with a church and a planned village could produce a place that would attract residents. He foresaw two villages, one Indian, one Eskimo, on opposite sides of the river, "where these hereditary enemies might live side by side in peace and harmony under the firm yet gentle influence of the church."

Villages on both sides of the river were called Alatna in 1921. The Alatna post office would be established in 1925 on the south side of the river, and renamed Allakaket in 1938. Today north-bank residents (where Dad and I lived) live in Alatna, south-bank residents in Allakaket.

The time I spent at Alatna with my dad helped me to understand and know him better. He didn't party or drink. He was a good cook and we ate good food. We lived in a well-built log cabin that remained cozy and warm throughout the long Alaska winter. Dad read a lot, and, I was surprised to notice, he worried a lot about his health and his trading business. Trading was not very lucrative.

I made many new friends at Alatna, and I attended school about 150 yards from our cabin at St. John's-in-the-Wilderness Episcopal Mission, where at the age of six I received my first real schooling in reading, writing, and arithmetic. Before my year at Alatna, at Anvik mission I had been taught to say the Lord's Prayer, and other religious teachings, and I had learned to put blocks together and to play color-coded games, but I hadn't been taught how to read.

At Alatna my teacher was Ireland-born Miss Amelia Hill, who served at the mission for thirty years as nurse, teacher, preacher, and administrator. The readers we used showed children living with their parents in elegant houses in the States, with a funny looking dog named Spot. Those houses didn't resemble the log cabins I was accustomed to, and Spot sure didn't look like a sled dog—I wondered what he was good for. People rode in cars. I had never seen a car and I wondered how fast they moved.

Dad and John Evans were often gone from the Alatna trading post on short trips to take orders or to deliver supplies. When Dad was gone, Edwin Simon, a Koyukon Indian who was to have a great influence on my life, was Dad's right-hand man. Edwin's father, a famous medicine man, had unusual white skin and blue eyes and was bald from birth. Edwin's sisters had blond hair when they were young. Edwin, a fine-looking man, had the usual Athapaskan light-brown skin and black hair. Having a sense of place and time and understanding how the Athapaskan world was changing, he proved to be a bridge for me and others between the old prewhite days and the modern ones. His wry humor and solid philosophy endeared him to many. He often acted as an interpreter when Athapaskans who spoke little or no English needed to communicate with whites.

Edwin was a traditional Athapaskan in many ways. Among his stories was how his mother chose his first wife in an arranged marriage. "Her family is good from way back," she told Edwin. "They treat their husbands good all the time." He accepted the woman as his wife in the old way, and it proved to be a good marriage.

Although Edwin knew where gold was likely to be found in the Koyukuk, he refused to prospect for it or stake any claims. This resolve came from an experience of his older brother, Andrew, and another Athapaskan named Alfred Isaac who had staked claims on Indian Creek near Hughes. Later Alfred sold his claim for $1,000, and Andrew got nothing.

"No, I won't look for gold. White man just take it away from you. There's no sense in looking for gold for someone else," Edwin said, meaning that whites usually swindled Indians out of good claims.

After I had been at Alatna for several months, Dad's illness erupted, and friends took him to Tanana for medical help. My heart sank as I saw him leave, lying in a dogsled, wrapped in furs. He looked helpless and weak, and I feared I would never see him again. A doctor at Tanana referred him to the Mayo Clinic in far-off Minnesota for treatment, and he was away for two and a half months. While he was gone, I lived with Kitty Oldman, John Oldman's wife, at Alatna. (We had picked up John Oldman in the Canyon on our trip upriver to Alatna.) The Oldmans' son, Abraham, was my age, and we became good friends.

Dad had recovered somewhat by the time he returned to Alatna, but because he was sick so often, he felt it best for me to return to the mission at Anvik where I could be with Jimmy and our sisters. Dad took me back to Anvik that June.

The next several years at Anvik passed quickly. Dad visited us for a couple of weeks each year, and we slowly grew up, living the routine of the mission on a day-to-day basis, and not really thinking of the future.

In 1925, losing money as a trader, and because of his failing health, Dad sold his share of the trading post to John Evans. At the same time he decided that Jimmy and I needed better schooling, so he arranged for us to go to the Eklutna Vocational School, operated by the Bureau of Indian Affairs (BIA), near Anchorage.

6

EKLUTNA

✸

The steamboat's shrill whistle nearly deafened Jimmy and me as we stood on deck watching the Anvik mission recede. That long blast signaled a new life for us, that autumn of 1925, for we were aboard the government-owned *Jacobs* bound for the Eklutna Vocational School near Anchorage. I was ten and Jimmy was eight. Dad had been at Anvik a couple of months earlier for his annual visit with the four of us, and had returned to Alatna, a 920-mile round trip. We didn't get to see him again before we left.

Carrying mail, passengers, and freight, every two weeks the *Jacobs* steamed from Nenana 200 river miles down the Tanana River to the broad, silty Yukon River, and then 400 miles down the Yukon to Marshall, returning by the same route. Another government steamer, the *General Jeff Davis*, ran the same route on alternate weeks. In this way, residents along the Yukon River received mail and freight once a week in summer. Villages along the Koyukuk River received mail only once a month during summer, and then only when water was sufficiently high for steamer travel. The Koyukuk steamers were much smaller than those on the Yukon.

The Yukon was the major summer route to the Interior for freight, mail, and passengers. By 1900 there were forty-one sizable steamers, fifteen smaller vessels, and thirty-nine barges competing for the Yukon River traffic. There was a shipyard at St. Michaels, near the mouth of the Yukon, where these shallow-draft river boats were built. As the gold rush subsided, privately owned Yukon River traffic decreased. To continue the service needed by residents, about 1915 the federal government started running Yukon River steamers.

Winter was another matter. The Yukon was still a main highway, but travel was by dog team, and all mail, light freight, and passengers were hauled on the ice of the frozen river. Bulky and heavy freight awaited summer and the steamers. During the 1920s, airplanes gradually assumed the mail routes previously traveled by dog teams, and by the 1930s, there were only a few dog team mail routes in all of Alaska.

For Jimmy and me, a couple of bush kids, the trip to Eklutna was high adventure. On the *Jacobs* we were assigned a stateroom with two bunks. Sleeping between cold, clammy white sheets was a strange experience, because we had never slept under anything but pure wool, and our skin was accustomed to sometimes scratchy but warm blankets. Food on the *Jacobs* was wonderful; never had we eaten so well. The several dozen passengers were friendly, and many knew our dad. We were seldom out of sight of anyone who wasn't keeping a helpful eye on us.

The boat stopped at Koyukuk Station. There I met Ella Vernetti, a beautiful half-Koyukon half-white woman who had just married Dominic Vernetti. I didn't see Dominic then, but he was establishing a trading post there, where he was to remain the rest of his life.

At Nenana we saw our first "iron horse" pulling what appeared to us to be about a mile of boxcars, and we first heard the thrilling whistle of a steam locomotive. The 470-mile Alaska Railroad was built and operated by the federal government. Completed only two years earlier, it connected the saltwater port of Seward to the interior town of Fairbanks. Railroads had penetrated the western states in advance of population growth, and people had followed. Optimists in Congress believed that a railroad would do the same for Alaska. While awaiting the miracle of population growth, the railroad was to provide access to the Interior for gold seekers and others. It didn't happen that way; most of Alaska isn't farming or livestock country to be settled like the western states.

Steam engines pulled both passenger and freight trains for the railroad, and for the next two years while we lived at Eklutna, we were to hear the haunting sounds of their whistles daily as they rumbled by.

We transferred to a passenger train at Nenana, and eager to see everything, I rode with my head out the window. I inhaled a lot of coal smoke, and cinders collected in my hair and spattered my face. Jimmy was half sick with undiagnosed tuberculosis and, to complicate matters, he caught a cold. To my frequent, "Look at this, Jimmy," when I saw something new and interesting, he could only look and nod dully.

From the train we could see the high rugged Alaska Range and Denali, which to us were like another world. Denali—The High

One—is the Indian name and the state of Alaska's official name for North America's highest peak. Non-Alaskans call the 20,320-foot-high mountain "McKinley," after a politician who never saw Alaska. It had been named by prospector A. W. Dickey in 1896, only twenty-nine years earlier.

At Curry, the end of the train run for that day, we stayed at a hotel operated by the railroad. We felt like royalty. The wide double bed assigned to us was pure luxury. We spent most of our stay watching animals at a nearby fox farm.

The train continued south the next morning, stopping occasionally for mail and passengers. The Alaska Railroad has always prided itself on stopping to pick up anyone, anywhere, along the tracks, and several times, far from normal waypoints, we ground to a halt so passengers standing beside the tracks could board.

On the second day after boarding the train, we reached the Eklutna school. The shop and gymnasium were still under construction. Built mainly in 1922 and 1923, this Bureau of Indian Affairs school was originally at Tyonek, an Indian village on the west side of Cook Inlet. It was moved to Eklutna (which was more a place than a settlement) to take advantage of the railroad transportation for students, mail, and freight, and for the cheap coal hauled by the railroad from Alaskan mines which heated the half-dozen large buildings of the school. The student body consisted of twenty-five boys and thirty girls—Indians, Aleuts, and Eskimos from all over the Territory.

We had been at Eklutna about fifteen minutes when one of the boys gave Jimmy a rough shove. "He's sick. Leave him alone," I warned.

"How about you, are you sick too?" the bully asked, mockingly.

"Try me," I taunted.

He swung at me, and I leaped in with flying fists. He had all he wanted in about twenty seconds and we separated. About then one of the supervisors growled, "You boys there. Stop that fighting."

Next was our first shower. Jimmy and I washed away the ashes, cinders, and coal dust, having fun adjusting the running water. We lingered, enjoying for the first time the sensation of hot water running over our bodies. Until then, we had known only baths, mostly in big galvanized washtubs. After we dressed, a bell rang, and all the kids started running. We followed.

"What's the bell for?" I asked, as we trotted along.

"Chow time," was the answer, which meant nothing to me. I had never heard the word "chow."

We joined the line of students waiting to be served. Within moments a big kid shoved Jim. Weak and frightened, Jimmy clutched me.

"Leave him alone," I warned the second bully we had encountered within an hour.

"You want to try boxing?"

I had never heard the term.

"What's that?" I asked.

"This," he said, and he punched me, hard.

I wasn't going to take that, so I pitched into him. He was being pretty professional—dancing about, guarding himself, and "boxing." I simply waded in, hitting him wherever and whenever I could, and I was doing pretty well. Then, unexpectedly, I hit him on the throat. He gasped and fell to the floor.

The matron in charge of the cookhouse yelled in alarm. Her husband shouted and grabbed me. I had been at school about an hour and already I had been in two fights. An Eskimo boy came to my rescue by explaining how the fights had started to the superintendent, Charles Briffitt, a part-Indian from the States, and he promised after-dinner paddlings for the bullies. I had never witnessed a paddling. Nothing like that had ever happened at Anvik Mission. But I wasn't frightened or horrified by it: I was pleased to see those two kids get what they had coming.

As soon as the school nurse realized Jimmy was sick, he was hospitalized for about six months because of the tuberculosis. Despite being isolated, he managed to make many friends, who visited him, and I was allowed to visit him frequently. He was fortunate to recover. Being half-white, he probably had more resistance to the disease than full-blooded Natives, who commonly succumbed to tuberculosis.

The excellent food at Eklutna also contributed to Jimmy's recovery. Hospital patients always received fresh milk, and sometimes all the students had fresh milk. There were also fresh vegetables from the fine school garden. One spring I helped Oscar Loft, one of the supervisors, plant the garden. At times there was meat on the table, including pork, beef, moose, mountain sheep, and caribou.

The five or six supervisors were also teachers. Except for Superintendent Briffitt, they were all white men. There were two supervisors of the boys and of the shop, and one in charge of maintenance and gardening. There were also several women teachers.

My reading, writing, and arithmetic studies, begun at Alatna, continued at Eklutna. I enjoyed learning and was a good student.

In our free time we students went on long hikes, and often fished for trout at Eklutna Falls. We could check out guns for hunting rabbits and spruce grouse, which were cooked in the school mess. Sometimes we camped over a weekend and cooked our own meals, including rabbits we shot. The school provided ammunition, and we never returned any of it; if we didn't use it killing game, we shot at targets.

It was on one such outing that I saw my first moose, a small bull shot by Augie Mack, one of the older students. Also, soon after I arrived at Eklutna, while on a hike I encountered a huge, hulking brown bear near the railroad tracks. It went on its way peacefully, while I retreated rapidly in the other direction.

During my second autumn at Eklutna, I went with a group of students on a big game hunt for Dall sheep and caribou. We rode the train to Broad Pass, high in the Alaska Range, and camped near the railroad tracks. Flocks of sheep on the nearby peaks looked like tiny moving patches of snow. White-necked caribou floated over the rough terrain of Broad Pass as they browsed, moving so gracefully that they seemed almost to be without legs. The bull caribou carried huge straw-colored antlers; cow caribou antlers were smaller.

Some of the older boys and a volunteer professional hunting guide killed about ten sheep and several caribou. The game was dressed and kept in an Alaska Railroad freezer car for use at the school. That good, fresh meat at Eklutna was new to Jimmy and me; the only meat we had eaten at Anvik had come out of cans.

We often visited nearby homesteaders, spending nights away from the school. At the homes of these friendly people for the first time I saw home-canned foods put up in jars—vegetables and wild meat, including moose, ducks, and geese killed along the shores of nearby Cook Inlet. I learned from these hardworking families how to make preserves out of wild raspberries, blueberries, and cranberries. Some of the homesteaders had animals that were new to me—cattle, pigs, goats, and chickens—and I always enjoyed seeing them. The home-steaders, who lived simply in small homes, were clearing land, developing farms. It was backbreaking work, but I never heard any of them complain. Even I, with no knowledge of farming, could see that years of work were needed to develop land so that it would be suitable for crops and grazing.

During my second year at Eklutna, in 1927, with several other students I made the twenty-five-mile trip by rail to Anchorage, then a "city" of about 2,000. Originally established as construction head-quarters for the Alaska Railroad, Anchorage's population had peaked at 6,000, and then after completion of the railroad, the population had diminished. I had never seen a place with so many big buildings and so many people. It was on that trip that I saw and rode in my first automobile, a Ford Model T owned by Dr. Howard Romig, a much-loved physician who came to Alaska as a missionary in 1896. I also saw my first movie, a silent, called *Taxi, Taxi*. It was an exciting trip.

At the school, Eklutna John, an old Indian trapper, was paid to teach the boys of fourteen and older how to make snowshoes by a method that was probably centuries old. Sent out to trading posts and stores all over Alaska as fast as they were made, the shoes sold for about eight dollars a pair to trappers, guides, and to tourists who bought them as souvenirs. Although I was too young to make snow-shoes, I was able to watch what he did, fascinated.

To select wood for the snowshoes, Eklutna John examined the inner bark of a birch tree to determine the growth pattern and grain of the wood before felling the tree. He left trees with unsuitable grain standing; most people would have had to cut into a tree to determine the grain.

Splitting the birch logs with wooden wedges, he hewed the pieces down with a small axe, then used a crooked knife to reduce the pieces to drying and bending size. The crooked knife is a traditional tool in the North, and when they were first available, they were often handed down from generation to generation. All early Alaska Natives trea-sured the metal blade.

The bent blade of this knife is sharpened on one side for a right-handed man and on the opposite for a left-hander. Used as a drawknife, it is pulled on the cutting stroke, never pushed, and cutting is accom-plished at the bend of the knife. It neatly removes fine shavings, and produces a smoother finish than can a straight-bladed knife.

Eklutna John didn't soak the wood for making his snowshoes, but worked it dry while it was still green. He took a raw new piece and gradually worked at bending it to make the sharp-angled curve for the front of a snowshoe. Finally, using his teeth, he finished the bend in the wood at a place where it had become very pliable. I never saw him or any of his students break a piece of that beautifully grained birch while bending it.

The form on which he built the snowshoes had one crosspiece, just back of the front end of the shoe, another piece across the top to reinforce the shoe, and there was one short pole to make the turn up at the front of the snowshoe. He used his crooked knife to finish the wood, shaving off fine slivers. He never used sandpaper. This old Athapaskan expert ground his own rocks for pigment and with it painted the wood an attractive rusty red.

The rawhide snowshoe filling, front and back, was of calfskin, the most suitable hide available, which was shipped up from Washington State. Eklutna John taught his students to soak the hide, remove the hair, and scrape the rawhide to uniform thickness. His gauge to then cut the rawhide into threadlike strands of proper thickness was a notch cut in his left thumbnail. He held a razor blade in his right hand and, as one of the students pulled it, he let the rawhide flow between his thumbnail notch and the razor blade resting against his left thumbnail. The rawhide had to be wet and soft to prevent his thumb from rubbing raw.

I saw the same method used for making rawhide strips from caribou and moose hides in the Koyukuk country years later. After I left Eklutna, I had no difficulty in making my own snowshoes, using methods I learned by watching Eklutna John. In the bush, when available, moose rawhide is used to fill the footpad, although beaver skin is also suitable. When available, caribou rawhide is used for the toe and heel areas.

My only problem at Eklutna was getting into fights. I frequently had black eyes from running into other boys' fists and a sore rear end from the paddle. The paddle, which had a tapered handle, was a three-foot piece of oak flooring, three-fourths of an inch thick, with rounded edges.

Each supervisor had a different way of applying this heavy stick. How often a student was paddled depended on the strictness of the supervisor. A first offense normally drew three swats. We were forced to bend over and hold our ankles with both hands—a position that was supposed to lessen the chance of kidneys and leg bones getting hit. The highest number of swats I received was ten. Sometimes the swats were so hard they knocked a student on his head, even when the paddle was being held with one hand. Supervisors were allowed to use two hands on the paddle when punishing students who were fourteen or older.

Sometimes a paddling became a beating. I saw a girl and a boy who were caught in sexual intimacy take sixty-five swats each, full swing. Neither could sit for a month; they had to stand to eat. That boy's bottom, which I saw, was a mass of black blood. It was whispered at the school that before my arrival a boy had died from kidney problems resulting from paddling.

The paddling was barbaric and cruel. Times were different then, and such punishment of children was accepted as necessary. My paddlings did me no permanent damage, although at one time my resentment was pretty strong. I think generally it was your own fault if you got paddled. But regardless of the paddle, I never gave up my right to protect myself by fighting.

Federal BIA schools such as the one at Eklutna fulfilled their role of teaching young Alaska Natives the basics of reading, writing, arithmetic, and hygiene. They educated these youngsters so they could fit into the world of the dominant white society. Eklutna, like many other BIA schools, also taught shop and building methods to the boys, and sewing, nutrition, and cooking to the girls. Without these schools, many Natives would never have learned how to read, or how to cope with modern society.

There are no longer any BIA schools in Alaska. The Bureau of Indian Affairs has assumed another role in educating Alaskan Natives by helping students go to schools of higher learning through grants and scholarships.

The single most valuable skill I learned at the Eklutna school was how to read. Reading opened a new world for me, and enabled me to educate myself in any subject. That alone made my stay there worthwhile.

After we had been at Eklutna almost two years, Dad wrote, telling us to return home to the Koyukuk. He seemed to be getting sick more often. He felt that if we were to survive in Alaska, we also had to learn to make a living from the land, and it would be best for him to teach us that.

Jimmy and I left Eklutna in May 1927. I was twelve years old and had completed third grade. That was the end of my formal schooling. Now I was to receive a different kind of education.

7

NULATO

❁

Jimmy and I felt we were old hands at traveling when we left Eklutna to return to the Koyukuk. Two years at the school had left their mark; we had gained confidence, and we'd made many friends—some whom we would encounter repeatedly in our travels about Alaska for decades to come.

One of the superintendents took us to the Eklutna station and helped us board the train. We got off before we reached Nenana to stay with John "Happy Jack" Felix, one of Dad's early prospecting partners. We were to travel downriver on the steamer *Alice*, which would leave as soon as the ice went out. While we waited, Happy Jack telephoned Nenana daily to learn about ice conditions in the Tanana and Yukon rivers.

After about a week the ice was gone, and Happy Jack put us on the train to Nenana, where we stayed over another day until the *Alice* was made ready for use. As we waited under the care of another of Dad's old friends, we met Mr. Coghill, a longtime Nenana businessman who insisted that I put on a pair of boxing gloves and spar a few rounds with his son Jack, who was about my age. (Jack Coghill, who still lives at Nenana, later became Alaska's lieutenant governor.)

When we were on our way aboard the *Alice*, Captain Adams let Jimmy and me ride in the wheelhouse as we steamed down the swift Tanana River. Because of the many sharp turns, the paddlewheel was in reverse much of the time. The two barges we pushed, one ahead of the other, needed to swing corners to remain in the channel. Backing down allowed the leading barge to swing around bends with the current; otherwise it would have rammed the bank.

The *Alice* stopped at Galena, a tiny Indian village of twenty-seven people, of which only two were there; the others were at muskrat hunting camps. It was the last possible opportunity to make money from furs for the year. Muskrats, hunted with a .22 rifle and taken with traps, were a major source of income for most people in the area. Because muskrats are taken in the spring, this brought cash to live on through the summer. Most residents had to depend on selling furs, for jobs were few, and only a handful of the more fortunate younger men had work on the government-owned riverboats at $60 a month and board, which was big money.

When the *Alice* reached Koyukuk Station, one of the first sights I saw was John Evans and Dominic Vernetti, busy buying muskrat skins for their trading posts. As usual, all of the residents had come to welcome passengers and to watch the *Alice* land. The steamer carried the first fresh produce since the final boat the previous September. Oranges, apples, potatoes, onions—all had been en route from Seattle for slightly more than a month. Anything less than two months old was "fresh." The bacon and ham also were considered fresh, even though both supported a luxuriant growth of mold. Yukon River residents who could afford twenty-five cents a pound were happy to get that ham and bacon, as well as four- or five-week-old eggs. Bottled root beer was a welcome treat, too.

I hadn't seen Dominic Vernetti since I was four, and he kept hugging me and telling everyone how I had saved my dad's life, "as a baby boy." To my intense embarrassment, he proclaimed loudly in his inimitable Italian accent, "Dis keed is wort' his weight in gold."

The *Alice* remained at Koyukuk Station for two days as the crew unloaded freight, some of which went aboard Sam Dubin's *Teddy H.* We remembered this little steamboat, for it had rescued us when our mother died. Captain David Tobuk was waiting to run the *Teddy H.* up the Koyukuk River to deliver freight to various mining camps, stores, and villages.

Jimmy and I attracted attention because people remembered the circumstances of our mother's death, and most knew our dad. Several Indians we didn't know shook hands with us, praising us for surviving, and assuring us that they would never forget us.

One's course in life often pivots on small incidents. At Koyukuk, I wandered into John Evans' store, where I feasted my eyes on the wonderful array of guns, hardware, clothing, and foods. I studied the items, similar to those my dad had offered in his trading post. A shiny new pocketknife caught my eye, and I picked it up. Suddenly the knife was in my pocket and I walked out of the store without paying for it.

I carried that knife for a day and a night. I couldn't sleep from worrying about it. I knew what I had done was wrong, but I was afraid to tell anyone. At the last minute before the *Alice* sailed, I went to Dick Livingston, the purser, and told him I had stolen the knife and wanted to return it to Mr. Evans. "Would you go with me?" I asked.

John Evans and his wife were watching the boat prepare to leave when Dick and I walked up. I felt as if the whole world was watching when I pulled the knife from my pocket and handed it to him. "I stole it from your store. I'm sorry," I stammered, tears coursing down my cheeks.

"Why, Sidney," was all he managed at first. Then he asked, "Why did you steal it?"

"I thought I wanted it," I murmured, studying my shoes.

"Well," said John, "that's the first time anyone has ever returned anything they stole from me."

I thought I was going to get a paddling like those I had experienced at Eklutna, but John said, "Son, I have heard nothing but good about you. You are very brave and honest for returning the knife. Because of this, I am going to give it to you."

I couldn't believe my ears until he placed the knife in my hand. Then, lifting my chin, he bent over to look into my eyes and said in a firm voice, "Sidney, if you ever really need anything, let me know. We can always work something out."

I treasured that knife for years, a reminder of my terrible mistake as well as of John Evans' promise and generosity. As Dick walked me back to the gangplank of the waiting *Alice*, Andrew Pilot stopped me. He was an important medicine man who was influential among the Koyukon people of the Lower Yukon. "You are a good boy. We will always remember you," he said, shaking my hand.

As the *Alice* ran the twenty miles to Nulato where we were to wait for our dad, I had a lot to think about. I was surprised to realize that people all up and down the Yukon and Koyukuk rivers knew who I was. Words of praise from John Evans, Indians I didn't know, Andrew Pilot, and Dominic Vernetti echoed in my mind.

I was at a pivotal time in my life, for I was still insecure, although I was beginning to lose my distrust in people. The praise I had received came when I truly needed it. The kind words were more effective than all the scolding and punishment I had had at Eklutna. Those words helped instill in me a feeling of pride in myself and reinforced my determination to succeed. I wanted to justify the faith these important people had in me.

At Nulato, Dick Livingston took Jimmy and me to Bill Dalquist, a friend of our dad's who was to care for us until Dad and his partner, Charlie Swanson, arrived from their trapping grounds far up the Koyukuk.

I made many friends in those intervening weeks. Jimmy and I played baseball with local kids. It was strictly hardball, no softball, which was considered "girly ball." I met Cosmos Mountain, a Koyukon as fascinating as his name. He was grinding the valves of an eight-horsepower Kermath boat engine, and I helped him for a few days. I had wanted to learn about engines and how to use tools, and this was a good chance. Cosmos played the violin at local dances with Aloysius Demoski, Alfred Dalquist, and others. Dances were the main form of entertainment in the villages.

I helped Cosmos peel poles and crosspieces to be used in building a fish wheel. While working, Cosmos told me exciting stories of Koyukon hunts. From him I gleaned the beginnings of appreciation for the culture of the Koyukon people.

I also met the Sommers boys, John and Bill, who were about my age. Their father, an old-country German storekeeper, had assigned them to the cordwood detail—cutting, splitting, and stacking firewood. I helped them with the firewood for several days, and I helped them unload a couple of barges that arrived with stock for the Sommers' store. Their father, John C. Sommers, was good to both Jimmy and me. We often ate at the bountiful Sommers table.

Dad and Charlie Swanson finally arrived with their thirty-two-foot riverboat *Vixen*, powered by a Model T Ford engine. Lean and tough from a winter of trapping, Dad was cheerful and optimistic.

Charlie Swanson, a Swede, had left the old country in 1897 to look for gold in the Klondike, so he and Dad had that in common. He was a grizzled, gray-haired old man who talked little, and then with a strong Swedish accent. He had a strong personality, and we always understood clearly where we stood with him. Soon Jimmy and I regarded him as we would a kindly but strict uncle.

We pitched a large wall tent on the Nulato beach to live in while the four of us built a cabin on the *Vixen*. Although the boat was only six feet wide, it then became our Nulato home where we slept and sometimes ate our meals.

One day I watched Charlie Mountain, father of Cosmos, come down the Yukon River, paddling his canoe beside a big log. One leg was in the canoe, the other gripped the log. In this unusual fashion the old Indian pushed that log onto the beach where he tied it. Then he paddled off and returned shortly with another log.

There was a demand for logs, and I began imitating Charlie. Using Dad's fourteen-foot canvas muskrat hunting canoe, I spent long hours bringing in logs that I found either drifting down the river or hung up along the shore. Soon I had logs scattered all along the beach. Joe Stickman, later famous as one of Alaska's great racing dog mushers, asked me who I was getting the logs for.

"No one," I answered.

Joe handed me six big, shiny silver dollars for six logs he had selected for his fish wheel raft. That sale was a big event for me, for I had seldom had as much as a dollar at a time in my pocket.

I gathered more logs, and sold a few more at a dollar each. No one wanted to buy the others, although they looked fine to me. I asked Bill Dalquist why. "They're green, Sidney. No good for fish wheels. You have to use dry logs to make a fish wheel."

Eventually I gave all the logs I couldn't sell to Charlie Mountain.

On one warm, peaceful spring day, as the brown Yukon flowed endlessly past Nulato, the residents were out enjoying the sunshine and readying boats and fish wheels for the coming fishing season. I sat on the beach, a wide-eyed twelve-year-old, taking it all in. Suddenly from upriver came a loud volley of rifle shots.

"People coming down," someone yelled.

With that, Indians ran in all directions. Excited men rushed to the beach, stuffing cartridges into rifles as they ran. They stood in a loose line, watching upriver, rifles ready.

I grew frightened and ran to Bill Dalquist's nearby cabin. "What's happening?" I asked, fearfully.

"They're getting ready to greet the Koyukukers," Bill laughed.

Relieved, I returned to the water's edge to watch. Soon another volley of shots sounded from upriver. Then the Nulato people opened up with a barrage; every man with a rifle fired into the river. An answering volley came from upstream, resulting in more shooting from the Nulato people. The ceremony was a carryover from an earlier time when the emptying of a muzzle-loader demonstrated peaceful intentions when two groups of Indians met.

A raft of ten boats lashed together drifted around a bend of the Yukon. The Indians in the boats fired their last shots as they came in sight. They were from Koyukuk Station, Galena, Ruby, Kokrines, and other upriver villages.

Most of the Nulato people sat on the board sidewalk along the riverbank to watch the approaching visitors and I sat with them. When the visitors came ashore, each walked the full length of the sidewalk and shook hands with every person. Not one word was spoken. There was no greeting of any kind, not even between long-separated brother and sister. No one hugged. They simply shook hands in a formal ritual that must have had its origin decades earlier when showing emotion was regarded as weakness. When the hand-shaking ceremony ended, people loosened up. Hugging and back-slapping began, as old friends and relatives came together.

The visitors had come to attend the funeral potlatch for old man Demoski, who had died a few days earlier. In 1922, when Dad and I had been in Nulato, Demoski had taken us to the Nulato River where the famous massacre of February 1851 had taken place. While he and Dad had talked, I picked up a few blue Russian trade beads nearby where the riverbank had caved in. Demoski told Dad the story of the massacre, and I have since heard versions told by other descendants of the Koyukuk and Nulato Indian participants.

A Koyukon chief and medicine man was the instigator. Koyukon people who know the oral history of their people have told me he was called *"Lolee-ann,"* or something pronounced close to that.* He was their most famous chief.

> The first Russians to arrive on the Lower Yukon wooed Lolee-ann's people, the Koyukon Indians, wanting to trade for fine furs. Relations had been peaceful for several years, but two incidents sparked the animosity that led to the massacre.
>
> The first involved Lolee-ann's daughters. One lived with Derzhavin, commandant of the Russian fort at Nulato. Then a second daughter attracted Derzhavin, and she too moved in with him.
>
> Lolee-ann demanded the surrender of at least one daughter. Derzhavin refused, saying that she was serving as a concubine for a visitor at the fort. After the visitor left, perhaps one of the chief's daughters would be returned.

---

* He is called Larion by both Peter Freuchen in his fictional account, *The Law of Larion* (1952), and Hubert Howe Bancroft in his *History of Alaska 1730–1885* (1886). William H. Dall, *Alaska and Its Resources* (1886), called him Larriown.

The second incident occurred when Lieutenant Barnard of H.M.S *Enterprise* arrived in Nulato in search of information on the fate of the 1845 arctic expedition of Sir John Franklin. Franklin and his men had disappeared, and for years the English sent many expeditions to the North American Arctic in attempts to learn their fate. Barnard, blunt-spoken and unaware of the Koyukon Indian character, remarked that he intended to send for Lolee-ann, who was about twenty-five miles away at an annual festival.

Barnard's remark was overheard by a Koyukon at the fort, who passed it on to Lolee-ann. Lolee-ann, a man of great power, was not one to be "sent for." The Russians, aware of this, always respectfully "requested the honor of his presence" when they wished to see him.

Lolee-ann's pride was hurt by Derzhavin's refusal to return one of the daughters. Barnard's intention to "send for him" was an insult that could not be endured. He called a council meeting, and swore that blood of the foreigners would flow. At that moment a dogsled driven by a Russian named Ivan Bulegin, accompanied by a Koyukon worker from the fort, appeared on the nearby Yukon River.

Lolee-ann's warriors killed the Russian, cut strips off the body, then roasted and ate the flesh. The warriors, on snowshoes, then set out for Nulato.

In darkness, half a mile from the Russian fort, they came to three large winter houses in which slept about a hundred Nulato men, women, and children. The Nulato people were then traditional enemies of the Koyukons. Lolee-ann's warriors found forty or fifty birchbark canoes nearby. Working stealthily, they broke up the canoes and thrust the pieces into doors, chimneys, and windows. Then they set the three buildings afire.

The inhabitants frantically tried to push through the flames. Some of the men hacked through the walls with axes, but arrows of the attackers felled them. Many Nulato people suffocated. A few women were captured as slaves, and one or two children survived by fleeing into the woods.

A young Nulato man named Wolasatux escaped. Koyukon oral tradition has it that he was permitted to escape: Nulato oral tradition says he was fleet of foot and escaped because he was faster than his pursuers. Russians inside the half-mile-distant fort slept through the fire and the attack.

After burning the three buildings, Lolee-ann's warriors went to the fort. It was morning, and Commander Derzhavin had just arisen and was sitting behind a house. The attackers forced a Koyukon employee at the fort to kill the Russian with a knife. A Russian interpreter witnessed the murder and chastised the Indian for it. Moments later he fell dead, pierced by seven arrows.

The attackers rushed inside and found Lieutenant Barnard on his bed, reading. The Englishman reached for his gun, but as he fired, the weapon was struck upward and the charge hit the ceiling. Again he fired, and for the second time the gun was struck upward. Lolee-ann killed Barnard with a knife. In that house, a mother and three children were also killed.

The attackers then tried to get into a room where workers, including two Russians, lived, but the occupants barred the door and fired through the window, killing one of Lolee-ann's warriors.

William Dall, a naturalist and explorer, wrote that the Russian American Company "never took any measures of retaliation for this massacre," and "presents were sent to the Koyukon chiefs, and there the matter ended." He concluded his account, "...a stockaded fort was soon built on the present site, and the graves of Barnard and Derzhavin lie a stone's throw behind it."

Now, shortly after his burial, upriver Indians had arrived for the memorial potlatch for old man Demoski (I believe his name was Joe), and for the annual spring gathering of the Lower Yukon and Koyukuk Indians. The potlatch, set for nine o'clock that night, was to be an old-style, formal ceremony, with feasting and a dance.

The potlatch is a traditional celebration among Alaska's Athapaskans. It may include feasting, gift-giving, music, and dancing. This traditional gathering, which varies from area to area, can be a thanksgiving ceremony with a communal meal in a public place or in a home. Or it can be a demonstration of respect for the dead at a funeral or memorial gathering, where the participants eat foods harvested from the land—fish and game, berries, salmon.

I wanted to attend the Demoski potlatch, but one of the younger boys of the village told me, "They don't allow halfbreeds from the Koyukuk in the hall." I thought he was serious, but he was just needling. All were welcome to the potlatch. I was beginning to realize that I was neither all Indian nor all white. I was a Siwash, or a "breed," as many people contemptuously called people of mixed blood.

I asked Cosmos Mountain and his wife, Vivian, if I could attend. "You go to the store and buy some hardtack. Then go with me. I'll take care of anyone who bothers you," Cosmos promised.

We arrived at the hall carrying our contributions; I had hardtack and a bundle of dried muskrat meat which Cosmos had given me. Vivian carried two bundles of dried ducks. Cosmos had a bucket of duck soup. We added our food to the pile on a clean canvas tarpaulin spread on the floor. Others had brought dried beaver meat, dried salmon, fresh meat, canned fruits, crackers, cigars, and a variety of other items. By the time everyone had arrived, the food pile had become a mountain.

Soon the 300 or 400 people in the hall became so quiet I could have heard a button drop. An elder went to the center of the hall, and sat on his feet.

"Who's that?" I whispered.

"They call him Peter Chief," Cosmos answered. He was once a chief of Nulato.

In a few minutes, Olin, one of the older Koyukon Indians from the town of Cutoff, stepped forward and sat on his feet, facing Peter Chief. The two took turns speaking. They often waved their arms, and they stared at one another. Each seemed to challenge the other. I thought their performance looked and sounded like a contest.

"What are they talking about?" I asked Cosmos.

He said he couldn't understand them either—that they were using "high words" not generally understood by the average Koyukon Indian. Once in a while one elder would confound the other with an unfamiliar high word. At that, their speech contest would stall until the other came up with an acceptable high word or statement. The "high words" were known to only a few of the Koyukon people; some words represented the meaning of an entire sentence. The debate was long and heavy. I don't know who won, if anyone did.

We turned to the food, and it was a great feast. Later, dancing began, and everyone in the village attended. Violins and guitars provided music for waltzes, fox trots, and square dances. My dad, skilled at calling square dances, called until he was almost hoarse. Everyone had fun.

Before the arrival of whites, Koyukon potlatches were primarily a ceremony to honor the deceased, with meat being eaten for spiritual communion with the dead. When whites arrived with their special holidays like Christmas, New Year's Day, Easter, the Fourth of July, and their version of Thanksgiving, celebratory potlatches evolved in some places.

Occasionally, preparations for an elaborate and costly potlatch may take several years. At Hughes, in the winter of 1934, I attended a potlatch in honor of my uncle Little William, a much-loved person (he had given me the snowshoes when I was a child). More than twenty Koyukon Athapaskan songs were composed especially to honor him. These songs, and stories of his accomplishments told at the potlatch, were farewell gifts to Little William.

The amount of food served at Little William's potlatch was staggering. It included sledloads of moose and caribou from the Melozie River, as well as dried Dall sheep from the upper Alatna River. There were dozens of dried ducks and geese. The dried meat came from animals killed the previous fall and prepared specifically for that potlatch.

It required a full week to cook all the food for the big feast that took place on the final night of that potlatch. Included in the foods were straps of fat from about ten black bear which had been cut into pieces two inches wide and more than a foot long—a prime delicacy. I received four strips of that fine fat myself.

Composition of songs to be sung at a potlatch, which are generally based on the accomplishments of the departed, may begin months ahead of time. To arrange just the right words for a song may take weeks, even months. The composer commonly takes advantage of the peace and silence of the trapline to do his work. Without distractions he can devote much time and thought to the new song and concentrate on making it exactly right. Many of the old favorites have real meaning to Athapaskans. Some of the words in songs of long ago are "high words" from a language that only the better educated Indians knew. Few people today understand many of these old words.

The famed Nulato stick dance, a sacred Koyukon memorial to the recent dead, is known throughout Alaska. I have seen and participated in the stick dance several times. The "stick," a long spruce pole wrapped with ribbons and crepe paper, is placed upright in the hall.

Celebrants dance around the decorated pole. The originator of the first stick dance composed thirteen songs, honoring the family he had lost. Even today, those songs are the opening songs of any stick dance, although very few people know all of them. Nowadays a tape recorder is used to lead singers through the full repertoire as the stick dance begins.

At the stick dances I attended in the 1930s, some of the singers could almost raise the roof of that old Nulato village hall with their voices. It is an emotional experience for a Koyukon to attend the Nulato stick dance.

In prewhite times, all clothing of the Indians was made from skins of wild animals. Occasionally at a potlatch, even today, the old way of dressing is memorialized when, during the ceremony, individuals who have been of great service to the deceased are dressed in new fur clothing from head to foot by the family of the deceased. More commonly today, clothing given may come from Sears or Penney's, except maybe for fur caps and mittens, and moccasins from the leg skin of moose or caribou.

Early missionaries opposed potlatches because they thought the ritual was based on superstition. They also objected when, during a potlatch, a new widow was stripped of all her possessions. This practice has ceased, and now overtones of Christianity are often intertwined in the ceremonies.

I believe the American Thanksgiving evolved directly from the potlatch, or a similar East Coast Indian ceremony. According to the standard version of how Thanksgiving began, the Pilgrims feasted to give thanks for the bounty of their new land. But I have a theory.

Many Pilgrims died during their first winter in the New World. During the following spring, summer, and fall, I presume, the Indians taught the Pilgrims how to grow corn and harvest wild game to prepare themselves for winter. My guess is that the Indians became concerned because the Pilgrims had not honored those who had died the previous winter, and without a ceremonial feast, the dead had not been shown proper respect. I think the Indians convinced the Pilgrims to make a potlatch, as we say. The Pilgrims probably considered this superstitious nonsense, so instead of calling it a potlatch, they covered their tracks by calling it Thanksgiving.

8

THE BATZA RIVER
TRAPLINE

❂

It was midsummer when the four of us left Nulato in the *Vixen* to travel upriver on the Koyukuk to Batza River where we planned to spend the winter trapping. The sturdy riverboat would be pushing a barge holding a year's supplies.

As we readied to cast off into the swift and muddy Yukon, a crowd gathered on the Nulato beach to wish us well and wave farewell. We cranked the Model T Ford engine, and the *Vixen* chugged into the stream, pushing the heavy barge. A few tears were shed, both on the boat and on shore, for we didn't expect to see these friends again for almost a year. Then, there were few people living in the Koyukuk and Lower Yukon, and we knew almost everyone, so friendships were close.

Our outfit included gasoline for the boat engine, which burned one gallon an hour. We covered about five miles an hour, so traveling the 250 miles to Batza required fifty gallons of gas. We needed an extra fifty gallons for short trips, and enough for the return trip downriver the following spring. Dad had bought six sled dogs in Nulato, paying as much as $15 each, which was top price for a good dog at the time. They, too, rode on the barge.

We had 700 pounds of flour, 300 pounds of sugar, 150 pounds of several varieties of dried beans, 50 pounds of dried vegetables (potatoes, onions, and other varieties), 150 pounds of rice, 100 pounds of dried fruit (apples, peaches, apricots, and raisins), 60 pounds of coffee, 25 pounds of black tea, 70 pounds of shortening and lard, 100 pounds of oatmeal, 100 pounds of cornmeal, 2 cases of corned beef, a case of wiener sausage, a case of minced clams (for chowder), a case of salt, and 30 pounds of hard cheese.

For the dogs we had bundles of dried salmon, harness, collars, and chains. There were axes, hammers, saws, wrenches, nails, bolts, putty, rivets, sheet metal, sheets of glass for cabin windows, and colorful oilcloth for the kitchen table.

Each of us had three changes of clothing, enough socks and gloves for a year, and a good windproof parka. Wool was the warmest fabric available (and is warm even when wet), so we had woolen jackets and heavy Sheffield wool underwear and pants. Each of us had raingear and Indian-made winter boots or mukluks. Fur mukluks, worn with heavy wool socks, vary in length up to knee-high, and are supple and warm. In them we used dried grass as a discardable, absorbent, and warm innersole. There was ammunition for Dad's .30-40 rifle, shotgun shells, and .22 rifle cartridges. Included with the hardware were many traps and animal snares.

Dad and Charlie had cached similar items at their trapping cabin and some supplies had been left over from the previous winter. If we forgot something, we had to do without.

The Yukon River ran high, and we had to dodge many drift logs as we traveled the first four-hour leg of our journey to Koyukuk Station. At the time, Koyukuk Station was a dangerous place for a boat when a south wind blew, although since then the river has formed a sheltering island in front of the village. Over the years I saw many boats sunk there by sudden winds and accompanying large waves. We had planned to bypass that village, but the weather was calm when we arrived, so we went on in.

Dominic and Ella Vernetti talked Dad into staying until morning, and that evening we ate a wonderful spaghetti dinner cooked by Dominic, a master at preparing Italian dishes. Someone suggested we have a dance, and soon everyone in the village had gathered and the dance roared on through the night. But about three in the morning, a breeze started from the south, and we rushed to the boat and headed out.

"If the wind blows too hard, pull into the slough about a mile above the bluff," called Andrew Pitka, a friend of Dad's.

Soon we saw a 500-foot-high bluff looming ahead where the Koyukuk joins the Yukon. After we rounded it, the wind picked up, and waves started to roll over the gunwales of our barge. To escape them we fought our way into the sheltered and calm slough Andrew had mentioned. We had escaped the wind, but at considerable cost: millions of whining mosquitoes greeted us in the slough.

We spent the entire day in our bunks sleeping and resting inside our bed nets to escape the mosquitoes. When the wind calmed that evening, we headed on up the Koyukuk. In a few hours we stopped where huge flocks of ducks and geese had gathered. With a shotgun, Charlie killed a couple of geese and made a tasty soup. The birds provided the first red meat Jimmy and I had had since we had left the steamer *Alice*, and it was wonderful.

For bush residents in those years, beans commonly took the place of fresh meat, providing protein in summer when there was no way to freeze meat. After a month or more of beans we were tired of them, so Charlie's soup was especially satisfying. The farther we traveled upriver, the more wildlife we saw and the fewer beans we had to eat. We saw ducks and geese by the hundreds of thousands, as well as foxes, lynx, and otters.

At the old village of Cutoff, we found my uncle Hog River Johnny. "Are you planning to return to Hog River?" Dad asked him. He shook his head sadly and said, "I wouldn't stay there now, not since Anna died."

Our Aunt Eliza Attla was at Cutoff too. She hugged me and Jimmy and fussed over us, giving us tasty tidbits to eat. While it embarrassed us, both of us missed mothering, so we loved the attention. During our boyhood years many of the warmhearted, motherly women of the Koyukuk eased our loneliness with such attention.

"Do the boys have mittens and moccasins?" she asked Dad.

He told her that we had some that had come by mail order from Outside. But that wasn't good enough for her.

"Stay over a day and let me fix these kids up," she requested.

The next day, she came aboard the *Vixen* with moosehide moccasins and rabbit-skin socks for Jimmy and me, as well as two beautiful pairs of moosehide mittens lined with wool from a Hudson's Bay blanket. She had sewn a band of beaver fur on the outside of the mitten cuffs for brushing our cold noses on. She also brought a pair of fine, warm, fur slippers for Dad.

"How much do I owe you, Eliza?" Dad asked.

"I do that for Anna, my sister. Maybe sometime those boys might help me," she answered. That was the generous, loving way of life on the Koyukuk in those days. She must have worked all night.

Shortly after we left Cutoff, Dad spotted a shiny, fat black bear poking along the beach ahead. Hastily, he beached the *Vixen* and went ashore with his rifle. We waited, excited. Soon we heard the crack of a shot, then another. Dad appeared and signaled to Charlie to bring the boat and barge on up the river. When we rounded a bend, Dad was kneeling on the sandy beach, skinning the bear. That black bear provided some of the sweetest meat I ever tasted. We feasted on it for many days until it began to spoil in the July heat.

At Hog River, we stopped at Mom's grave. After we cut away the grass and small willows crowding the tiny site, we prayed. Our thoughts were melancholy, and there wasn't much that could be said. Seven years had passed since she had left us, but our memories of her were still vivid and our hearts were heavy.

The Hog River country is beautiful, with clear streams flowing through spruce and birch forests. Hudson Stuck described it well. After he drove a dog team from the Koyukuk drainage into the Kobuk in early February 1906, crossing two headwater forks of the Hog, he wrote, "As we came down a steep descent to the little east fork, it showed so picturesque and attractive, with clumps of fine open timber on an island, that it remains in my mind as one of many places...where I would like to have a lodge in the vast wilderness."

Batza River, our destination, pours into the Koyukuk thirty river miles upstream from Hog River. We arrived there late one evening, and immediately Charlie and I took the fishnet skiff downriver and set two short gillnets at an eddy. I had helped my mother with gillnets, and now Charlie taught me more about them. They were both empty the next morning, which told us that we had arrived before the salmon.

Dad and Charlie lived in a fourteen-by-sixteen-foot log cabin they had built the previous winter. It was too small for four people, so we cut logs to build a twelve-by-sixteen-foot addition. With a whipsaw, Charlie and I cut enough lumber for floors, doors, and other features. I had helped Bill Dalquist whipsaw a shaft log for his boat at Nulato while waiting for Dad and Charlie to arrive, and now Charlie taught me more about using this tool that was almost indispensable in the Alaska wildlands.

A whipsaw is about one-eighth-inch thick and perhaps ten inches wide at the upper end, tapering to four inches wide at the lower end. Total length may be five to seven and a half feet. A permanent long handle is attached to the top end. The lower, adjustable, handle is generally a block of maple. A frame is built so a log to be sawed is above the head of the man at the bottom of the saw, who pulls down when cutting and guides the blade of the saw to keep it on the lower line. The man below is liberally sprinkled with sawdust and anything else that comes off the log with every stroke. The man on top pulls the saw up on his cut, guiding it along the line marked on top of the log.

The addition to our enlarged log cabin became our bedroom. The front room was a combined kitchen, workshop, and living room where we skinned fur animals, made sleds and snowshoes, and repaired and made new dog harness with webbing and rivets. Charlie, a good sheet metal worker, made several stoves there.

There was plenty of work. All of us did whatever was at hand, with no separation between kid's work and adult's work. Dad wanted us to learn how to take care of ourselves, so the best way was for Jimmy and me to pitch in and help with every task.

We built two small, windowless log outcabins that summer—one downstream, about halfway to Hog River, the other about ten miles upriver. We used them for overnight stops or for short daytime rests while running our traplines. Each was a ten-by-twelve-foot windowless shelter with a small stove. The doors were only three feet high, barely big enough to duck through. To enter, we had to step over the lower three logs of the cabin; this type of threshold reduces the amount of cold air that pours through an open door in winter. At each of these outcabins, we kept matches, candles, a small supply of food, and a week's supply of dry firewood ready for use.

The salmon run was poor that summer, so we caught and dried only 500—hardly enough to feed our six dogs through the winter. We split and dried the fish in the usual way. It appeared likely that we would end up having to feed our dogs rabbits, if there were any.

One of our last jobs before freezeup was to pull the *Vixen* out of the water. About a mile and a half downstream we found a back slough that looked safe. River ice hadn't pushed inland to bend the larger six-inch-diameter willows along that slough for many years, and some of those trees must have been ten to twenty years old. Pulling the boat out of the water at the slough saved five or six days work, because we didn't have to make a Spanish windlass to pull it up a steep bank. Dad and Charlie agreed that our boat would be safe in the slough from the destructive power of ice during breakup.

So the dog team and sled could travel easily, Jimmy and I spent hours widening trails and shoveling them smooth where they climbed the banks of the river.

When the lakes froze over and snow came, we began to notice mink, fox, and some lynx tracks. Marten were scarce, and marten season, closed several years earlier, remained closed.

That fall, Jimmy and I trapped our first mink, and when we went to retrieve it, it sprayed us with its skunklike scent. We had mixed feelings when we arrived at the cabin carrying that mink. On one hand we were proud of our catch, but on the other we knew that we didn't smell very good.

And sure enough, when we stepped into the cabin carrying our mink, Dad whooped, "Get out of here, quick. You kids stink!"

Sheepishly, we left the cabin, still carrying our catch. Dad made us strip to our birthday suits and scrub down. Charlie skinned the mink and found the skin to be a blueback (bluish color inside the skin), which indicated that the fur was not prime. From that we learned it was too early to trap other furbearers, so we waited for another month before setting more traps. By then the fur on all the animals had reached its longest, sleekest, and densest condition—in other words, it was prime and the bluish color inside the skin had disappeared.

Cold came on fast in October, freezing the Koyukuk River over in just a couple of days. Dad, Jimmy, and I crossed on the ice to scout the country on the far side. We camped in the open, without a tent. Searching for tracks, we found mink, marten, and fox sign on the big grassy lakes. Dad and Charlie hadn't trapped there the previous year.

We broke a dog team trail across the river and cut a swath through the brush to the hills. Here we set some traps for marten. According to Dad, the bootleg price for marten was $20—big money in 1927. (My views on illegal trapping have changed, but I'm not judgmental about what happened more than half a century ago when only a few Indians or others living like Indians resided in the Koyukuk and Yukon valleys and they did what they had to do to survive. There were few people, few trapping regulations, and little enforcement of hunting and trapping laws.)

When trapping season was open and we were ready to catch furbearers, we followed the trails we had brushed out during summer with dog team and sled, through areas attractive to foxes, lynx, mink, and marten. We set our traps along these trails, some of which ran ten or fifteen miles. With some sets we used bait to attract animals, and with others we made blind sets—that is, we set the traps where an animal was likely to step blindly into them. Some traps were placed in cubbies—little brush or bark shelters that are attractive to furbearers, especially marten. Sometimes we hung a ptarmigan or duck wing over a trap so it would entice a marten to investigate.

We ran these traplines regularly to remove the trapped animals. In the normal below-zero winter temperatures that occur in the Koyukuk valley during trapping season, the animals died within hours, but if their frozen bodies remained in the traps for more than a couple of days, ravens, jays, shrews, or other animals were likely to eat them, damaging the furs.

Money didn't mean much to me then. Accomplishments did. I spent every spare hour outdoors working. I made my first dogsled out of split birch, lashing it together with *babiche* (rawhide). I cut my own bedroll out of the skin of the black bear Dad had shot. And I ran my own trapline. It was the most fun I had ever had.

By Christmas, we had twenty lynx, ninety foxes, thirty mink, and twenty contraband marten. Marten, a sleek brown tree-climbing relative of the mink, appear to have very long cycles of abundance and scarcity. One winter, about 1895, my grandfather, the trader, caught more than 500 marten with deadfalls—primitive traps set so that logs fall on the animals that trigger them. He received twenty-five cents for each skin. At that time, and in earlier years, marten were not only a fur producer to the Indians of the Koyukuk, they were also a food animal. After the 1920 federal ban on the trapping of marten, Koyukuk marten didn't return to real abundance until the late 1970s and early 1980s, although trapping was reopened about 1930.

By March, Dad decided that he and I had to take our furs to Tanana to sell them before prices dropped. He worried that a depression was near, and of course he was right: the bottom dropped out of the economy the next year.

One cold, clear morning in March we waved good-bye to Charlie and Jimmy, and headed down the glistening white trail on the start of our 300-mile round trip. My snowshoes hardly sank on the hard-packed route as I walked ahead of the dogs. Temperatures had moderated, and daylight hours were increasing noticeably. I was living with my dad, doing man's work at the age of twelve. Daily I learned more about surviving and succeeding as a North Country trapper—which appears to be a simple existence, but in reality is a complex and challenging profession. My life was beginning to come together.

We mushed twenty miles, reaching Little Sammy's camp the first day. Little Sammy, married to my aunt Big Sophy Sam, one of Old Mama's daughters, welcomed us for the night. He was a good-natured Koyukon Indian who played violin at village dances; he played by ear, and he was really good at it. The life of every party, he was a sincere Indian who followed the old customs.

We reached Hughes the next day, where we stayed with Old Mama. As usual, she cried, fussed over me, cooked a special meal, and gave me new mittens she had made. I truly loved that wonderful lady. After my mother died, Old Mama was the nearest substitute for a mother that Jimmy and I had.

About six inches of snow fell that night. In the morning we headed over the mountains to Indian Creek. At first we progressed well, but then we had to break trail in deep snow over a stretch that no one had traveled for many weeks. Dad knew the trail, and the government had marked it, so we didn't go astray. Nevertheless, the eleven miles from Berry's mine to Utopia were awful. Because of the deep snow, the trail had no bottom and the dogs had no footing. When dogs can't get traction to pull, they wallow around, tire quickly, and need help in moving the sled. At such times the musher is the hardest working dog in the team.

I had to double-break the trail—I tramped ahead half a mile on snowshoes and then returned to repeat the process, with three snow-shoe tracks compacting the snow enough to give the dogs footing and allow the sled to move more easily. By the end of the day, when we arrived at the Utopia mail cabin, I was exhausted. To travel the eleven miles, I had walked thirty-three miles back and forth.

Ernie Wingfield, a former prospector, was trapping at Utopia Creek. He had heard from other travelers that we were coming, and the previous day he had walked halfway to 70-mile Cabin and back, breaking trail over the route we were to follow. And he was planning to use the trail we had just broken on the following day, so our trail-breaking efforts balanced. Travel was easy to 70-mile Cabin on the trail that Ernie had broken; I had to double-break trail only the last six miles.

Every night on that trip we had to cook dog food. To do this, we had to cut firewood, start a fire, melt snow, and cook rice or cornmeal, and then cool the mush before we could feed our hungry animals.

We hit a fresh trail at the 70-mile Cabin. Tony Kokrines, a Tanana-born Indian who hauled mail from Tanana to Wiseman on a govern-ment contract, had gone through with his big dog team, headed for the Koyukuk. As we traveled, I learned the history of the mail route from the people we encountered along the trail and from evening talk. The Koyukuk mail run by winter trail began in 1906. Bob Buchanan was the first to fulfill the monthly mail contract from Tanana to Wiseman. Ed Allard hauled mail for the next eight years, then John Adams for the following four years. Next, trader Andy Vachon of Tanana won the contract and sublet it to old man Kokrines. He and his sons Anthony, Andrew, and Bergman Kokrines hauled the last of the mail by dog team over that trail. After that, about 1930 or 1931, the airplane took over. I knew all these drivers except for the earliest, Bob Buchanan.

The monthly mail run was the sole contact with the outside world for miners and prospectors who lived in the Koyukuk in the early 1900s. There was no radio. There were no airplanes. Dog teams carried everything in winter, riverboats carried everything in summer. Before regular mail routes, prospectors or miners carried mail to the mining district it was bound for and left it at a trading post. Letters from loved ones, magazines, and newspapers were treasures beyond value for these isolated men. In remote villages and mining camps, I've seen magazines with loose pages, the print worn from handling, treated as if they were valuable documents, as they were handed from man to man. Small wonder that mail drivers were considered special.

We moved swiftly down the trail that Tony Kokrines had broken, arriving at 32-mile Cabin that night, having covered thirty-eight miles in one day. Dad rode the sled downhill, and I had fun running on my snowshoes. We stayed the night at the cabin of John Larson, a longtime prospector. Tanana was only thirty-two miles from his cabin.

With an early start the next day, we reached Tanana before dark. Many residents were recovering from flu after an epidemic in which seventeen people had died. The town had been quarantined, and if we had arrived two days earlier, we would have had to return to the Koyukuk.

Tanana was a community of about 600, about seventy percent Athapaskan. It had two roadhouses, a pool hall, three general stores, a sheet metal shop that made stoves, and other small businesses. Soldiers from adjacent Fort Gibbon helped to build and maintain the telegraph line from Fairbanks to Nome. (The telegraph line was to be maintained until 1943 when wireless [radio] replaced it.)

At Tanana, Dad bargained for the best price for our furs. Finally he sold part of them to Ole Shade of the Northern Commercial Company and then shipped the remainder to the Seattle Fur Exchange auction. My season's catch of four lynx, many foxes, many marten, and one wolverine, sold for more than $1,000.

Though our stay was short, we saw Edwin Simon. I hadn't seen him since the year I had lived with Dad at Alatna, and it gave both Dad and me great pleasure to see his beaming face again.

We headed home on a fast, hard-packed trail. I walked and ran all the way on the level and uphill, and rode the sled going downhill. We reached Hughes, 120 miles, in four days, and we met Little Sammy on the trail. He had moved to the Melozitna River headwaters to hunt moose, as there were no moose in the Koyukuk River valley. He had come to Hughes to tell Chief John that a cow moose had left the Melozitna River and headed over the divide into the Koyukuk.

Little Sammy noticed that I had worn my snowshoes ragged. "That growing kid, he needs new snowshoes," he said. "Man, he walked all the way to Tanana and back on those old ragged ones. I just made these for myself, he can have them. We can't hold him back with bum snowshoes." With that, he handed me his newly made snowshoes and I proudly accepted his generous gift.

We traveled easily in the trail broken by Little Sammy, but after about ten miles on my new snowshoes they started to hurt my feet because the harness wasn't broken in, and I had to put on the old ones. We arrived back at our Batza River cabin the following day to find that Jimmy and Charlie had collected more fox and marten furs.

We hadn't taken the contraband marten to Tanana. The game warden for the region, Frank DuFresne (later a nationally known outdoor writer), patrolled from Tanana, and Dad didn't dare chance being caught with all those marten furs.

After we had been home a day, I was curious to see how Chief John was making out on his hunt for the cow moose. We had seen the tracks where he had turned off the river about forty miles below Hughes, so I presumed he would be at the lakes below there.

Chief John was half-brother to Old Mama and my great-uncle. He was a small, tough man who had once killed a grizzly bear with a spear. He would not admit to this feat. If he had, it would have been considered bragging, which was not acceptable in the old Koyukon culture. While he wouldn't admit to the exploit, others somehow knew about it, and he was held in high esteem.

I walked upriver on my new snowshoes for about two and a half hours and came to his trail where it led down through the lakes, following the moose tracks. I went home, and the next morning the weather was clear and around 0 to 10 degrees, so I headed downriver, figuring maybe I would intercept him. In three hours I found him camped with his wife, Big Mary. They had tracked the moose for a couple of days until they caught up with it and shot it. The moose hide was stretched out on the snow, and they were scraping both sides of it with a curved piece of trap spring tied to a short stick for a handle.

That's the way it was then. Whenever a moose showed up in the Koyukuk, someone would find its trail and stay with it until he killed the animal. Once the moose was taken, camp was made, and every bit of the animal was used.

Chief John and his wife had banked the base of their tent with moose hair for insulation, and they had made a moose-hair bed for each of their five dogs. Chief John had found rocks at a nearby bluff with which to break the bones so they could boil out all the nourishing fat and marrow. They had skimmed the fat off the top of the water and with it made a soup. It was surprising how much fat they got out of those bones. I ate with them, and with a little added rice, that soup was delicious.

Some of the meat was cut into strips and dried into jerky. They cooked and ate all of the intestine parts and the large blood vessels. All the meat from the head (some of the sweetest meat on a moose) was removed, cooked, and eaten. No usable part was wasted.

"Need help going back?" I asked.

"No. We stay three more days to finish the skin and cook all the bones. We take our time. Maybe stop at spring muskrat camp on way back to Hughes—after breakup. No hurry," old Chief John explained.

They were living real Indian style, enjoying life. They planned to consume the all-too-rare treat of fresh meat in leisure while basking in the warming spring weather. There was no need to hurry.

Caring for the valuable moosehide took them several days. First they removed the hair by dry-shaving it with a sharp knife. Then the hide was stretched out on a smooth place in the snow and pegged down so it would freeze evenly. As soon as the hide was frozen solid, they scraped the remaining meat and fat off the flesh side, which was a full day's work.

After the flesh was removed, the stakes were pulled and the hide was turned over, and the hair side was scraped to remove the black tissue until the hide was white. This was another full day's work.

The skin was then dried and rolled until it could be tanned, sometime during summer or fall. To tan it, the hide would be soaked in a mixture of water and rotten moose brains. Sometimes a bar of brown soap was added. The hide was wrung dry by fastening one end to a tree or stump, and twisting the other end with a five-foot pole. Then it would be hung up and scraped with a sharp flat rock. Again the hide would be soaked in the brains solution and scraped. The harder one works at scraping after wringing the water out, the softer the finished product. The hide was held with one hand while it was scraped with the other. This required hours of patient work.

The hide was then sewed into a pouch or tube, and a canvas or skin tube was sewed around the bottom to provide a pipe or conveyer for smoke. Then it was smoked on one side, with the smoke wood never allowed to flame. The smoking gives a moosehide a beautiful golden brown color. The longer it is smoked, the darker the finished product. Preferred smoke wood is bone-dry rotten spruce. The Koyukon people pick such wood up in the woods whenever it is found, for it isn't common. The resulting tough but soft, golden brown tanned moosehide is suitable for making pants, shirts, jackets, moccasins, and mittens.

Chief John gave me a piece of moose meat and pointed out a shortcut portage that reduced my trip home by at least an hour. The next fall I named that portage Chief John Portage (and so it is called today).

When I went back to their campsite a few days later, Chief John and Big Mary were gone. Nothing remained to show that they had killed a moose—no bones, no skull, no hair. Everything was cleaned up or buried.

9

DEEP COLD

During the winter of 1927–28, I spent an unforgettable day running part of our Batza River trapline when the temperature was −78 degrees Fahrenheit. During the 1920s and into the 1930s, such extremely low temperatures were not uncommon, and we often ran our trapline in −50 to −55 degree temperatures. That winter, between Thanksgiving and New Year's Day our mercury bottle remained frozen solid, meaning the temperature remained at −42 degrees or colder. Dad wouldn't let Jimmy or me go out for any length of time when the temperature was below −60. "Too risky," he warned.

He didn't need to remind us what could happen at such temperatures if we became wet in overflow, a common phenomenon of the North. When rivers freeze to the bottom and groundwater continues to flow, pressure builds and the force from groundwater sometimes is strong enough to lift the ice. The water may break through the ice and spread along the frozen surface—this is called overflow. Sometimes the water gushes through the ice like an artesian well, rising several feet above the surface of the ice. Overflow may be a fraction of an inch deep or a foot deep.

We had frequently heard Dad tell how one December with a big dog team, he was hauling mail to Fort Gibbon. As he drove his dogs up the Yukon River on a day when the temperature was −78 degrees, two soldiers who wanted to go to Fort Gibbon for Christmas asked if they could travel with him. He couldn't take both, for adding 90 pounds or so of duffel for each soldier would have been too much added weight on the sled, but he agreed to take one of the men.

"You'll have to walk," Dad told the soldier. Everyone understood that walking was part of traveling with a dog team pulling a heavy load. Dad was walking himself. The dogs moved at walking speed and on downhill slopes they went a little faster.

"Stay away from water. Don't mess around trying to tiptoe through overflow of any kind," Dad warned the soldier.

When they reached the Tozitna River, which had frozen to the bottom, overflow was running on top of the ice. The water was barely an eighth of an inch deep, and the soldier, ahead of Dad and the team, walked across the skim of water. Immediately the bottoms of his boots froze as solid as iron.

Dad turned the team and traveled an extra hundred yards to go around the water, then returned to the trail to rejoin the soldier on the far side of the overflow.

"My feet are getting cold, Jim," said the soldier.

"Did you walk across that water?" Dad asked.

"Yes. But I seem to be warming up now. I think I'm in good shape," the soldier answered.

In a few miles they reached the cabin of Monkey John, Dad's friend, where they stopped to warm up.

"How are your feet?" Dad asked the soldier.

"Fine. Don't worry," he answered.

"Why you ask, Jim?" Monkey John wanted to know.

"He stepped in that overflow on the Tozi, at 78 below," Dad answered.

"Too cold. Me *atsukee* (scared)," said Monkey John, feeling of the soldier's feet.

"Solid froze!" he said.

Monkey John harnessed his dog team and raced to Fort Gibbon to get an Army detail with a doctor to retrieve the man.

In the meantime, Dad and others brought snow inside the cabin to put the man's feet in. Snow was a popular remedy then. It was often even rubbed on frostbitten parts before discovery that such crude treatment could do further damage. The Army men with a doctor and dog team hauled the soldier to the Fort Gibbon hospital. He eventually lost both legs. So Jimmy and I knew enough to stay away from overflow during the deep cold.

An important part of our trapline equipment was a fine Taylor thermometer calibrated to −98 degrees Fahrenheit. We paid ten dollars for it, when a good quality thermometer that registered to −50 or −60 degrees sold for fifty cents. That January, the Koyukon "month of the days going from short to long," I had been stuck in the cabin for days, impatiently waiting out a long cold spell. The reading on the Taylor thermometer edged up to −58 degrees and Dad said it was warm enough for me to go out. I dressed in my warmest clothes. Over my wool union suit I wore a pair of heavy wool pants and a heavy wool shirt. Over the shirt I put on a wool jacket, and on top of that I wore a cloth parka with a hood with a wolverine fur ruff. I pulled wolf fur socks over my wool socks, and packed a clean innersole of dry local sweetgrass in my moccasins before putting them on, then pulled on a pair of Alaska Indian-type moosehide moccasins, which folded and tied at the ankle.

My mittens were the moosehide ones made by my Aunt Eliza, lined with Hudson's Bay five-star blanket wool. Beaver fur was sewed to the inside of the gauntlets, which kept the heat in yet allowed enough circulation to prevent sweating. Beaver fur was also attached to the outside of the gauntlets, giving me a place to wipe my nose, for the inescapable nose drips one gets in the extreme cold.

I carried an axe, and in my packsack I had a closed can holding kerosene-soaked burlap rags with which to start a fire if needed. (Even today in my snow machine winter survival kit I include a supply of starter burlap rags. I cut them into six-inch squares, pack them tightly into a can, pour kerosene or No. 1 diesel oil over them, and then close the can with a tight lid. One of these rags under dry sticks as a fire booster can be a lifesaver.)

I left about 8:30, well before daylight. Around my neck and over my face I wrapped a five-foot-long wool scarf, a gift from Ella Vernetti. Moisture from my breath would freeze on the scarf, so I occasionally turned it to a dry spot. As I walked, my exhaled breath made a crackling noise as it hit the super-chilled air, a sound that starts occurring at about −50 degrees.

Jimmy and I had experimented earlier that winter with boiling water. At −55 degrees, a cup of boiling water hurled into the air makes a great *whoooosh* and instantly turns into a cloud that drifts off slowly; no water falls to the ground. And when we opened the door of our warm cabin at such temperatures, the cold air rushed in and condensed the moisture of the room, and the condensation rushed along the floor like escaping steam.

That cold day as I ventured out to check some traps, animals were not moving—there were no tracks. I knew that foxes were curled up in dens or buried in deep snow, their noses covered by white-tipped tails. Beaver and muskrats were snug and safe under the ice of rivers and ponds. Mice scurried about under the snow, where they too were insulated from the terrible cold.

I found two marten in traps, removed them, and reset the traps.

This success encouraged me to snowshoe on. I came to a frozen red fox in a trap. His fur was beautiful. I reset the trap, but left the fox to pick up on my return. I had kept my mittens on while removing the three animals and resetting the traps; bare hands begin to freeze in seconds in such cold.

I sensed that the temperature was dropping, but I didn't feel cold. Only my fingers were icy from carrying the axe in my hand, so I put it in my pack. The axe is a necessary tool on a trapline, for limbs and small trees need to be cut around a set trap, and sometimes brush must be cut in a trail. In an emergency when one must have a fire or build a temporary shelter, the axe is indispensable. A trapper on the trail without an axe would be like a carpenter without a hammer.

As I approached the next trap, a blind trail set, I saw disturbed snow from some distance. Steam was rising from the breath of some animal, which growled ferociously, threatening me when I neared. A puff of steam erupted from his jaws at each growl and with each breath. The hairs on the back of my neck tingled, and I almost lit out for home.

Firmly caught in a No. 3 Newhouse trap was a wolverine, one of the most fearsome of Northern mammals, and he had been in the trap only a short time. Usually solitary, and never very abundant, the wolverine is the largest land-dwelling member of the weasel family in North America. The Koyukon people consider the wolverine's spirit to be the strongest of any animal, and they treat it with great respect. One of the Koyukon words for the wolverine is *doyon*, coming from the Russian *toyon*, which means chief or great man. The strength of this beady-eyed, low-slung, heavy-clawed animal is difficult to believe. Sometimes a wolverine steals animals from traps, and occasionally one breaks into a trapper's cabin or cache in search of food. The destruction this powerful thirty-pounder can wreak in a cabin is renowned in the North.

It was my first encounter with a live wolverine. I was certainly afraid of it, as it roared and threatened to eat me alive, but I was anxious to take it home, for the fur was valuable. We had quite a struggle, which took me some time, but I managed finally to put an end to it with a heavy club, without damaging the beautiful fur.

Removing it from the trap, I put it in my pack. I noticed its glossy brown fur, with the two pale lateral strips that converged at the base of his bushy tail. But I didn't linger because the encounter had tired me and I began to feel the cold. It was time to go home.

Snowshoeing as rapidly as I dared, just short of causing me to break out in a sweat, I headed down my backtrail. I picked up the fox and carried it in my mittened hands for a time, but my fingers started to grow cold, so I buried it in deep snow at the edge of a lake and marked the place with a stick. I was tiring fast and growing steadily colder. For the first time that day, I felt the cold through my pants.

At −50 degrees and colder in the Northern wilds, complete silence reigns. The only sign of life may be an occasional raven flying overhead—his wings make a loud noise in the dense air. There is the occasional startling rifle-shot crack of a tree freezing and splitting, or the eerie drum of ice giving off a loud *spaaaaang*, with the sound echoing and rumbling away underwater.

I realized the cold was becoming more intense as I shuffled homeward. I must have walked for two hours, and, despite my heavy clothing and physical exertions, I had become cold from head to toe. I knew that I had to keep moving because no amount of clothing would keep me warm if I stopped. Yet I moved slowly, knowing that if I overexerted and started to sweat, the perspiration would freeze on my clothing and allow the cold to penetrate.

The wolverine was heavy, but I didn't want to leave it behind; besides, it kept my back warm. When I came to the river I couldn't see across it because a thick fog was hanging over it. Our cabin was across the river. As I went down the riverbank, I felt the difference in air temperature: with each step it felt as if I were wading in a cold river.

Just before I reached the far bank, dimly through the fog I saw the shadowy forms of Dad, Charlie, and Jimmy, waiting for me. Weakness gripped my body, and I dropped my pack with the wolverine in it before climbing the bank. Even without the wolverine on my back I had difficulty reaching the top. Kicking off my snowshoes, I hurried directly into the cabin. The others followed. No one spoke.

I sat on a wood block we used as a stool. Charlie cut my moccasin strings and yanked off my moccasins and socks. "No frostbite," he announced. His welcome words were the first any of us had spoken. Other than minor frostbite on my cheeks and on the tip of one of my little fingers, I was fine.

"Dammit, Sidney, I've told you never to go out when it's colder than sixty below," Dad scolded.

"It was only fifty-eight below when I left," I said, defensively. "You said it was all right."

Eagerly, I told him about the wolverine, the two marten, and the fox. I knew my take was valuable; the four furs would bring about eighty dollars. My report helped take some of the pressure off. My wolverine was the first we had trapped that winter, and its fur alone was worth ten dollars from a fur buyer—more if traded or sold to an Indian or Eskimo fur seamstress.

"You know how cold it is?" Jimmy asked. "It's 78 below right now!"

Charlie gave me a cup of warm water to drink and made me rest on my bunk. Soon my cozy warm bearskin blanket and the heat inside the cabin made me drowsy, and I fell asleep. When I awoke a few hours later, I still felt exhausted. Charlie said he had felt the same fatigue from deep cold in the Dawson country of Canada when he was market hunting for moose in 1897. "Fighting the cold takes the energy out of you, fast," he said.

"Beware if nothing is moving in the woods" became ingrained in me after that memorable bone-chilling day. If animals aren't moving, the weather isn't likely to warm soon, and the absence of fresh tracks in the snow should have warned me to return home and stay indoors that day.

The Koyukon old-timers I came to know later taught me not to fight the cold but to be cautious. They knew how to forecast the weather, which told them when to stay home. I have known of a few Koyukon Indians who died in the cold, but they were usually young fellows who had ignored the advice of the elders.

For more than two weeks after that, temperatures of −60 degrees and colder continued. I've experienced only two deep cold spells that lasted longer—one in 1929 and one in 1930.

In 1929, Charlie Irish from Wiseman, on the Middle Fork of the Koyukuk River, took the census along a stretch of the Koyukuk River, interviewing each person in the district. When Charlie drove his dog team to our cabin on December 28, the temperature was −65. He and George Butler, his Indian guide, had set out thirteen days earlier, but −60 temperatures had delayed them from the time they had left Wiseman. Their runs were slow and short—not much more than ten to twenty miles a day. Travel in extreme cold is hard on dogs, so they had no choice.

Charlie and George remained with us overnight, and the next morning they took off for the mouth of Hog River, fifteen miles away by trail. They were gone five days, during which time the temperature never climbed above 60 below. They had to keep moving, because they were running out of dog food. When they arrived back at our place, their dogs were near exhaustion, and some had bleeding feet.

I'll never forget that night. Our thermometer outside registered

−67 degrees. When Charlie's team was still miles away, our dogs barked a warning because sound carries great distances in cold dense air. Jimmy and I put on our parkas, mittens, and warm moccasins, and went outside with a lantern. We heard the sled runners squeaking across the snow and the jingling of dog harness, and as we held up the lantern, the dogs trotted around a bend in the trail and into the light. The team looked like a steam locomotive—the frosty breath from the eight animals and the two men formed a small cloud around their heads and swirled in their wake. Dogs and men were covered with sparkling ice crystals.

Jimmy and I had grass beds ready for each of the dogs and firewood ready for cooking their food. We lit the fire, carried water already hot from the stove in our cabin to fill the cooking kettle, and quickly cooked food for the weary animals.

"We can't pull out for a while. The dogs need rest, and tomorrow will be real cold. This cold will last quite a while," said Butler.

"How do you know?" Dad asked.

"Did you see the sun today?" he asked. "It was copper-colored and hazy, with a ring around it. That always foretells a long cold spell."

"We'll see," said Dad.

See we did. Until the twenty-fifth of January not a single day was warmer than −72. Charlie eventually ran out of dog food and had to use some of ours. Since we were short ourselves, he promised to buy dog food for us at George Light's store at Hughes, and he soon sent us a sledload of dog food with Little Sammy.

Unfailingly, clear winter days in the Interior of Alaska are cold and cloudy days are warm or at least warmer. During that cold spell, the skies remained clear, and anytime I went outside I saw smoke rising straight up from our stovepipe into the still, frigid air, where it immediately lost its heat and settled slowly to the ground and spread out in a blue haze.

January 26 warmed up to −60, if you can call that warm, and Charlie and George prepared for an early departure the next morning. When they left, the temperature was −58. They planned to make it to Little Sammy's camp, twenty miles upriver. But if it grew colder, they might have to return to our cabin.

Temperatures remained warmer for three days. We learned that Charlie had reached Hughes before the next cold wave hit. With temperatures in the −70s, they were stuck in Hughes for another eight days before they could leave for Wiseman.

When George Butler had been at our cabin, he'd told us he hadn't felt well even before that trip. The deep cold took its toll; he died of tuberculosis before the ice ran that spring.

Until 1989, the last truly deep cold spell that I remember came in 1939. I was at the old town of Cutoff, where it was −70 or colder for twenty-eight consecutive days. In January 1989, record low temperatures were set for dozens of official weather stations throughout Alaska's Interior. Some temperatures along the Yukon and Koyukuk rivers repeatedly fell below −80 degrees for a week or so. We'll never know exactly how cold that spell was, for the official government thermometers issued to weather stations in Alaska do not register colder than −80 degrees Fahrenheit.

10

MY FIRST BOAT

It was March, and the increasing daylight hours and milder temperatures started me thinking of breakup, when ice on the rivers would leave and we could travel by boat again. If I had a boat, I could use Dad's three-horsepower Evinrude outboard motor. I was nearly thirteen, had learned a lot that winter, and I saw no reason why I couldn't build a boat. Dad encouraged me. "Don't let anything stump you; you can do whatever you set your mind to," he told us frequently, and his wise advice stayed with me.

I had no lumber, no nails, and had never built a boat. The previous fall I had learned how to whipsaw lumber, so I knew that with hard work I could produce my own lumber. We hadn't planned to build a boat, so we hadn't brought enough nails. Undaunted, I pulled nails out of all our wooden cases, and I also pulled whatever nails could be spared from our cabin walls.

Dad and Charlie told me how to build a boat, but insisted that they had no time to help. I would have to build it by myself, but that was fine with me.

I went into the woods near our cabin and selected two straight spruce trees that were about twelve inches at the base. I sawed them down, and, with the help of Dad, Charlie, Jimmy, and our dogs, dragged them along the snowy trail to the whipsaw pit. Before rolling the logs up onto the sawing frame, I peeled the bark off with an axe and a drawknife.

The previous fall I had worked the whipsaw standing under the log, with Charlie on top. Now, Charlie said, since this was my project I had to learn to lead the whipsaw from the top. Charlie and Dad worked beneath the log.

Learning how to feed the saw from the top didn't take long. I was physically strong, and in good shape from steady outdoor exercise. Charlie, working in the pit and manning the lower end of the long saw, usually tired after a while. Then he would have to have a smoke of his Old Westover Plug, which took some preparation. He would pull the aromatic plug of tobacco from his hip pocket, whittle a few shavings off, and grind the chips in the palm of his hand. These he poured into his pipe and tamped down with the fingers of the other hand. Only then would he light up. For a few moments his weathered face would be wreathed in smoke, and he resembled a chimney ablaze. When the blaze subsided, only the smoke and the good, strong smell marked Charlie's location.

The first two cuts on a log are slabbing cuts—a slab is removed from each side, leaving a log with two flat sides. When we had finished slabbing our first log, I had to figure out how many boards I could cut from the log and how thick each could be. With a pencil I marked lines on both sides of the now-flattened log and discovered that six cuts would give me seven boards—enough for the boat bottom. The other log would provide enough lumber to make the sides. I figured I should be able to make the ribs out of the slabs, after sawing the slabs into the proper thickness.

I was in a hurry to finish sawing my lumber. One day while Charlie puffed on his pipe I tried a few impatient strokes of the saw by myself, but it was difficult. Then Dad helped with a dozen or so pulls.

But Charlie warned Dad, "Better lay off, Jim. Trying to keep up with Sidney on the saw will kill you."

Dad had been half sick all winter. And because Jimmy had had tuberculosis at Eklutna, we wouldn't let him work too hard. We sure didn't want to lose him. Despite us, Jimmy was determined to be active.

"How am I going to get tough if you don't let me work?" he demanded one day, when Dad told him he couldn't work on the whip-saw. "You let Sidney do anything he wants," he said, tears streaming down his cheeks.

I came to his defense. "You're hurting Jimmy worse holding him back all the time. Let him at least try," I urged Dad and Charlie.

That convinced them, so they let Jimmy help me whipsaw my boat lumber. First Charlie instructed him to stand to the side and watch how he handled the saw from the bottom. He carefully explained how to avoid jamming the saw in the narrow cut, how to keep the saw directly in the cut, and how to follow the line.

Then Charlie rested. Dad took over for a few strokes but he tired, so Jimmy grabbed the handle. I pulled up for a stroke, but he immediately jammed the saw when it was at its highest point. I lost my balance and flew off the log down into the sawpit with Jimmy.

Then Charlie showed Jimmy where he had made the mistake. He had overfed the saw on the downstroke, and Charlie explained that the man on the bottom must feed the first half of the saw, while the top man feeds the last half of each downswing.

Jimmy and Charlie took turns working with me, but Dad quit. It was my own fault. One day while he was helping me saw, I called down, "Dad, take off your boots, will you?"

"Why?"

"So I don't have to lift them too when I pull you and the saw up!" I answered.

He exploded. "Saw it by yourself, smartass," he said and stalked off. I apologized, explaining that I was trying to be funny. At my age I wasn't really aware of the aging process. I had no way of understanding how difficult it is when a once-strong man loses his strength to ill health and the passing years. About then I started to learn to keep some of my thoughts to myself.

We finished sawing up the first log in about two and a half days. With Jimmy in the pit, each stroke of the saw cut from three-eighths to half an inch of lumber. Jimmy improved as he learned how to handle the saw, and he gained strength from the exercise. We completed the second log in two days, even though it was bigger. It yielded eight boards, plus some gunwale pieces. I made a drying rack for the lumber and placed thick sticks between the boards about every four feet so air would pass between them.

Planing and jointing the boards didn't take me long. Then I had to select another log on which to build the boat, a lofting platform—a solid floor on which I could draw the lines of the boat, and which I could nail to. I found a dry, light log that was easy to work and hand-hewed it with my axe to flatten it.

Next, marking out the boat bottom took quite a little doing. Charlie, who had built double-ender boats, watched without a word as I planned and marked. Finally he said, "Mind if I show you something? We worked hard sawing that lumber. Be a shame if you spoiled the bottom—that's the critical part of any boat."

I had been hardheaded about that boat. I was building it, and I wanted to build it all my way. "OK," I agreed, reluctantly. My lines did look rather strange, and I wasn't sure what I was doing.

After he showed me what he had in mind I erased my many lines.

My boat was to have a twenty-foot-long bottom. Charlie told me to divide that by three and then use that figure plus eight inches. "That's where you should start the bend, the curve to the bow stem," he said.

That was a big change from my drawing. After that I asked for his advice and Dad's too on other aspects of the boat. They advised, but neither would work on the boat. I didn't realize then just how determined Dad was that Jimmy and I learn to take care of ourselves while he was still around. The way to learn to build a boat, of course, is to build a boat.

Once the lumber was reasonably dry and I had marked my lofting log, my boat progressed quickly. Jimmy helped me all the way and, of course, he learned too. The boat was clinker-built, meaning that we put the bottom sideboard on and lapped the next board over that about an inch and a quarter and so on up the side. Lapboard construction of this type is easy because there is no caulking. Many clinker-built boats are riveted, but I had no rivets, so I clinched the nails and they held.

I made a few mistakes. The sides of the boat were too thin, for in planning for the thickness of the boards, I hadn't allowed enough for the saw cut and for shrinkage in drying, so the completed boards were only three-eighths of an inch thick. That's enough for a boat on the Koyukuk River, but it is a little thin for the rough waters of the Yukon.

We had two gallons of linseed oil left over from building two canvas canoes, so I painted it on as waterproofing and as a preservative, and it did a nice job of sealing the wood. I wanted to turn the boat over almost before the oil dried, I was so eager to add the gunwales, floorboards, and the two seats.

I built the stern square to accept Dad's outboard. But I hadn't allowed enough pitch in the stern, and when the outboard started, it caused the stern to squat too much. I corrected the problem later. I also learned that the old outboard was too heavy for the width of my boat.

I finished my boat just three days before breakup. I have never been prouder of anything I have accomplished than I was of that boat.

11

THE FLOOD

Usual breakup time for the Koyukuk is mid-May, but in 1928 it was late May when at last the ice began to move slowly down the river. But it jammed and stopped moving almost immediately. Those huge, thick, rough blocks of ice, many weighing dozens of tons, were simply too big to float easily downstream. The extremely cold winter had frozen the ice to an unusual thickness and it piled up in a shifting, grinding mass.

Next day the ice moved again, but downstream from our cabin the blocks formed a dam, causing the frigid, rushing water to flow over the bank. "Getting dangerous, Jim," Charlie said, anxiously watching the rising water.

"Sure is," said Dad. "Let's get everything out of the cabin. Put what we can on the roof, the rest in the cache." We scurried, and in an hour the cabin was empty.

Our bearproof cache was a platform fourteen feet above ground in a large spruce tree that had a trunk about two and a half feet in diameter. We always kept some food, and usually a few furs in this cache. When the flood threatened, we stored more food, winter clothing, caribou-skin sleeping bags, an extra stove, traps, tools, and guns there. We knew these valuables would be safe, for that tree had to have been growing there for a century or more.

Our cabin perched on a point of high, gravelly ground, well above any flood level within memory. With the huge ice jam, we figured water might reach the cabin door, maybe even flood the floor. In case the water rose high enough to force us to leave, we put emergency supplies in my new boat and chained the dogs nearby. We had cut a trail to the lakes behind our cabin. That trail could provide an escape route to a hill three-quarters of a mile away, beyond the lakes.

The ice dam shifted. For about three hours, a whole river of ice rushed past our log home. The sight was spectacular. Thick chunks as big as a house tumbled by, rolling, grinding against one another and against the river bottom. Geysers of water spurted high. Ice chunks, forced onto the bank, sheared trees like matchsticks. The sharp edges of ice and the force of the current plowed the bank away. Some giant pieces of ice ran as far as ten feet up on the bank. The noise was a continuous rolling thunder. Jimmy's eyes were as big as egg yolks and mine must have been too.

Again the ice jammed downriver. The rising water soon floated huge hunks of ice and spread them out along the riverbanks. Trees snapped like toothpicks and crashed into the jumble of ice and flooding water. As the water reached our cabin, we boosted the dogs ahead of us and climbed onto the roof.

Before our astonished eyes the water rose swiftly to the level of the roof. Hastily, we piled everything we could, including the whining dogs, a .22 rifle, some clothes, and a little food, into my new boat, the fishnet skiff, and into a canoe. We could scarcely believe that the river could rise so rapidly; it had come up the last four feet in less than two hours. As we paddled toward the hills, we knew that our cabin would soon float. We didn't worry about our cache, for that big tree had survived many a flood.

Upon reaching the hill, we unloaded the supplies we had hastily gathered and waited for a few hours. Then we tried to paddle back to the cabin, but the current, even in the lake, was too swift for us. Muskrats rode swirling ice chunks along the shoreline. They too had been washed out of their houses.

Returning to the hill, we spent two days and a night listening to the destruction. It sounded as if Hell had broken loose along the Koyukuk. Trees crashed to the ground as they were struck by the ice. Great chunks of ice collided and scraped against one another, creating a never-ending roar. Ice rubbing against ice produced high-pitched screeches and low growls.

Suddenly ice downstream broke free and the water dropped swiftly. The level fell so fast—six feet in a few hours—that we wondered whether there would be enough water to float my boat (the heaviest of the three) back through the portage. We loaded up and headed back, reaching the portage without difficulty. I went first, paddling the canoe, but a tangle of fallen trees and huge ice chunks blocked the way.

We went back to another short portage and a creek that flowed into the river half a mile above our cabin. That route was clear, so we followed the openings. Flood water was just emptying from the creek when we arrived at the river. Ice chunks, some as big as our cabin, were stranded high along the banks among the scrubby streamside willows. As we waited on the wet, sloppy shore, our boat nearly went aground. As the water dropped we had to keep moving it into deeper water.

Despite the sogginess we found some half-dry wood and coaxed a fire into burning, to heat some food and coffee and to drive the damp chill from our bones. The river was still choked with ice, so we had to wait for it to clear. Along the banks, ridges of debris indicated that the water had been eight feet or more above normal high-water mark. Tired, we dozed off, sprawled atop our gear in the boat because the ground was too wet to sit on or lie on. We walked down the bank of the Koyukuk, hoping to see our cabin downriver, but piles of ice blocked our view.

Early next morning we maneuvered out of the creek and into the Koyukuk, which was now clear of big ice chunks. Drifting downstream, we avoided the smaller pieces of ice that still floated about. Charlie figured the ice that pushed onto the banks was now sliding back into the river.

Where our cabin had been, we found only a huge pile of ice. And the cache tree had disappeared. Everything we owned, except what we had in the boats, was gone—furs, food, traps, guns, tools, winter clothing—everything. Gone. A clean wipeout: even the gasoline for the *Vixen* was gone.

We were in shock. To Jimmy and me it was almost as if the world had come to an end. We had accomplished so much in our winter on the trapline, and now everything we needed to survive as trappers was gone. Fortunately, we were carrying the money received from selling furs at Tanana.

We drifted downstream to where we had stored the *Vixen* and she too was gone. We found the frayed end of her bow line attached to a freshly splintered spruce stump. Gone too was the barge that we had pushed upriver.

The scene along that desolate stretch of river remains etched in my mind. Broken branches, splintered stumps, downed trees, mud, freshly gouged cutbanks, melting dirty ice chunks—all gave the impression that the world was now a broken-up, filthy, miserable swamp. We were all silent.

We drifted thirty miles downriver to our old cabin at Hog River, where Mom's grave was. No ice jams had formed along that part of the river and water hadn't even gone over the banks. Old Mike Laboski and Ben Keilly had lived in our cabin there while trapping along Hog River that winter, and were getting ready to pull out when we arrived.

"Well, we've at least got a cabin now," Dad said to us, with a sad smile. "That's a start."

Mike and Ben had extra food which they agreed to leave. Charlie examined the supplies, looked the cabin over, and made up his mind.

"I'm going to stay and prospect here this summer. You and the boys go on out and get us reoutfitted," he suggested to Dad.

They talked briefly and decided that the three of us would take the small boats downriver to Nulato where we would try to acquire another power boat for our return. Somehow, we had to catch enough salmon to feed the dogs for another winter. Charlie was unenthusiastic about fishing on the Koyukuk. Fishing on the Yukon was far easier and much more productive.

"Let's see what happens," Charlie said. "I'm sure everything will come together before fall. You have lots of good friends. I'm not going to worry." We decided that in the fall we would fix up our old store and cabin at Hog River where we would live during the next few years while trapping. We left our lead dog with Charlie for companionship and took the others with us.

"I think it's awful to leave Charlie behind like this," I said to Dad.

"Charlie has the gold bug," Dad explained. "He's wanted to find gold ever since he hit the Dawson country thirty-five years ago. He wants to prospect Sun Mountain." Sun Mountain was a nearby ridge that Charlie had often talked about.

We left old Charlie on the riverbank as we drifted downstream. He wore a wide-brimmed hat, a canvas jacket, worn pants, and rubber-bottomed leather shoepacks. His gray hair showed below his hat, and his weathered face showed calm determination. I hated to leave him, and wondered if we would ever see him again. He waved once, then stood watching until we rounded the first bend. I thought he looked lonesome.

Drifting downstream we stopped at likely lakes and back sloughs to hunt muskrats with the .22 rifle. At Koyukuk Station we learned that Nulato and Koyukuk Station residents had also experienced a bad flood at breakup. We weren't surprised, for breakup floods aren't unusual along the Yukon River.

Trader John Evans told us that Joe Stickman had pulled a boat off the ice that might be the *Vixen*. Encouraged, we went on to Nulato to see Joe. He owned a large powerboat with a twelve-horsepower four-cylinder Universal engine—a big engine for those days. He had used it to pull the runaway boat ashore below Nulato. Sure enough, he had salvaged our *Vixen*. She had been found perched atop a drifting block of ice. One side was caved in, the propeller and rudder were sheared off, and the pilot house was gone, but the engine seemed undamaged.

"How much do I owe you, Joe?" Dad asked.

"Is $10 too much?" Joe asked. Joe had paid two men $5 each to help him, and he had used some gasoline in towing the *Vixen* ashore.

Ed Allard was about to take the mail boat up the Koyukuk on its first trip of the year, so Dad sent along some grub and a note for Charlie. We pitched a tent on the beach beside the *Vixen* two miles below Nulato and set up a saw pit so we could whipsaw the lumber we needed. John Tilley and Bill Dalquist loaned us tools and we worked long hours to rebuild the ice-battered boat.

Joe Stickman liked the twenty-foot boat I had built so well he asked Dad if he could buy it. "It's Sidney's boat. You'll have to talk to him about it," he told Joe.

I was playing baseball with the Nulato team one day when Joe came to see me. "I'd like to buy your boat, Sidney," he said.

"How much will you give for it?" I asked.

"Old Ambrose makes big gas boats for $150. Your boat's a lot smaller. How about $100?" he offered. One hundred dollars was a fortune to me.

"My wife wants that little boat pretty bad. She wants to use it for fishing."

I thought about it. His wife, Lucy, was always good to us. Just that day she had treated us to a big feed of fried king salmon. And Joe had helped us by saving the *Vixen*. Nevertheless, I hated to sell my boat.

My turn came to bat. After my base hit, a line drive into left field brought me around second and third bases. Joe caught up with me again after I crossed home plate.

"How about it?" he asked.

"All right," I said. "I don't really want to sell it, but you helped us. Now it's my turn to help you."

I was learning that life wasn't all dollars and cents—that business can be tinged with feelings for the other guy. After all, I could build another boat.

In about five days we launched the *Vixen*. Her engine ran fine, and she didn't leak. She had no cabin, but that could wait.

A trader at Nulato, Pop Russell, knew we had been wiped out and that we were low on cash. He had heard we were going to fish for salmon, so he offered to buy dried dog (chum) salmon from us for six cents a pound. He had a mail contract, and he needed enough dried fish to feed his mail team.

Russell's offer was an opportunity for us to earn money, but we would have to work hard. We knew nothing about making a fish wheel, which is how we planned to catch our fish. Johnny Sommers and Charlie Evans offered to help us. Local fishermen agreed that Devil's Island would be a good site for a fish camp, and no one claimed the island, about four miles below Nulato, as a fishing location.

In two days we collected raft logs for the fish wheel, as well as some green poles. With plenty of help and advice from experts, we built the fish wheel the next day.

The fish wheel is a simple device. Two wire baskets and two paddles, like four spokes on a wheel, radiate from a large wooden axle. River current turns the device, and as it rotates, the baskets scoop fish from the river and deposit them in a collecting box. The fish wheel is effective because salmon follow the riverbank as they swim upstream toward spawning grounds. When placed directly over a place where salmon pass, each revolution of a basket has a chance of picking up fish.

We used the *Vixen* and our canoe to move the fish wheel to Devil's Island, where we cut brush to clear space for a camp and a smokehouse. The story of our being wiped out at Batza Creek had spread up and down the river. Travelers on the Yukon stopped to see us and have coffee; many pitched in to help for a while. In a few days we were ready to fish.

We set the fish wheel to turning and almost immediately started catching chum salmon. Charlie Evans taught us how to cut the fish for dog food and Jimmy and I quickly learned the technique. We cut and split the fish and kept Dad more than busy hanging them on the drying racks we had built. With practice we were able to process 800 six- to eight-pound salmon a day. One dried male chum salmon from the Yukon weighs from a pound to a pound and a half; females weigh from six to eight ounces. A salmon's weight varies with the distance the fish is from salt water. By the Fourth of July, we had 5,000 salmon dried or hanging on the drying racks. We smoked some of the choicer fish to eat ourselves.

Jimmy and I wanted to participate in the festivities of the Fourth of

July at Nulato. That morning we began working very early and cut and split 500 salmon. Then we paddled our canoe upstream to Nulato, where we competed in races, baseball, jumping contests, and other games.

A dance that night capped the celebration. "It's time you started dancing, Sidney," said Lily Stickman, Joe's younger sister, as she grabbed me by the collar and dragged me onto the dance floor. And dance I did! After that they couldn't keep me off the dance floor.

Jimmy and I paddled back to camp late that night. It was light, so we immediately set about cutting and splitting the afternoon catch of 350 salmon. The days of July fled, and soon we had prepared 10,000 chum salmon. We needed at least 2,500 to feed our own dogs during the coming winter. The remainder were promised to Pop Russell.

A friend gave me two fine young sled dogs. Toby Patsy gave Jimmy another. (Patsy wrote "Eagle Island Blues," a song popular along the Yukon, and eventually a popular recording all over the United States.) With the addition of these three our team numbered eight, which Dad thought was too many, so Jimmy and I split and dried another 500 salmon to make sure we would have enough food.

We bundled up Pop Russell's 6,000 pounds of dried fish and hauled them to his warehouse. Our income from the fish was about $360. We were still short of the $3,000 needed to pay for a year's outfit (roughly the equivalent of $25,000 today). We had about $2,000 combined from sale of furs at Tanana the previous winter and from the salmon sold to Pop Russell. Dad didn't want to ask for credit, and decided we should try to manage on what we could pay for. We could go to Hughes for supplies by dogsled if need be.

When Dad gave Pop his list, Pop snorted, "Hell, I thought you said you lost everything last spring. This won't take you through half the winter."

"I don't want to put anything on the books, Pop," Dad said.

"Don't worry about it. I'll give you what you need. Pay what you can. I'll catch up with you next spring. Keep some money so you can buy winter gear if you need to," he advised. We left Nulato owing him $1,400, a huge debt in 1928. Pop Russell was a prince.

Another bit of sweetening came when my uncle Hog River Johnny found our barge in a back slough at Cutoff. He arranged for Ed Allard to tow it to us with the mail boat on his downstream run. My uncle had heard we were fishing to make a stake; he knew we would need the barge on our return to Hog River.

We left Nulato on the first day of August, our barge loaded with a good winter outfit, plenty of good dogs, good grub—everything. As usual, everyone in Nulato was on the beach to see us off. We traveled day and night, moving northeast up the beautiful Koyukuk. Dad, Jimmy, and I took turns steering. Memories of the sodden, ice-smashed desolation we had left the previous spring grew dim. The riverbanks now appeared normal, with high green grass, leafed-out trees, clear tributaries, and clean-washed sand and gravel beaches.

We arrived at Hog River in four and a half days. Charlie recognized the Model T engine's steady roar long before we came into sight. Wearing a mile-wide smile on his weathered face, he stood on the bank waiting in the exact spot we had left him the previous spring. He was thin, and his long uncut gray hair almost flowed over his collar, but he cheerfully said, "I never doubted that you'd come back with a good outfit."

I often think back to that challenging year filled with learning experiences for two boys, and realize how from those events I learned that hard work and determination pay off. Eventually, I began to view that period as a wonderful time.

12

SNARING A GRIZZLY

✦

After arriving at Hog River, we prepared for the winter ahead. We built or rebuilt four cabins, and cut enough firewood at all of them to last through the winter. We girdled nearby trees so that dead, dry trees would be available for firewood in the future.

When the fall waterfowl migration was on, we killed many fat geese and ducks and dried the meat for winter use. Of the dozen or so varieties of wild berries found in the Koyukuk, we commonly used about eight—blueberry, lowbush cranberry (lingonberry), highbush cranberry, bog cranberry, bearberry, crowberry (also called black-berry), cloudberry, and rosehips.

That fall we picked forty gallons of blueberries and preserved them with layers of sugar in wooden kegs. We picked another ten gallons of lowbush cranberries for preserves, plus an assortment of other vari-eties. We picked and dried a large supply of mushrooms. In late fall we were still catching a few pike, whitefish, and worn-out salmon in gillnets set in back eddies along the Koyukuk River. We split and hung these fish to dry, since besides being excellent dog food, they made good bait for marten and mink sets.

One night a large animal raided our fish supply, knocking down fish racks, scattering fish, and carrying some off. Our chained sled dogs raised a big ruckus. At daylight I followed the animal's tracks and found where it had prowled back and forth within view of the fish racks, probably deciding on a safe route to the tempting food.

"A black bear, Dad?" I asked.

"I don't think so," he said, thoughtfully, peering at the indistinct tracks. "Black bears are eating berries now, getting ready for den-up. I think it's a grizzly."

A grizzly! The strongest, most dangerous animal in the region, grizzlies were uncommon in the broad valley of the Koyukuk. They are larger, stronger, and generally more aggressive than black bears, and the Koyukon people treat them with great respect. I had caught a brief glimpse of a grizzly a few miles from our cabin a few weeks earlier. Perhaps this was the same one.

"I'm going to catch it, Dad," I said.

"Go ahead," he encouraged.

I searched my mind for a plan, and recalled the steel cable that warden-pilot Sam White had given me. One day the previous summer while we were at Nulato, a Swallow biplane had roared down the river, circled the village, and then, because there was no airport, landed at the ball field. White, one of Alaska's pioneer aviators and the world's first flying game warden, was liked and respected by almost everyone—a rare game warden indeed. Unfortunately for Sam, the Nulato ball field was too small for his Swallow; in landing, he ran into the ballpark fence, bending his propeller.

I helped him straighten the prop and find items he needed for the repairs, and I ran errands for him when he needed it. When his prop was repaired, he unloaded his plane to lighten it for takeoff. Included in his castoffs was some 3/16-inch steel airplane control cable, which he gave me. I watched, fascinated, as Sam took off from the ballpark and flew on upriver. Airplanes were a rare and exciting novelty in 1928.

To attempt to catch the grizzly, I fashioned a snare out of some of the cable Sam had given me and set it between two birch trees where the raider had walked. That night we listened tensely, waiting for the fish-stealer to return. The night remained silent, and we finally went to bed.

At dawn we were suddenly awakened by the roars of a bear, yelps of the dogs, and snapping of brush and trees. I hotfooted it out of the cabin, grabbing Dad's .30-40 Winchester lever-action rifle that had been propped next to the door. The snared bear was mowing down birch trees like grass. I had securely fastened the end of the steel cable to a stump.

As I rushed to the spot, all I could see was a mass of brown hair flying back and forth. The bawling of the furious bear raised the hairs on the back of my neck. Trees and branches snapped and whipped about. The dogs screamed and lunged at the ends of their chains. It was bedlam. I fired the big rifle into the lunging bear. For a thirteen-year-old the .30-40 kicked like a mule, but I didn't even notice. The charging slowed. I worked another cartridge into the barrel, aimed, and fired again.

"Shoot again, before he charges!" Dad yelled.

I stood staring at the bear in awe, wondering why it was still on its feet, and then fired several more shots into it. Finally the bear fell, and I started to run toward it.

"Stop! Sidney, stop! Keep back!" Dad shouted.

I then received a forceful lecture on why one should not approach a dangerous animal immediately after shooting it. To emphasize the point, Dad wouldn't let Jimmy or me go near the bear until we had eaten breakfast. I didn't eat much, and what I ate went down fast.

The bear appeared huge to me, but Dad said it was a small grizzly. The animal was old, with worn teeth and a deeply scarred face. We skinned him and tried to eat some of the meat, but the flavor was so strong that we couldn't handle it. Even our sled dogs didn't want it. We finally tossed the unused meat into the river.

Just before freezeup, Little Sammy and my aunt Big Sophy Sam came by and spent a night with us. Little Sammy spotted the skin of the grizzly. "Where you get?" he asked Dad.

"Sidney got him," Dad explained, relating how I had set the snare and then shot the bear.

"You're pretty foxy, Sidney," he said to me. "You use head. You slow big animal down so you can shoot. You pretty young to get big animal already. I was much older before I killed one. That's when they said I could have a partner—a woman to live with."

Not once did he use the words "brown bear" or "grizzly bear." He was a traditional Koyukon who followed the old ways. No respectful Koyukon ever spoke directly of a "grizzly" or "brown bear." It was always "that big animal."

I didn't know what Little Sammy was driving at, but I think Dad suspected. After much talk about the boat I had built, the salmon I had caught on the Yukon River, the furs I had trapped the previous winter, and, finally, the "big animal" I had snared and shot, Little Sammy came to the point:

"You are young, but we have to say that you have earned the right to have a partner, a woman, anytime you want."

My jaw dropped, and Dad and Charlie grinned. Little Sammy had made his point and dropped the subject. For months afterward I was teased about Little Sammy's comments.

"Ya got your lady partner picked out yet, Sidney?" Charlie would ask, with a grin. Dad and Jimmy had their fun, too. Girls were still a mystery to me, and I didn't appreciate their teasing.

One cold winter day my uncle Weaselheart arrived with our mail from Hughes, and to pay a visit—so we thought. Actually, he had made the trip to inform Dad that he and other family members had selected a woman for me. Little Sammy had told him about the grizzly.

Weaselheart, one of my mother's brothers, was about four feet eight, heavy set, with bluish-colored lips. The name "Weaselheart" was a literal translation of his Koyukon name. He was originally known as "Little Peter from Hog River." He was a man without fear.

As soon as he arrived at our cabin, Weaselheart asked me to tell him about the grizzly. After I had modestly recounted the incident, he asked, "Have you ever caught a black one?" (meaning a black bear).

I had killed two black bears—one in its den during the winter when I had stumbled onto it while setting marten traps, the other while blueberry picking. "Two," I told him.

"Good," he said.

Then he told Dad about the "woman" he and other family members had chosen for me. She was a twelve-year-old girl. "This is the Indian way, Jim," Weaselheart explained to Dad.

Dad exploded, "Indian way or not, he's just out of diapers. How in hell is he going to support a woman, let alone himself? Let's at least wait until he's dry behind the ears. It's up to Sidney to decide who and when."

"But Jim," Weaselheart said patiently, "I've paid $5 to the girl's parents for Sidney's right to marry her, because he is qualified. He has proven himself to be a man."

The custom of granting the privilege of marriage to a young man when he killed a "big animal" was a carryover from the days when a Koyukon man killed a bear with bow and arrow or spear, thus proving that he was brave and capable—a far cry from what I had done.

It wasn't common for relatives to arrange a marriage without speaking to the father of the groom. That's probably why Weaselheart talked to Dad the way he did—he knew Dad wasn't intimately familiar with the custom and he thought that Dad might accept the arrangement if it were completed in advance.

I knew the girl but had never thought of marrying her. I stuttered a bit, and finally said, "Thank you, Uncle, but I think Dad is right. I'm not ready to support a woman yet." For some years after that, the girl would hardly speak to me. She was forced to marry an old man, and she blamed me because I hadn't accepted her as my partner.

Forced marriages generally occurred when young girls were given or sold to older men who had lost their wives. There was generally no shortage of women. Arranged marriages, such as the one Weaselheart organized for me, were also fairly common.

Again I was subjected to much kidding from Dad, Charlie, and Jimmy, and now they had a name to throw at me. "Sidney, do you suppose Dorothy (not her real name) likes her eggs sunny-side up or over easy?" Charlie might ask at breakfast as I was dishing up his food. Or Jimmy would crack, "Your parka is torn, Sidney. Better get your wife busy with a needle." I was glad when they tired of it.

Trapping that winter was poor, and our furs brought only $2,800. Fur prices had plunged, due to the Depression. If the preceding winter was cold, that of 1928–29, if anything, was colder. There were weak chum salmon returns to the Koyukuk in 1932, and for a few years after that—probably due to the terrible winters of '27–28 and '28–29. Many of the creeks had frozen to the bottom, killing salmon eggs and fry that were in the gravel.

The first sign we saw of the Depression came in the spring of 1929 when the value of muskrat skins suddenly dropped. Dominic Vernetti, who was having a hard time himself, offered a dollar for three muskrat skins in trade, or twenty-five cents each, cash. Trappers who had built up credit with him the previous year would get a dollar for a skin, the price for a muskrat then. Traders often acted as bankers for residents of the Yukon and Koyukuk. Folks could leave cash credit on the books and take it out later in either trade or cash for the amount they had sold him at the time.

Hard economic times had little impact on our lives, for we depended largely upon the land for our food, shelter, and heat. We planted potatoes, cabbage, carrots, and other vegetables at Hog River. I convinced Dad that I knew how to make a fish trap like I had seen built and used at Anvik, so we built one under my supervision. We fished with it at the mouth of nearby Clear Creek, a tributary to Hog River, to catch our dog food as well as for our own food. There wasn't sufficient current at Clear Creek for a fish wheel, and we were after whitefish, pike, and burbot—fish that a fish wheel seldom catches.

At Koyukuk Station we paid Pop Russell what we owed him, and left about $1,000 on deposit for our fall outfit.

"Order what you need—even more than a thousand dollars worth. I know you'll pay. Don't short yourself. I'll send it all up with Wilfred Evans on his last freight trip in August," Pop promised.

Despite stories of traders who became rich off the Natives along the Yukon and Koyukuk, few actually left Alaska with any money. Those I have known—John Evans, Dominic Vernetti, Pop Russell, John Sommers, Andy Vachon, Tom Devaney—died in their stores, and most died poor.

During the Depression, storekeepers had a lot invested in both Natives and whites, for "jawbone" (credit) was a way of life. Most trappers and rural residents paid their bills once a year, as we did. The traders often grubstaked prospectors, and more often than not they had no return on that money. Any profit storekeepers made commonly disappeared because they helped so many people by giving credit for which they were never paid.

People in Koyukuk country often said that Dominic would steal the shirt off of one fellow, and give the shirt off his back to someone else. Perhaps so, but when the chips were down, he was there to help. Once Koyukon Bobby Vent was so sick he couldn't walk, and was down to about ninety pounds. He had no money, and no one in the village of Huslia where he lived had any money to help. Several of us wrote to Dominic asking if he'd foot the bill to fly Bobby to the hospital at Tanana. "We'll pay you back next spring, or this winter, with fur," we all promised.

I put Bobby on the *Mudhen*, the name we had given to the mail plane, which flew him to Koyukuk. On his arrival, Dominic paid his way to continue on to Tanana, and even gave him some spending money.

Hard times or not, when someone needed help, Dominic, and most of the other traders I have known, could be counted on.

13

ON OUR OWN

✸

After freezeup in the fall of 1929, Charlie and I went upstream to
Batza River where we spent several days looking for fur sign. Trapping had been poor the previous winter, and we were looking for
better prospects.

One day we split up—I searched the country in one direction,
Charlie in another. In addition to fur sign, we looked for signs of mice,
because when mice are plentiful, fur animals that feed on them are
usually abundant. I found enough fur and mouse sign to be encouraged, but that night I also had other news. "I found a fresh moose
track today, Charlie," I reported. That was an event to celebrate, for
no moose then lived in the Koyukuk valley.

"We'll get that moose tomorrow," Charlie promised. He loved to
hunt, and often told stories of his market hunting days in Dawson
country in '97.

"How do you know that?" I asked.

"Did it run?"

"No," I answered.

"Did you see only one track?"

"Yes."

"It's a cow," he said.

Early the next morning Charlie led me up the Batza, not bothering
to follow the moose tracks. We stayed high on the south slopes,
watching the brushy north slope across the valley. By mid-morning we
hadn't seen the moose.

"They'll be lying down now," Charlie said. We made lunch and
rested until about 1:30. I was impatient, and wanted to continue with
the moose hunt.

"It'll be 2:30 or later before they get up," Charlie told me.

"What do you mean 'they'?" I asked. "I saw only one track."

"I'm sure it's a cow with a calf," he said, confidently.

About 3:30 we spotted two moose—a cow and an almost grown calf. Amazed at Charlie's intuition, I stared at him. We quietly worked our way out on a point closer to the moose, which were browsing on the opposite slope.

The cow seemed to sense our presence, for she looked alertly in our direction. "About 600 yards," Charlie muttered, as he raised the leaf sight on the .30-40. The distance looked to be about a mile to me—I couldn't imagine anyone shooting anything at that distance. Nevertheless, Charlie stood with a forever-long aim, the rifle resting against a little cottonwood tree. When he finally pulled the trigger, that old cannon roared, and the cow dropped like a stone. The calf fled.

"I got her right behind the ear," Charlie said, straight-faced.

"How do you know that?" I asked, awed by the shot.

"That's where I aimed."

Sure enough, the bullet had caught that cow right behind the ear, and for a time at least, I thought Charlie was the world's greatest moose hunter and shooter.

After I had a few years of hunting experience, I figured out his "miracle" shot. The front bead on that Winchester almost covered the entire moose at that distance, so there was no way he could have aimed behind the ear. When the moose fell like a log, it told him where the bullet had hit. As for predicting that it was a cow with a calf, Charlie knew moose habits. The infrequent moose that wandered into the Koyukuk in those years were mostly cows and cows are usually accompanied by a calf.

It was to be years before I saw another moose in the Koyukuk. We feasted on that fine fat cow all that winter. Having such good fresh meat was a welcome change from the small game, fish, and black bear we usually depended upon. The moosehide, hair on, made a warm, comfortable mattress.

That winter was milder than the previous two, but with the low prices for furs we made little money, although our catches were good. Dad's health continued to deteriorate, and there wasn't anything he could do about it. It was clear that he could not continue to live on the trapline because the work was too hard for him.

The trapping year of 1930–31 was like the previous year; fur prices were low, because the Depression was in full swing. We subscribed to *The Saturday Evening Post*, which I remember cost five cents a copy and a year's subscription of fifty-two issues was $2.50. We also subscribed to *The Literary Digest*. In these magazines we read about the many unemployed in the States, how men had to leave their families to bum their way around the country looking for work, and about lines of unemployed men at soup kitchens. I used to love Western story magazines, and I subscribed to three of these old pulps. When we picked up our mail each year, I always looked forward to reading the previous year's magazines.

During those lean years for others, we felt lucky, for we ate well, with most of our food coming from the land. We had our log cabin home and the equipment we needed to hunt, fish, and trap. While our furs brought little money, we certainly didn't suffer.

When we took the *Vixen* downriver with our furs in the spring of 1931, Dad announced that he'd decided to quit the trapline. "You've learned enough to take care of yourselves," he told Jimmy and me. "You can go back to the trapline alone if you want. I won't worry about you." He got a job as a guard in the jail at Nulato, and old Charlie Swanson left for Canada and disappeared from our lives.

Although this was quite a change for us and we would miss our Dad and Charlie, Jimmy and I loved the trapline life and we were excited at the prospect of being on our own. Trapping was an important and rewarding way of life; few other ways existed for making a living on the Koyukuk and Lower Yukon. And while I was only sixteen and Jimmy was fourteen, we knew we could manage.

Although Jimmy's health had improved, during that first year when we were alone, I always tried to do most of the heavy work. I ran the longer traplines, and broke trail when we traveled together and the going was tough. Jimmy hated it. "Why do you always baby me, Sidney?" he often asked. "I'm all right."

"I don't want you to get sick on me out here in the woods," I told him. We were many days from help by dog team or riverboat.

Jimmy seemed to get stronger as the months went by. We always ate well, for Dad and Charlie had taught us how to cook and instilled in us good eating habits. We had plenty of game meat and fish, and in summer and fall we always had an abundance of fresh vegetables from our garden. Both of us had learned how to make bread during our first winter at Batza River.

We shared work. One week I baked twelve loaves of bread at a time; the next week Jimmy did the honors. Whoever returned to the cabin first from the trapline or other work did the cooking. Neither of us ever waited for the other guy to do the work. And we kept tidy cabins. We acquired a lifelong habit of washing dishes immediately after eating. Our cabins were always comfortably warm, and usually we had plenty of rest. And with all the work we did daily that was necessary to stay alive, we got plenty of exercise.

And we had fun.

Spring was always a special time. In late April, snow still covers the ground in the Koyukuk valley. Then one day, suddenly, warm air arrives, and with it come the geese, ducks, cranes, robins, thrushes, and many other birds, and soon after that, breakup on the Koyukuk River occurs.

One day after breakup, but while ice was still floating down the river, I was in an especially exuberant mood, delighted that spring had arrived. I undressed and jumped into the frigid Koyukuk in front of our cabin. Jimmy joined me, and we swam among floating ice cakes, laughing at our silliness and enjoying the feeling of the cold water.

That spring we whipsawed lumber, hand-planed it, and built a thirty-four-foot cabin boat with a ten-foot beam which we called the *Ark*. It was a great improvement over the battered *Vixen*. We installed a twelve-horsepower Kermath marine engine, and built in bunks and a folding table. From that time on, when Jimmy and I traveled to various fishing or hunting spots on the Koyukuk River, we could live on the *Ark* instead of having to camp on the beach. With this big boat we could travel comfortably on the Yukon River as well. And we could push or pull a barge loaded with our sled dogs and freight. We used the *Ark* for more than a dozen years before losing her in the Yukon River flood of 1945.

During that spring of 1932 we practiced canoe racing on the Koyukuk in front of our cabin. We had one good fast canoe and a second, slower, load-carrying canoe. Koyukuk and Yukon canoes like ours were locally made in all shapes and sizes, averaging about fifteen feet in length. Commonly framed up with birch or spruce ribs, the sides were quarter-inch thick lumber whipsawed from spruce and the bottoms were about five-eighths-inch thick. Canvas was stretched over the wood and painted.

Jimmy and I took turns racing in the two canoes, but the one who paddled the fast one always won in a race. I didn't realize the skill we were acquiring as paddlers until that summer.

Jimmy and I ran the *Ark* to Nulato to sell our furs, to buy groceries, and to see Dad. No matter how many times we made these trips we always enjoyed them, and for the hundreds of miles we cruised the Koyukuk, we looked forward to seeing what was around the next bend. Black bears frequented the riverbank; ducks and geese were always overhead; songbirds sang among the trees and flitted around us. Beaver, muskrat, and otter often appeared in the clear river water.

We were at Nulato on July fourth, when the village celebrated with athletic contests, picnics and community dinners, and an all-night dance. Jimmy surprised everyone, including me, when he won the 100-yard dash. He was a bit shorter than I was, but he was wiry and quick. About twenty people entered the race, including adults. Jimmy got off to a fast start and stayed in the lead all the way.

The highlight of the day was a canoe race over and back across the broad Yukon River. Joe Stickman practically owned the Fourth of July canoe race at Nulato. He had never lost.

Our friend Toby Patsy asked my approval for him to loan his canoe to Jimmy for the race. I hesitated, still feeling responsible for my brother, and always trying to keep him from taking risks. "Look at my canoe," Toby suggested.

The slender, well-shaped craft had a seventeen-foot bottom, and was only about ten inches wide just aft of the center, with a nice long taper at both ends. I stepped in and paddled a short way. That canoe really moved when I leaned into the paddle.

"I know you'd win the race in that canoe, but I found it first," Jimmy piped up when I came ashore. That settled it.

Everyone in town was on the bank of the Yukon to cheer the paddlers on as about fifteen canoes of various sizes and styles lined up for the contest. Dad and I grinned at each other when, at the crack of the starting gun, Jimmy's canoe leaped ahead. He stayed in the lead all the way across, made a quick turnaround, and was half a dozen lengths ahead of the nearest canoe when he reached the shore at Nulato.

Joe was a good sport. "I never dreamed that a skinny kid like that would beat me," he said with a grin. "You Huntington boys are good at everything." For two youngsters who lived on their own, such praise was encouraging, especially coming from Joe, who excelled at everything he did. I get a warm glow when I recall those words.

Dad was proud of us too. He carefully inspected the *Ark* and pronounced it first class. "I knew you boys would do all right trapping. I didn't dream you would build a fine big boat like this though," he said.

Back upriver, we cut stacks of firewood for the coming winter at our trapline shelter cabins, which were roughly ten to fifteen miles apart. Because we had only five dogs that season, we walked most of the time. One of us would take two large dogs and a small sled and walk from trap to trap on one line; the other would take the three smaller dogs and a small sled and walk another trapline.

There is always something interesting to see on a trapline. A frequent companion was the tame little-headed hawk owl that is commonly out during the day. This friendly fellow perches atop small spruces, waiting until a traveler arrives. He then flies ahead and lands, waiting for the traveler to catch up. He'll go on in his silent way, to wait again, watching with his wise yellow eyes, swiveling his head about. Another friendly bird is the gray jay, or camprobber. Stop for lunch or to make camp, and suddenly, silently, a camprobber is there, perched nearby, watching, ready to steal food, seemingly curious to see what is going on.

By Christmas we had caught more than 200 mink, mostly good-sized animals. For some reason mink were everywhere that winter, eating anything they could catch, including one another. I couldn't figure out why there were so many, and thought then that perhaps they bred twice a year. I know now that mink breed only once a year. After that season, I never again saw them in such numbers. By spring we had 300 fine mink furs.

We lived by hunting, and we killed many bears during our years on the trapline, for we ranged far and needed much meat. The finest black bear meat comes from an animal taken in its den during winter. These bears also carry loads of highly treasured fat, which can be cut from the carcass after skinning, like removing a blanket, leaving only lean meat. Some blankets of bear fat weigh up to 100 pounds, although the average is probably around forty or fifty, depending on the size of the bear and the abundance of fall blueberries.

We rendered the bear fat—that is, we heated it on a stove until it melted and could be poured into containers where it would keep fresh for months, especially when frozen. Pieces of dried fish dipped into melted bear grease is a delicacy eaten like potato chips. We also ate melted bear grease with low-fat fish and with lean game meats.

Jimmy became fascinated by the traditional Koyukon Indian way of hunting for black bears in their dens. Dad was especially fond of black bear meat, which no doubt contributed to Jimmy's enthusiasm. He was proud of his bear-hunting prowess, much of which he learned from our uncle Hog River Johnny. I thought he took unnecessary chances, like the time he crawled into a den head first to kill a bear.

One shot in the dark, one bear. End of story.

The best bear den areas in the Koyukuk are in low, rolling hills, around big lakes, creek banks, wherever there is cover. Experts—and in time Jimmy became an expert—can quickly identify the sign that indicates a black bear is ready to den. Some can even tell how close a den is likely to be from such sign. Female black bears like to use blueberry bushes as bedding in their dens, hence a torn-up blueberry patch in early winter can indicate a female black bear den is near. Dark, shiny droppings of a certain consistency are typical of bears when they are ready to enter their den for winter.

Our uncle Hog River Johnny told us where to look for black bear dens. When we found one, we would walk close and stand by the entrance until the bear stuck his head out. Then we'd shoot him. When leaving a den, black bears are usually trying to escape, so there was seldom a confrontation.

The more aggressive grizzly bears were another matter. They may charge from their den and attack an intruder. We could tell what kind of bear we were dealing with by the color of the hair found near a den entrance, and sometimes by the tracks if they weren't covered by snow.

Jimmy found himself in real trouble at a black bear den one October. He found bear sign and followed the tracks to the den. He shoveled snow away with a snowshoe, but he still couldn't tell where the opening was. He probed with his rifle until it broke through the loose snow and into the den. Still he felt no bear.

He found a plug of dead grass and branches, which he pulled out. With more nerve than I would have had, he crawled into the narrow entrance, shoving his .30–30 ahead. Still no sign of bear. He stretched his arm and rifle as far as he could reach. That brought action.

A bear growled and slammed the rifle down, knocking it from Jimmy's grasp. Jimmy didn't argue. Leaving the rifle, he wriggled out, backwards. He could imagine all too clearly what would have happened if the bear had grabbed his arm.

Safely outside the den, Jimmy decided to use another age-old Koyukon technique to take the bear. With his axe he chopped an opening in the top of the den, expecting the bear to shove his head through the hole so he could kill it with the axe.

When the hole appeared big enough for the bear's head, Jimmy released the four dogs from his sled, thinking the dogs would keep the bear off of him if it broke out of the den. He climbed atop the den again and swung the axe into the hole he had made. The axe struck a bear, and the furious animal erupted from the den with a roar. Blood, dirt, and bedding flew. Before Jimmy could move, most of the angry, bleeding bear was out of the hole, within a few feet. Now in self-defense, he swung the axe, cutting deeply into the bear's head.

The dogs, yapping with frantic excitement, didn't come to help him. Puzzled, he glanced over his shoulder and saw that a second bear had emerged from the den and was on its hind legs, facing the attacking dogs. Jimmy saw it strike one dog with a powerful front paw and toss it fifteen feet through the air. The other three dogs tried to maneuver behind the bear to attack, where they could escape the slashing claws. Everything happened in split seconds. Before Jimmy could turn to deal with the bear in front of him, a third bear rushed from the den snarling.

Jimmy had his hands full.

The first bear, injured by the blow to his head, dropped to all fours. Swiftly, Jimmy chopped through its backbone, paralyzing the animal. Figuring the dogs would keep their bear occupied, Jimmy turned his attention to the third bear. The animal stood on hind legs, claws outstretched, ready to attack. Jimmy leaped to it and with a swipe of the axe split its stomach open, spilling bloody, steaming viscera onto the snow. The bear's claws ripped through Jimmy's heavy parka sleeve and tore his arm. Ignoring the pain, he whacked again at the bear's belly, completing the job of disemboweling it. Jimmy jumped aside as the animal fell forward in the snow.

The three dogs, growling and screaming, were still fighting the second bear. Jimmy leaped at the animal with his axe, and sliced its nose to the bone. Quick as thought, the bear slapped the axe out of Jimmy's hands, sending it end-over-end until it disappeared in the deep snow.

Weaponless now, Jimmy remembered his rifle inside the den and dove into the entrance. The dogs were still worrying the bear, but now the bear was after Jimmy. The enraged animal clawed Jimmy's boots as Jimmy crawled into the darkness, frantically feeling for his rifle and praying no more bears lurked inside the den.

Flat on his stomach, he located the rifle and half turned to face the bear, which now blocked the den entrance. The bear was close when Jimmy fired. The rifle blast inside the cave temporarily deafened him, but the bullet killed the bear.

It took some time and a lot of effort to shove the heavy carcass out of the way so he could crawl out of the den. The big, limp bear was like a cork in a bottle. The first bear, paralyzed with a severed spine, lay growling nearby, and Jimmy finished it with another shot. The dog that the bear had flung through the air was so badly injured that he had to shoot it to put it out of its misery. It was one of his favorites, and for months afterward he blamed himself for the dog's death.

Jimmy was covered with blood, and blood stained the snow for thirty feet around the den. Except for deep claw slashes on his arm, he was unhurt.

During the years on the trapline, I learned to love the challenge of building useful items. I made many snowshoes, using techniques I learned from Eklutna John. I also built many dogsleds of split birch. Dogsleds cannot be screwed, bolted, or nailed together because such joints will not withstand the twisting and jolting of the trail. Instead, *babiche* lashing is used. After soaking, the wet rawhide shrinks as it dries, tightening the joint. *Babiche* allows a sled to bend and twist without splitting the stressed wood as it bounces over rough trails.

Jimmy and I whipsawed many feet of lumber, planed it, and made sturdy tables, chairs, cabinets, and shelves for our cabin, as well as more boats.

I decided that I wanted to play a musical instrument. We had no battery radios in the early years, but we did have a windup phonograph with some hoedown records, the kind of music played at village dances where the violin and guitar are popular.

The Koyukon people began playing fiddles in the late 1800s, obtaining instruments from Canadian trappers. Later, Irish and Scottish gold rushers brought more violins and more fiddle songs. And Koyukon people composed many songs of their own. Most Indian fiddlers learn to play by ear; many never learn to read music.

I found time between trapping chores to make a guitar. It had a good sound, but it was not as handsome as a store-bought instrument. Next, I made a violin, basing my design on a picture in a Sears, Roebuck and Co. catalog. To make glue for it, I boiled a moose hoof. The handle was maple, the fingerboard ebony, the top was birch, and the back and sides were spruce. I colored the spruce by treating it with acid.

I worked for days steaming, bending, carving, and sanding, closely following the design of the picture. In the spring, I ordered strings and a bow from Sears. For many years, Jimmy and I played that violin at dances all up and down the Yukon. My moose-hoof glue didn't hold well, and in wet weather the violin started to come apart, so I bought some good commercial glue, reglued it, and we used it again for a while. But one summer I left it at our cabin at Hog River, and while I was gone the roof leaked and the violin got wet and came apart again, and I never reassembled it.

On days too stormy or too cold for working our traplines, and between trapping seasons, I used to study mechanical magazines, where I read about the universal inventors' goal of creating a perpetual motion machine. About 1931 I decided I could solve that age-old problem; my machine would run forever.

I spent months designing various parts, soldering and whatnot to shape a wheel-like contraption with arms that flopped out on one side and folded as they came up on the other. The weight and movement of the arms caused it to turn continually. My "invention" did quite well; once it turned on its own for almost an hour. But it wasn't really tuned up so it could continue running. I suppose I fared about as well as anyone else trying to invent a perpetual motion machine.

On the trapline, Jimmy and I shared many adventures. One winter afternoon we struck the fresh track of a marten—the trail couldn't have been over fifteen minutes old. We had often run down marten, forcing them into a tree where we could shoot them. I once killed three in one day in this manner.

That day the marten that Jimmy and I chased on snowshoes wouldn't tree. We nearly had him two or three times, but then we'd catch a glimpse of him bounding through the snow ahead. When we put on a burst of speed, the marten veered behind trees, or squirted through a patch of brush where we couldn't see him. We'd then have to go around the thicket.

By the time we picked up his trail again, he would be well ahead. The deep and loose snow made tracking that bounding little marten easy. Finally, just before dark, he treed, and I shot him with the .22 rifle we carried for the purpose and we had earned another twenty dollars.

"Which way to the trail?" I asked Jimmy. He shrugged and pointed. I figured the trapline trail was in a different direction. "OK, let's go this way," I suggested, compromising between Jimmy's guess and my own.

Jimmy was agreeable, so we headed across country, following what we thought was a shortcut back to our original trapline trail. The night was dark and cold. Because clouds blocked our view of the stars, we couldn't use the North Star as our guide, but the white snow reflected enough light from the sky to permit us to travel.

We had started out early that morning, and by nightfall, after chasing the marten for several hours, we had put in a strenuous twelve-hour day. We traveled single file, as is customary on snowshoes, taking turns breaking trail. After we had crossed two or three ridges and traveled for several hours, nothing looked familiar. The slope of the ground seemed wrong.

"Where are we?" Jimmy finally asked.

I didn't know. We figured out the next day that we had gone far back into the Purcell Mountains. We didn't have maps. (For many years we called this range of low mountains dividing the Koyukuk drainage from the coastal Kobuk drainage the Hog River Mountains.)

"Let's circle back, find our trail, and backtrack," I finally suggested. It was a last resort. We were hungry and tired to the bone. Neither of us wanted to spend the night siwashing under a spruce tree. We circled and after a long time found our tracks and retraced them. If we had gone by instinct we'd have probably traveled all night, farther and farther from where we wanted to be. At four A.M. we two exhausted kids arrived back at our cabin, too tired to eat a meal. We crawled into our bunks and slept until afternoon.

14

NO MAN'S LAND

✿

We were still trapping at Hog River in 1933 when I was eighteen. That fall I explored the Hog River-Pah River divide, part of what was called No Man's Land in the old days. The Pah drains into the Kobuk River in Eskimo country, and the divide between the Pah and Hog River is fairly low.

I found fair fur sign and decided to trap there. In November I put traps out along the upper Hog. A few days later, with thirty more traps in a backpack, I set out on foot from my Clear Creek cabin, planning to set more. I reached the last of my previously set traps about daylight. My traps had caught a few marten, which I hung in trees where I could pick them up on my return.

After I passed the portage trail, I started setting marten traps, following the right bank of the Hog. Hog River turns 180 degrees in a huge horseshoe; the Pah River portage takes off to the northwest from the approximate apex of the horseshoe.

By about three o'clock I had set all my traps. Encouraged by many fresh marten tracks, I headed home, backtracking and marking my trail with blazes on trees, broken branches, and other sign.

I didn't mind being alone. There was much to see—rabbit tracks, an occasional scurrying rabbit, a scolding red squirrel, a lethargic porcupine perched in a tree. A hawk-owl paced me in the treetops. Several ptarmigan leaped into flight along the stream. My snowshoes whispered through the dry snow, and I strode along, eyes busy, searching for tracks, which always told a story. The physical action felt good, and the icy winter air in my lungs was like wine.

I had nearly reached the Pah River portage trail when I saw strange snowshoe tracks. Someone had followed me a ways, then had taken off on a direct line for the portage lake where most travelers camped because of sheltering timber and plentiful firewood. His stride was too long for me to step in his tracks; he was either going fast or he was a big man with long legs. I yelled a few times but received no answer.

I followed the tracks, thinking he must be camped at the usual site. Dark was near. I began to have a creepy feeling, remembering stories I had heard of missing Indians in this mountainous No Man's Land. To my knowledge, it had been decades since any Koyukon had disappeared in No Man's Land, but there were still stories. Before the turn of the century, no matter what happened to an Indian in No Man's Land—a fatal fall, freezing to death, a lethal encounter with a bear— Koyukon Indians assumed that Eskimos were responsible for the disappearance, and another story was born. Likewise, Eskimos blamed the Koyukon people for every Eskimo who failed to return from No Man's Land.

Although I was a bit nervous, I kept going. Soon I saw smoke. Although dusk was near, no light shone where the smoke was rising. No sled dogs barked. At the campsite I found the smoke was from ashes dumped from a stove. A tent had been pitched nearby. Dog and sled tracks led toward the Kobuk side of the range. It was evident that as soon as the stranger had reached camp, he had knocked his tent down, loaded his sled, and left.

I puzzled over this on the long hike home. That night my way was lit by a brilliant aurora that writhed in a huge curtain overhead, like a gigantic twisting rainbow. The reds, greens, and purples were brilliant, and great searchlightlike flashes punctuated the movements. I have heard that some people fear winters in the Far North because of the long, dark nights. In the Koyukuk, where clear skies in winter are the rule, nights are seldom really dark. It's only difficult to see when occasional heavy clouds cover the sky or when thick snow falls.

The aurora lights many winter nights, and so does the moon. The beauty of a full moon on a sparkling snowy landscape is difficult to describe: it can seem almost like full daylight, with tree shadows. Even the stars provide plenty of light for traveling on clear nights. Alaska's crystal air seems to magnify the millions of diamond-bright stars in the northern skies, and there is no background of city lights to dim their brilliance.

The following week, I went to see whether the mysterious visitor to the Pah-Hog portage had moved his camp down the Pah River a short way or had left the country. I walked eight miles to the Pah, where I poked around for awhile, following his snowshoe tracks. I concluded that the unknown person had taken up his traps and departed, despite the abundant fur sign.

A few years later, Jimmy, our brother Fred, and I made a dog team trip from Hog River to the Eskimo town of Kobuk to buy supplies. As the raven flies it is about seventy-five miles, and twice that distance by dog team. At Kobuk, trader Harry Brown asked me where I trapped.

"Usually on the Hog River, sometimes twenty or thirty miles above the Pah River portage," I answered.

"Who goes with you?" he wanted to know.

"I go alone" (Jimmy seldom trapped the area with me).

"What!" he exclaimed.

"I trap alone," I repeated.

He then told me that several years earlier he had staked two Eskimos who had gone to trap at the Pah-Hog portage. They had soon returned, reporting "a big band of Indians traveling on the south bank of the Hog River."

"They said they had barely escaped with their lives," said Brown. "They told me that the Indians were hollering signals to each other."

I realized then that my yells had been heard, and like me, the Eskimos had remembered the stories of danger in No Man's Land and had fled. I wonder what their thoughts would have been had they realized that they had run from one youthful, medium-sized Indian, who was also somewhat spooked.

As a youngster I heard from my relatives and other Koyukon Indians many tales of the murder and violence of earlier years. Some of the stories dated to prewhite times, seven or eight decades before I was born. Many stories of murders by both Eskimos and Indians originated from the Zane Hills and Purcell Mountains, the rugged low mountains and hills that lie between the Koyukuk and Kobuk country—No Man's Land.

Neither Indian nor Eskimo controlled No Man's Land. Adventurous individuals who penetrated that remote area sometimes disappeared. Long before I was born, my uncle Frank, brother to my mother, went hunting in No Man's Land. Hog River Johnny, his brother, was to meet him there. When Johnny arrived at the meeting place, Frank was gone. Reading the tracks, Johnny could tell that Frank had arrived and met someone, but the trail disappeared and so did Frank. He was never seen again.

Years later a rumor drifted across the land: Eskimos from the

Kobuk Valley had heard that Eskimos from the Selawik district had "taken" (killed) a man from the Koyukuk River. Based on the rumor, hunters from the Koyukuk, seeking revenge for the loss of Frank, supposedly went up the Dakli River and waited for some Eskimos to enter No Man's Land. After some weeks an Eskimo family arrived. Local legend had it that the Indians killed every member.

Old Toby, a Koyukon from the Kateel River country in the Koyukuk valley, died at an old age more than seventy years ago. His son, Young Toby, was one of the last of the Indians from the Kateel. Young Toby was also one of the great Koyukon song makers. During the early 1930s Young Toby told me this story:

> About 1850, Old Toby, then a young man, was hunting with a partner at the headwaters of the Kateel. The two men found evidence that strange hunters had taken game there.
>
> They consulted other Koyukon Indians. The group decided to send two of their finest hunter/warriors into the Kateel area before the prime fall hunting season. The Indians selected Old Toby and his partner for this assignment. Old Toby, a six-footer, was unusually tall for a Koyukon Indian.
>
> The two slipped into the headwaters region of the Kateel, making every effort to conceal their presence. While lying hidden in a brushy area one day shortly after their arrival, they noticed unusual movements of caribou on a high ridge of the Kateel valley. The animals trotted about nervously, as if human hunters were near.
>
> The two warriors studied a thick stand of spruce trees at the end of the ridge, about half a mile from the river. Nearby was a large lake that held a beaver lodge. They suspected that hunters were hiding in those trees—not Koyukon Indians, but Eskimos.
>
> Old Toby and his partner prepared themselves for a long stay in their hiding place. Only after darkness fell did they move from hiding to stretch and get a drink of water. They ate dried meat and fish, and lit no fire. Carefully, they observed what was happening.
>
> On the afternoon of the third day after the unusual caribou behavior, a small bunch of the animals wandered off

the high ridge. When they reached the end of the ridge near the timber, all but one suddenly bolted. A remaining caribou staggered about for a few moments as if hit by an arrow, then it fell. As darkness came, the caribou remained where it had fallen, but by the next morning it had disappeared.

That night Old Toby's partner moved upstream so he could get a closer view of the other side of the river the next day. At the end of that day, after dark, he rejoined Old Toby. "I saw two Eskimo hunters feasting on the caribou they killed," he reported.

"They have made a foolish mistake, taking that animal in the open, revealing themselves," Old Toby said. He smiled at his partner and added, "They're not going to leave, because the beaver lodge in that lake has six beaver—two old ones, two medium-size ones, and two small ones. They won't leave those fat animals alone. We will have our chance if we are patient. But we must be careful."

That night the two Koyukon warriors schemed, basing their plans on the presence of the six beaver. Before daylight, Old Toby's partner crossed the river to await the opportune time. He and Toby believed that only one Eskimo hunter would go to the lake to take a beaver, while the Eskimo who remained behind stood guard.

Sure enough, toward evening on the third or fourth day after the Eskimos had killed the caribou, Old Toby saw an Eskimo sneaking near the timber at the edge of the lake. At that moment Old Toby, still on the south slope of the valley, showed himself. Both Eskimos quickly spotted him. Old Toby simply stood in the open, a tall, ominous, distant figure. This frightened the Eskimos.

The Eskimo who had started for the beaver lodge quickly disappeared. The Eskimo standing guard was too busy watching Old Toby far across the valley to worry about his partner. Realization that it was a trick didn't dawn on him until too late. As he started to look behind himself, an arrow pierced his back.

Old Toby, still standing on the south slope, heard the signal he was awaiting—one beat on a dry tree. This told him that his partner had killed the lookout. Old Toby then crossed the valley and went to the lake, searching for the beaver-hunting Eskimo. At first he saw no sign of him.

A large fallen tree lay half in the water. Old Toby walked to the base of the tree. Stooping, he discovered slight but fresh disturbances; something or someone had crawled out on the trunk of the tree. He studied the water, but could see nothing.

He walked toward the beaver lodge. Near the lodge a point of land extended into the water; reeds grew at the water's edge. The grass was undisturbed. He walked to the point and silently looked in every direction. Still he saw no sign of the missing Eskimo. The growing darkness was making it hard to see anything.

Then he noticed a movement of the water, ever so slight, at the end of the point. Had he imagined that the water lifted? No, the surface really was lifting and falling. Could someone breathing underwater cause the ripple by expanding and contracting his chest? Old Toby peered at the reeds that protruded from the water, stem by stem. Poised, with arrow ready to fly, he detected a single reed that was moving with a slight rise and fall of water. Old Toby strained his eyes as he peered into the depths. There, finally, he made out the missing Eskimo, lying on the bottom of the lake with his feet and body inside one of the tunnels to the beaver house. The hollow reed held in his mouth formed a breathing tube.

Taking careful aim, Old Toby let his arrow fly, thus ending the hunt for the Eskimo interlopers.

I have heard Eskimos tell similar stories, almost legends, about the old days, when enemy Koyukon Indians were caught in No Man's Land. After about 1900, as whites came into the country bringing their laws with them, "disappearances" of Eskimos and Indians in No Man's Land gradually ceased. Travel between the Lower Yukon or Koyukuk valley into coastal Eskimo country now requires only a few hours by snow machine, and Indians and Eskimos commonly visit back and forth without fear. The violent deaths, fear, and hate are vestiges of the past.

15

THE OLD
KOYUKON WAYS

❁

I developed an early interest in my Koyukon roots, and in the culture and history of the Koyukon people. With firsthand experience living from the land, I gained an appreciation for the abilities of my forebears who had survived in the Koyukuk country without rifles, modern traps, fishing nets, modern tools, processed foods, and ready-made clothing.

Interior Alaska's Athapaskans were the last of Alaska's Natives to come into contact with white men, when the Russian creole Malakof built a blockhouse at Nulato in 1839 (creole was a term used by Alaska's early Russians for those of Russian and Native ancestry). Malakof found that the Koyukon people had iron pots, glass beads, cloth, and tobacco that had reached them through trade with coastal Eskimos.

From Nulato, fur-seeking Russian traders traveled up the Yukon to the mouth of the Tanana River. The Athapaskans they found were eager to obtain blankets, axes, knives, muzzle-loading rifles, powder horns, lead balls, kettles, and files. They didn't care much for the clothing offered by early Russians and Hudson's Bay Company traders (who arrived at Fort Yukon in 1847), because their own skin clothing was superior in warmth, durability, and appearance.

In 1866, the explorer William Dall wrote, "The Koyukons are the most attractive in appearance of the Indians in this part of the Territory. The women do up their hair in two braids, one on each side. The original dress of the male Koyukons consists of a pair of breeches of deerskin, with moccasins attached, and a deerskin parka without any hood, long and pointed before and behind. They are fond of ornaments and gay colors."

Another early writer said that in winter the trousers of the

Athapaskans along the Yukon were of fur. Mittens and a hood or fur cap were also worn in winter. The clothing was often decorated with dentalium shell, a trade item from coastal Alaska, or porcupine quills. After white contact, trade beads were commonly used for decoration.

Change came swiftly to the Koyukon people after arrival of the Russians, and swift change has continued to this day. Edwin Simon, born in 1898, considered that he lived three lives in his eighty-one years. His "first life," until 1930, was mostly primitive by today's standards, and basically the same as that of his parents. He used birchbark canoes and poling boats for river travel. Candles provided light. Dogs pulled his sled as well as his poling boat while he poled or paddled. He carried a muzzle-loading rifle, bow and arrows, and an axe. Wherever the family stopped to live for a time, they built a sod *igloo* or house (*igloo* is an Eskimo word borrowed by the Koyukons; it means house). By digging about four feet underground, the house would be half below ground level. With the axe they cut poles and sod for walls and roof. A fire burned in the center of the floor, and smoke escaped through a hole in the roof. The family moved frequently to where they could most easily catch fish in traps they built, or where they could shoot game. Much of their clothing was made of animal skins.

As an adult, Edwin once asked his mother, "What did you do with all your things when you traveled all the time?"

"What things?" she replied. "We had nothing—a rifle, bow and arrow, one axe, and the clothes we wore. We didn't leave anything behind."

In his "second life," from 1930 to 1960, Edwin owned a gasoline-powered boat with an inboard engine. He used oil and white gas for lamps and lanterns. He wore manufactured clothing, roamed less, and lived in log houses. He was not entirely dependent on wild game and fish for food, because food could be purchased at trading posts.

In his "third life," 1960 to 1979, he enjoyed electricity and running water in his permanent log home. He owned a snow machine, a three-wheel all-terrain vehicle, a refrigerator, a freezer, and a radio. He fished and hunted game for food mostly within easy traveling distance of home.

Many of the old ways of the Koyukon are entirely gone, others are disappearing. Even the skills of hunting, trapping, and fishing in the old way are changing—altered or eliminated by outboard motors, scope-sighted rifles, and snow machines.

As a boy I admired the knowledge and abilities of many of the

Koyukon elders, and I loved listening to their stories of the past. I learned from them that during the 1800s the Koyukuk valley was poorer in fish and game than other areas in Alaska. In contrast, the Yukon River, with its great runs of salmon, was considered a paradise. At the time, if you didn't kill, you didn't eat; the people's very existence depended on fish and game, and they hunted and/or fished year-round. They didn't farm or grow crops. They harvested some berries and dried fish that they caught, but when they had to make long treks to go where game and fish were more abundant, they could carry only a limited amount of such food.

The following is a story told to me by Chief Henry (1883–1976), who had learned it from his grandfather. He believed it was based on an actual event. Chief Henry was famous for his story-telling, songs, and philosophy of life. For me it illustrates how precarious the lives of the Koyukon people were in the old days:

> Times were hard in the Koyukuk River valley in the 1820s and 1830s, with virtually no game and no fish. There were no moose. The Koyukon people had overfished the streams and lakes. They had blocked some of the streams with fish traps for too many consecutive years, wiping out returns of salmon to the Koyukuk River.
>
> Dulbi Slough and Dulbi River were the last two streams that still supported salmon runs. (It has only been in modern times that the Koyukon people have been aware of the life history of salmon: that the tiny fish, which hatch from eggs buried in the gravel of a stream, travel downriver to the sea, where they mature so they can return to the very stream of their birth.)
>
> Most of the Indians left the Koyukuk River to search for a place where they could find fish and game. Many moved to the Yukon River where they knew they could catch and dry enough salmon during summer to last through winter.
>
> Some of the Koyukon families that remained in the Koyukuk River valley starved to death, still hoping that fish would arrive. They could have moved to the fish-rich Yukon River with other families, but they had gambled and lost.
>
> Four springs passed. The people who had moved longed for their Koyukuk country homes. They decided that by this time the caribou would have returned to their old home. The rabbits, long gone, should be returning now, too. With such

thoughts, despite warnings of the elders who doubted that fish and game had returned in such a short time, some of the people left the security of the Yukon River and returned to Hog River.

Fall set in. At Hog River the fish traps that blocked the streams produced very few fish—not enough to see the people through the winter. In those days of famine, the Indians moved on their own legs, pulling a sled to carry only what they needed for existence. There were no dogs to pull sleds, because there was no food for the dogs.

With starvation near, some of the men went hunting in the nearby hills and mountains. They were away many weeks. Finally, in January, as days were beginning to lengthen, some of the men returned. Others did not. Perhaps they had starved to death.

Those who came back had found caribou a long way off in the headwaters of the Melozitna River. They brought with them some meat, but not enough to feed everyone. They had cached meat along the way, planning to eat it for strength as they returned with their families to the Melozitna headwaters, where they had left their main meat cache.

A young man who had qualified for a woman the previous year returned home from this long hunt. He found his wife with a baby boy born just after he had left.

The young father found his family hard-pressed for food. His mother, especially, was weak. Food she could have eaten she had given to her daughter-in-law, the mother of the newborn baby. Slowly but surely, she was starving herself to death, giving away her life's energy so her only grandson might live.

Everyone in the camp hurriedly prepared for the long move to the Melozitna, except for the old grandmother. "I cannot go, my son," she said. "I do not have enough strength."

"I will pull you in my sled. You raised me well; I cannot leave you behind to die," the son promised.

The mother did not speak for a long time. Finally, she called to him and his woman and asked them to listen to her. As she spoke, she cradled her grandson in her arms.

"Son, I am old now. I worked hard all of my life to raise you. We have had hard times for too many years. I raised you properly even after your father starved to death. We kept going. I can do no more. But even while I die, I am going to help you. Without me, you and your young wife and baby boy might survive. With me along, you would not survive. The trail is too long and hard for me to walk; pulling me on the sled would take all of your strength.

"You must listen to me. Use your head, not just your eyes to cry. Be a brave man, not the kind of brave that it takes to kill big animals. You must be braver than that to make me happy, and to let your wife and son perhaps live a longer life.

"I am sure they will not live long if you do not do what I ask you to do. I took good care of you. Now you owe me. Show me how brave you are. I will not go with you, and you must not leave me here to slowly starve and freeze to death."

Understanding what his mother had told him, he sadly left the igloo. He went to the leader, the medicine man of their little tribe, and told him what his mother had said. The leader explained to the young man that this had happened before. "She is right. Big animals are easier to take than the life of the woman who brought you into this world. I watched your mother raise you. She did a good job. She is still trying in her last hours to help you.

"You must be strong and brave. If you do not do what she asks of you, you will slowly put to death your young wife and your only baby. I know you are strong. You are not going to do something you have to hide from or be ashamed of. You will be doing something to make your mother happy, the mother who worked so hard to raise you, the mother who is still looking out for you. Are you brave enough to do this?"

The young man and his wife spent a sleepless night. If they were to survive, they must join the trek to the meat cache on the morrow.

Early in the morning after the young man and his wife had loaded everything in their sled, the mother walked out of her igloo with a coil of rawhide rope. She moved steadily toward a birch tree at the side of the trail. She put one end of the rope over a branch of the tree, sat down and put a loop over her head and around her neck.

Then she faced away from the trail and called, "I am ready, my son."

He pulled on the rawhide rope.

All of the Koyukon elders know this story, but, as one old woman told me, "We can't tell such stories because it is against our beliefs to tell these stories to others." For this reason, many of the oral traditions of the Koyukon people are being lost.

Many stories I have heard from Koyukon elders illustrate that all thoughts and energies were aimed at survival. After about 1850 when rifles and shotguns were available, starvation largely ended for Alaska's Athapaskans.

I caught a glimpse of how difficult early Indian life was from Johnny Oldman, a Koyukon elder. In 1934, he was seventy-two and I was nineteen. Just before Christmas that year, my brother Jimmy and I left Hog River with Johnny, his son, Abraham, and a four-year-old girl. With two dog teams, we headed for Hughes, where the potlatch for Little William was to be held. (Little William had made the snowshoes for me when I was a child.)

Temperatures were −50 degrees and colder during the day, and even colder at night. Jimmy and I helped to break trail for the two sleds, which were loaded with bear and moose meat for the potlatch. The little girl was bundled up in one of the sleds.

On the second day out, near dark, when we crossed a creek in the bottom of a valley the thermometer on my sled registered −68 degrees. "Leave the meat, go to the top of the ridge, and make camp. Put up the tent," Johnny Oldman instructed Jimmy and me. "It'll be warmer there."

As Johnny had predicted, the temperature was warmer on the ridge, only −52 degrees. Jimmy and I put up the tent, set up the woodstove, and quickly built a fire. The stove heated the tent rapidly. When Johnny and Abraham arrived, Johnny suggested that Jimmy, Abraham, and I return to haul the meat out of the valley that night to save time the next day. When we arrived back at camp with the meat, Johnny had finished cooking dog food and our supper was ready.

The mercury in my thermometer was now almost down to −60 degrees. When we got inside the tent we found the little girl inside, naked, her skin blue from cold. She had wet her clothes during the long day of riding the sled, and Johnny had hung them over the stove to dry. Feeling sorry for the poor girl, I started to wrap her in my spare long johns.

"Don't do that Sidney," Johnny said. "It's not really cold. She has to get tough. A long time ago Indians had to be tough to live. That's why a long time ago our people were strong. Only the tough boys and girls survived. The weak, the sick, and the crippled died. If we wrap up those kids all the time, how are they going to grow up to be tough?"

Twelve years later, when Johnny Oldman was eighty-four, Edwin Simon and I visited him at the Alaska Native Service Hospital at Tanana. Things weren't looking good for Johnny. He was in a bed in a small ward. His thinning hair was gray, and age wrinkles lined his face. His gentle brown eyes sparkled with intelligence, but he was thin and frail. He had little time left.

I talked with a nurse who cared for him. She complained, "His skin has to be at least half an inch thick!" She usually bent the needle of her hypodermic syringe while trying to force it through the thick skin of Johnny's buttocks. Johnny had spent most of his life out in the cold; I guess his body reacted by developing a thick, tough skin. The only way she could make the needle penetrate was to ram it, hard; sometimes she bent the needle, pulled it out, and tried again.

Many Alaska Natives were coming to the hospital for treatment. "You know, Sidney, too bad, but I can see the days of the good, strong, healthy Indian coming to an end," Johnny said, sadly.

"How's that, Johnny?"

He spoke slowly, in a weak voice. "Sidney, I'm almost at the end of my life, and I am ready to go. I have lived a good clean life. I know I did right in my life. You even show me that by coming to visit me before I die. I like to thank you for coming.

"You see all these people come here from all over Alaska? Many are very young. Even young women come to have baby. Young people these days are sickly. You can see they are not going to live long; only medicine keep them alive. Now look at me. That medicine don't help me because I'm stronger than the medicine they got. People are not strong anymore. Not long ago only the strong ones lived.

"They raise all the weak ones now, what we call 'misfits.' How can the good, strong Indians last when they breed with weak people? People used to be born from two strong, healthy parents who survived to grow up when things were tough, when nothing came easy. Koyukuk Indians were strong then. No more, Sidney. No more strong Indians," he said sadly, slowly shaking his head. Johnny Oldman died soon after our visit.

Although Alaska has a national reputation as a region of abundant wildlife, it is a poor land when compared with almost any other state on the basis of pounds of game produced per acre. The Koyukuk valley, which straddles the Arctic Circle, with its short growing season and harsh winters produces few pounds of meat (in the form of wildlife) per acre. Small wonder that the early Koyukon people perpetually wandered, always looking for places where there were game and fish in abundance.

Chief Henry told me of years when little or no game was available, which meant little food and no new clothing for the people, often for long periods. People saved their good winter clothing for cold weather because with everyday use the fur wore off, leaving nothing but leather to protect from the cold. "That's what we called being poor," he told me.

Women made all clothing from skins. There were no mosquito nets or insect repellents. Smoke was the only way to escape these pests, and during summer every family had to keep smudges burning. One early Athapaskan technique to escape mosquitoes while canoeing was to place a dish of wet moss, or a piece of bracket fungi, with a few hot coals in the bow of a canoe; when the canoe was in motion the smoke surrounded the paddlers and discouraged insects.

Matches were not available, and there were few or no metal tools, no steel traps or snares. And all medicines came from plants.

Braggarts were looked down upon by the early Koyukon people, and hunters went to extremes to present a modest front. A hunter who had killed two large moose might return to the village and say, "I finally caught two calves," to give no hint of bragging.

Chief Henry and other elders believed that all animals have personalities, and they treated them accordingly when shooting, trapping, or snaring them. If you didn't treat an animal properly, its spirit was offended. Then that animal would refuse to be caught in your snares or traps. These beliefs and values still linger among many of the Koyukon people.

At one time there were Koyukon songs that honored each and every species of wildlife. A few people still know some of those songs. No old-time Koyukon would laugh at an animal, or speak disparagingly of it. They believed that you had to be careful in talking about the animals, so as not to offend.

You never said you were going hunting; you were just going for a walk, or for a ride in your canoe to see the country. In this way you didn't let the animals know your intentions. Even after killing an animal, the Koyukons had certain ceremonial obligations. For example, a hunter or trapper carrying a wolverine home would sing something like, "...a rich person (or a chief) is coming to the house." A good blanket was spread on the floor next to a wall of the house or of a tent, and the wolverine was placed in a sitting position, its back propped against the wall. Each person who visited the house placed a small food item near the wolverine. The wolverine was to be well treated and not offended in any way.

A small piece of dried fish or other food would be placed in the mouth of a fox, a marten, or other small game, and grease or lard was smeared over the nostrils so the animal would not be offended by the smell of the inside of the house.

Wolverine and wolf carcasses were burned, not simply discarded or buried. Unused brown (grizzly) bear meat and other parts were buried or burned to destroy the spirit. Beaver and otter bones were returned to the water with a request to "make more" (of those animals).

You never would point your finger at an animal to indicate where it was because he would feel your finger pointing at him and walk away.

A wolf in a trap might be spoken to: "Wolf, I ask that more of you come to my traps," and only then would it be killed. Any trapped animal was killed as quickly as possible to reduce suffering, and trapped animals were always treated with respect.

Spirits of birds were also catered to. A hunter might say that he had "bothered" some ptarmigan when he had hunted them, indicating that he had inconvenienced the birds.

When talking about hunting or trapping, people might say, "I am going to hunt for nothing," to not offend any animal by specific mention. They believed that one should always sound humble toward animals. Being too confident and acting as if shooting or trapping animals were easy wouldn't show proper respect. If you behaved respectfully, animals would allow themselves to be caught in your trap or shot by your gun.

Hunting provided not only meat for early Indians, but also clothing, bedding, tents, rope, string, sinew for sewing, and bones for making tools and needles. Caribou bones are the hardest, and make the best scrapers and other tools. Caribou skin makes the warmest winter parkas, pants, boots, and mittens, but the animals have to be killed when the hair is just the right length.

To obtain good caribou skins for clothing, early Koyukon hunters traveled 50 to 100 miles or more to the hills and mountains seeking fawns in late July and early August. Some year-old caribou were killed, but their skins made clothing of only fair quality. Nothing could beat the quality of fawn skins. When taken at that time of year, the hair of fawn skins is strong: it doesn't break off and shed as does the hair of older caribou. Also, the leather, as light and as soft as chamois skin, can be worn against the skin.

"How did the people keep warm in winter?" I once asked Chief Henry. "You never keep warm," he replied. "We had to be tough, and use a good head and watch ourselves."

When Chief Henry was very young, his family moved from the Koyukuk River to the Yukon to fish for salmon because salmon had stopped coming to the Koyukuk. He said his parents saw famine coming, and their medicine man told them to move.

"You must not stay in one place too long. When you do, you kill all the fish. There is no game to eat. You must not take a chance and get caught at freezeup in the wrong place, where there are no fish," he warned.

Winter was the critical time to the Koyukons. The deep snow, the extended periods of extreme cold, the iced-over rivers, the few hours of daylight—all make life difficult in the Far North. The regular winter home of the early Koyukon people—the half-buried sod house—must have been dank and dark, even with a fire burning most of the time.

When the Koyukon people camped out or needed temporary winter homes, they erected a tepeelike igloo made of spruce poles and insulated with moss. A fire in the center of the floor was likely to create a smoky interior, but you could sleep on the floor under the smoke where it was warm. According to old-timer Louis Golchik, you could even sleep without blankets if a fire burned. I once visited Golchik's comfortable spruce-pole igloo. It was dark, but it was warm, roomy, and comfortable.

At times the early Indians had to ration fish. Even the skins of fish were saved, for they were valuable as food.

In some years, the cyclic snowshoe hare was important food. This creature, which is brown in summer and white in winter, literally floats on loose snow because of its huge feet. Roughly every ten years it becomes abundant in some places, and the lynx, foxes, marten, wolverine, and owls feast. In the old days, so did the Koyukon people, for the hare is easily snared and the food is good, although it has virtually no fat. Rabbit skin is fragile, easily torn, so the people used to cut it into long strips, which they wove into blankets and sometimes clothing.

The spirit of the snowshoe hare was considered to be rather weak. Nevertheless, people would break the legs of hares when they brought them inside to cut up, keeping their spirits from running around loose.

When hares suddenly erupted in great numbers, Koyukon elders explained that the winter-white animals had "fallen from the sky with the snow."

———

No matter how clever or careful the Koyukon people were, they sometimes got caught without food. If they didn't migrate soon enough, starvation was not uncommon. To be effective, moves away from the Koyukuk had to be made across the last crust of the spring snow. Wearing snowshoes, they moved swiftly, making it possible for them to reach the Yukon in time to build a fish trap before the summer runs of salmon began. Salmon were regarded as lifesavers. The Koyukon people usually eventually returned to their Koyukuk valley home, commonly after years of living on the Yukon.

When the whites arrived, they brought flour, valuable for mixing with other foods—meat, fish, skin—to make gravy. Flour stretched what little food the Indians had. When caribou were scarce, meat was dried until it crumbled and then it was mixed with flour and water to stretch it to the maximum.

The coming of whites—and the fur trade, which was long Alaska's economic mainstay—also brought a new type of economy to Alaska's Natives. Their subsistence economy was converted to a trade economy in which store clothes and white man's food replaced skin garments and, in part, the food derived from the hunt, fish traps, and the trapline.

Gradually, periodic moves by the Koyukon people seeking better hunting and fishing grounds ceased because supplies were available from traders. By 1900, a trading post could be found in most of the larger Native villages along the Yukon and Koyukuk rivers. During the last half of the twentieth century, more and more villages came into existence and the perpetual wandering of the people ceased. Schools, churches, and permanent year-round homes were built, and a new way of life was set for the Koyukon people.

16

SIWASH

When I was thirteen years old, I became aware of prejudice against half-breeds. At Nulato I had joined a soccer game in progress on the mission playground. Suddenly one of the kids on the opposition team poked his face into mine and sneered, "You half-breed Siwash." I continued to play, not realizing that the boy had intended an insult.

"What's the matter with you, Sidney. Are you afraid of him?" a friend asked.

"No. Why?"

"Didn't you hear him call you a half-breed Siwash?"

"Yeah. What's that mean?" I asked.

"Those are awful dirty words to call you. He wants to fight you, I think."

I ran to the guy and asked, "What did you call me?"

"Half-breed Siwash," he answered, with a mocking look.

"What do you mean by that?" I asked, genuinely puzzled.

"Don't you know that means you're a dirty coward?"

I understood "dirty coward" all right. He immediately had a fight on his hands, even though he was a couple of years older. I had had plenty of practice fighting at Eklutna school, so I gave him more than he had bargained for.

Other boys started to come to his rescue, but Father Mac, the Catholic priest who had been watching the game, held them off, allowing me to finish the job. When the kid had had enough, I let him up from the ground.

"What happened, Sidney? You don't look for trouble," Father Mac asked.

I told him what the boy had called me, that I hadn't understood "half-breed Siwash" as fighting words. "But," I told Father Mac, "I understood 'dirty coward' and I was only trying to accommodate him."

"I'm sure he understands that now," said Father Mac, with a barely repressed smile.

My dad, who in 1897 toiled his way over Chilkoot Pass into the Klondike gold fields, claimed that Indians around Skagway were called Siwashes; he thought it was a tribal name. As he traveled into the headwaters of the Yukon River, he saw more Indians.

"What Indians are those?" he asked another gold rusher.

"Oh, they're Siwashes," was the answer.

The next step to "lazy Siwashes" or "damn Siwashes" came easy. When something was stolen, even if a white man was the thief, some "low-down Siwash" took it.

To the Athapaskan Indians along the Yukon and Koyukuk rivers, by the 1920s and 1930s the term certainly had a negative connotation. Call someone a "Siwash" and you had an instant fight on your hands. It was even more of an insult than "son of a bitch" was among whites.

At Koyukuk an Indian once called me a son of a bitch, and I lit into him with both fists. He backed off, claiming I was fighting him for no reason. "I only called you a son of a bitch," he explained.

As stampeders from the Klondike gold rush moved down the Yukon River, "siwash" became more degrading. I've seen terrible fights among Indians who were careless how they used the word.

My dictionary says that "siwash" comes from Chinook jargon (in the Columbia River country, Chinook was a *lingua franca*), with its root the French "sauvage," meaning wild, or savage. One definition is, "To camp, live, or do things after the manner of an Indian; esp., to travel without equipment."

"Siwashing out" is a commonly used term in Alaska and elsewhere for tough camping with minimal gear. It probably came from the reputation, deserved or not, that Indians ("Siwashes") have for being able to survive in the woods under extreme conditions.

Some folks' version of siwashing out is pretty tame compared with real "siwashing." I have known many Koyukon people who often siwashed out when conditions were really tough—people like my uncles Weaselheart and Hog River Johnny, Edwin Simon, Johnny Oldman, and others. Most of them later in life paid a heavy price for exposure to extremes. As they grew older, arthritis or rheumatism crippled them with constant pain.

Many modern Alaskans consider sleeping out under the open skies, even in a $300 down-filled sleeping bag, as "siwashing out," but that's the easy way. In my younger years, Koyukon elders told me to avoid siwashing out unless I had no choice. "Only when you are all played out, or lost," Edwin Simon warned. I made up my mind that I would never siwash out, but of course I couldn't avoid getting caught a few times.

Edwin told me what to do if I had to siwash out during winter when all I had with me was the clothing I wore and an axe. His words probably saved my life.

One night in early February 1935, when I was a tough nineteen-year-old, I learned about siwashing firsthand in the Hog River country behind Sun Mountain. I frequently ran marten down, but I often got into trouble in doing so.

Interested in establishing a new marten trapline, I decided to scout new country. I left my Clear Creek camp on Hog River about 4:30 in the morning, and drove my dog team to the foothills, where I tied them.

It was breaking daylight when I put on snowshoes and set out to search the hills. Snow was deep, but none had fallen for several days. If marten were around, I knew I would see their tracks, made since the previous snowfall. I soon found good sign, with marten tracks here and there. I toured among the big hills and covered many miles. Late in the day, I ran into a fresh marten track. To test its freshness, I slid the head of my axe into the snow under the track and tried to lift it. Disturbed snow sets after a time, and an old track remains intact when lifted with an axe in that manner. This track crumpled, which indicated that it was fresh. The marten was traveling in the opposite direction I wanted to go, but I didn't worry about that.

Part of the satisfaction of the trapline was the excitement I felt when on a fresh trail. But sometimes I would forget to be smart. I forgot the dog team I had left tied. I forgot that I had traveled hard all day. I forgot that darkness was near. I forgot that I hadn't eaten since breakfast. I took off on a run, snowshoes flying, following the fresh track over a ridge and down into a steep valley, thinking I would catch him quickly. His tracks, instead of meandering, with short leaps, changed to a straight line with large leaps, so he knew he was being trailed. Finding no big trees to climb, he ran faster.

Floundering in the deep snow in that steep-sided valley, I slowed

SHADOWS ON THE KOYUKUK

my pace but continued to follow him along the creek. The chase lasted about an hour. Finally, after several miles, I caught up with him. He treed and I shot him with my .22. His fine pelt was worth about $20, big money in 1935, when a good day's wage was about $5.

Within a few hours that $20 seemed like small potatoes.

When one makes his first mistake in the woods, other mistakes usually follow. When I had left my cabin on Clear Creek more than twelve hours earlier, the temperature had been −34 degrees, with no wind, a fine temperature for traveling. Until the marten chase, I'd remained comfortable because I was properly dressed and kept moving. The marten chase had made my clothing damp with sweat, and damp clothing combined with cold is a lethal mixture.

Rather than climb the steep slope, I decided to head down the valley, which seemed to turn in the direction of my dog team. I walked for about an hour, left the creek where the bank wasn't so steep, and climbed out of the valley. Both darkness and cold deepened.

Reaching the top of the ridge, I decided to follow it out, expecting to intersect my snowshoe track at any time. I was growing very tired, and darkness under the heavy spruce timber made it difficult for me to see any distance. I came to an open place, but I didn't see anything that looked familiar. I crossed the ridge into a new valley, scanning the snow as I went, searching for my own tracks. The snow seemed deeper and the cold more intense. I was dog tired.

I decided to build a fire, rest, and dry my damp wool underwear, for I could feel the penetrating cold sapping my strength. With my axe, the most important survival tool in wooded country, I cut dry wood and started a fire atop the snow. The heat felt good and I could feel the moisture leaving my underwear. The flames quickly thawed a hole in the snow that eventually became more than four feet deep. Using a snowshoe for a shovel, I dug in around the edge, away from the fire, following it down. I wasn't thinking of siwashing out, only drying off.

I dozed in front of the fire. Then I remembered Edwin's warning: "Look out if you get sleepy. Go to sleep and you can fall into the fire. You can be burned so badly you can't do anything, and then you will die. Take care of yourself before you let yourself fall asleep."

I roused myself, suddenly realizing that I was going to have to siwash it for the night. I cut a few larger trees, some green boughs, and three-and-four-inch-diameter dry poles. Soon I had a large pile of wood.

I built up my original fire. By this time it had melted its way to bare ground. I placed the green spruce boughs near the fire, where they thawed, dried, and warmed, ready for later use. Then, using my snowshoes, I dug a second hole in the snow for another fire, near my original fire, which by now was burning down. I scooped all the hot coals and partly burned wood from the first fire and placed them on my new fire, and then I piled wood high on the new fire.

I laid my supply of now-dry green spruce branches over the spot where the first fire had burned. Steam arose from under the branches, for the ground was still hot. I remembered Edwin's instructions: "Lie down with your parka over you for a blanket, and you'll get two, maybe three, hours sleep. When the cold wakens you, the other fire should just be going out."

Edwin also said I would be stiff all over, but rested. Everything proved to be true to the last detail. When I lay down on my pile of green spruce boughs with my parka on top of me, the warmth from the heated ground felt heavenly. I was asleep in moments. When I awoke I was rested, but no more heat was rising from the ground beneath me, and the cold was beginning to penetrate. My muscles were so stiff that I could hardly get the kinks out. The damp steam seemed to have settled in my joints.

My second fire was nearly out, but by piling dry wood on the coals I soon had the flames leaping high. I huddled near the life-giving heat and thoroughly dried my clothing, damp from the steaming ground.

I waited for daylight before moving on, for I knew I was lost. With the first faint light, I worked my way high on a ridge in search of a landmark. As I peered across country, I discovered that after killing the marten I had walked toward the Koyukuk River, away from Hog River where I had left my dog team.

I spent almost that entire day hiking back to my dog team and driving the dogs back to my cabin. After thirty-six hours without food, the dogs and I were ravenous. Based on that experience, I did my best to avoid having to siwash out during winter again.

Do I get upset nowadays if someone calls me a half-breed Siwash? I haven't let anything like that bother me for years. Besides, I can always look anyone who does straight in the eye and say, "You're absolutely right, friend. Now, what's your background?"

17

KOYUKUK GOLD

✪

Because of the Depression, during the early 1930s a silver dollar looked as big as a full moon in October. Fur prices were low, and we saw little cash, but we continued to live as trappers and from the land. Despite the tough times, we were happy and lived well.

Dad's health continued to grow poorer. In 1934 he left his job at Nulato and entered the Alaska Pioneer's Home at Sitka. After a year there his health had slightly improved, and he was restless.

When I was eighteen I spent much time at Koyukuk Station, where a girl named Jenny Luke lived. We were married in 1934, when I was nineteen, and we lived at Hog River. Jimmy lived with us for a year after we were married.

In 1936 Jimmy married Celia Olin at Cutoff, about eighty river miles from Hog River, and he lived most of the time in that Koyukuk River village, close to her family. During some winters he returned to trap with me at Hog River.

After he had been in the Pioneer's Home for a little over a year, Dad wrote to Jimmy and me, "Whether I die lazing around the Pioneer's Home or digging for gold in the Koyukuk makes little difference. I might as well be doing something, so I've decided to try digging for gold at Bear Creek."

Trapping, freighting, and trading were only sidelines as far as Dad was concerned. Gold was what he came north for, and the search for it continued to be his passion. He had faith in the Koyukuk gold fields, and with good reason: from 1900 to 1930 about five million dollars worth of gold came out of the Koyukuk, mostly from the headwaters area, seventy-five miles upstream from Bettles.

Bear Creek, about forty miles northwest of Hughes, a headwater tributary to Hog River, is one of Alaska's sixty Bear Creeks. Gold was found there in the 1920s and earlier by Dominic Vernetti and others, but not in large amounts.

Most of the area surrounding Bear Creek is permafrost—permanently frozen ground—but Bear Creek ground is wet, not frozen, with only a few spots of permafrost. Permafrost forms when the average annual temperature is below freezing, and in some of the colder regions of the arctic, permafrost is hundreds of feet deep.

Because of the wet ground at Bear Creek, early miners couldn't sink a hole to bedrock where the gold lies without being what they called "drowned out." Dominic Vernetti and Ernie McCloud and a couple of others managed to take $2,000 worth of gold out of a frozen pit at Bear Creek before being drowned out. After that, Ernie McCloud worked at Bear Creek for years, trying unsuccessfully to develop a way of mining the area before he was starved out.

But Dad was convinced Bear Creek was worth another try. "No one has mined Bear Creek right," he said. "If we can get down to bedrock and prove gold is there, we can either sell out, or mine it ourselves."

So in January 1935 Jimmy and I headed across country to Bear Creek with our dog teams and built Dad a fine twelve-by-sixteen cabin out of dry spruce logs. We put up a good roof, digging under the snow for sod to insulate it, and we mudded the walls to eliminate drafts and installed a good window and a door.

At the time I had a wife and was starting a family. Jimmy was busy trapping and had no money. Financing a mining venture was out of the question for us, but we could help some. We took Dad to the cabin and left him there more or less on his own, and hauled food and other supplies to him periodically. Bear Creek wasn't far from the end of one of my traplines, so I checked on him every few days.

Dad staked claims for himself and for friends and small investors who had provided him with power of attorney, then he gradually froze a prospect hole down into the wet ground.

First he dug down three or four feet, chipping away the frozen ground, making a hole about three feet wide and five feet long. When he got down about five feet, he chipped out the frozen earth, filled a bucket, climbed the ladder out of the hole, winched the bucket up, and dumped the spoil. That he did again and again. The process was slow and strenuous for a sixty-eight-year-old in poor health.

When he reached wet ground, he sometimes waited days for it to freeze. Then he dug a test hole to see how far down it was frozen. When he was sure six or eight inches had frozen, he chipped out the frozen ground, leaving a frozen crust thick enough to prevent ground-water from entering.

Each week he dug down another six inches or so, and eventually his hole was almost eleven feet deep. One day when he dug out some frozen dirt he noticed dampness. He figured it would freeze, since the temperature was around −30 degrees. But the next morning he found the hole almost full of water—the wet spot had given way. Dad had been drowned out, like all the others. Two months or more of hard, patient work had been destroyed overnight. He didn't say much about it, but I knew he was bitterly disappointed.

He didn't live long enough to know that he had dug to within a foot and a half of bedrock—and millions of dollars worth of gold! That summer he sold partnership shares in the ground he had staked. His various partners were all mining people, and they arranged for the United Smelting and Refining Company to drill prospect holes, with an option to lease or buy.

Shortly after that Dad died at Fairbanks.

I went to work for the mining company in 1937. We flew the first drill to Bear Creek in a small plane, and then a little D4 Caterpillar was driven in. While I worked at seventy-nine cents an hour to help set up the drill and to move it around, my wife, Jenny, lived with our kids in a log cabin at the mouth of nearby Clear Creek.

That winter I saw good fur sign, so I quit the mining company and went trapping. I went back one day to visit the drill crew. They fed me and were cordial, then one of the men told me, "Sidney, your dad would turn over in his grave if he knew what we have found." They had drilled a prospect hole next to Dad's eleven-foot-deep hole. In the bottom of their six-inch-diameter hole, they had panned $16 worth of gold. Later, when a dredge was brought in, more than $3 million in gold came from that one claim alone.

After drilling, the exploration company acted on their option and bought all the claims. For our inherited shares, Jimmy and I each received $15,000—a fortune to us.

Almost twenty years later, in 1955, a gold-mining dredge was brought, piecemeal, up the Koyukuk River. I worked as a foreman, clearing the road that ran twenty-eight miles from the river back to the mining camp. In the fall and winter when the ground was firmly frozen, we hauled in the dredge parts and reassembled this machine-filled floating behemoth—a floating building that could be dragged along, scooping up the gold-laden earth. The buckets it swung could pull gravel to the surface from as much as sixty feet below ground level. At the site, we had big Caterpillars and graders, pile-driving equipment, and other heavy machinery.

I was paid well—$600 a month, plus room and board, so I worked there a year. But I missed my wife and kids.

One of my jobs was to use a surveyor's transit to lay out a seven-mile ditch for bringing water to the dredge. I had to follow contour lines through the hills so the water fell at a maximum rate of about one-half inch per 100 feet. At the end, the water dropped straight down for 142 feet, providing pressure for a hydraulic nozzle. Since I was self-taught as a surveyor, I enjoyed this challenging job. Later, the company engineer resurveyed my ditch and found that I was off only one-half-inch in the seven miles.

I also helped to run the dredge. One day the man who was panning on the dredge quit. "Sidney, would you mind panning for a while?" a supervisor asked. "We'll leave your salary at $600 a month."

I agreed, but reluctantly. The panner, who pans a sample of the dredged-up material every twenty minutes or so, guides the dredge all day. He judges which direction the dredge should travel and the dredgemaster follows his instructions. Until then, with the work I was doing, I had been able to get out of the noisy contraption from time to time.

The gold came in steadily as I panned during that first day. On hand were nine buckets of pure gold, each weighing between 90 and 100 pounds. When I removed the mercury amalgam with a retort outside of the dredge, the gold looked just like butter.

Until then, working the dredge on Dad's claims hadn't bothered me, not even the one where he had been drowned out. But as I panned the gleaming yellow stuff, I suddenly realized that all that gold I was seeing had been my dad's—I was making others rich with Huntington gold.

I put the pan down, found the foreman, and said, "Call Sam White for me. I'm leaving." Sam White had left his job as game warden, and was the Wien Airlines bush pilot at Hughes.

"What's wrong, Sidney?" he asked.

"I'll tell you some other time. I have to leave. I have no gold on me." They were careful to make sure that people leaving the dredge carried no gold.

To my knowledge, $20 million worth of gold came from the Bear Creek claims on which Dad filed. I never returned to the dredge.

18

SLED DOGS

✦

One May day in 1937, Jenny and I drove our dog team up Clear Creek. The dogs pulled a twelve-foot basket sled equipped with a gee-pole. Wearing skis, I straddled the towline and guided the sled through the deep snow with the gee-pole, a spruce pole that projected from the front of the sled.

Jenny was pregnant and rode on the rear of the sled. We started to cross a deep gully, and as we pitched down the steep cutbank, Jenny stepped on the brake, a simple hinged claw on the rear of the sled. But the brake didn't catch and the heavy sled picked up speed and got out of control. The rear end whipped around and threw Jenny clear across the gully onto the opposite bank and she sustained serious internal injuries.

I put Jenny on the sled and drove her back to our Hog River cabin. Leaving her there, I drove several miles to my uncle Hog River Johnny's place, found his wife Molly at home, and brought her back to nurse Jenny.

I waited for a day, but Jenny didn't improve. She was in considerable pain and Molly advised that I get her to the hospital. "I've never taken care of anyone hurt like this," Molly said.

Jenny was in no condition to ride a dogsled to the hospital. I had to get an airplane. The nearest plane was at Koyukuk Station, so early the next morning I took off from Hog River with my eight dogs. My leader was Dakli, a lovely animal with upstanding pointed ears and a beautiful gray coat. She resembled a wolf. I've never had a better leader.

That day that grand dog team averaged more than ten miles an hour for the 120 miles from Hog River to Koyukuk. Those dogs loved to run. Happily carrying their tails high, their feet pattered on the hard trail, steam puffing from their mouths, with the sled runners singing their song—a song that changed pitch with speed and with changes in the trail.

That evening, I found bush pilot Herman Lerdahl at John Evans' store. "How much will you charge to fly Jenny from Hog River to the hospital at Tanana?" I asked. "I don't have much money, but I have some marten skins, and I think I can get some cash."

"I'll help Sidney with money if he needs it," John Evans said.

"OK, I'll fly her tomorrow," Herman said. "You can pay me when I come back."

The next morning he flew his Curtiss Robin on skis to Hog River, picked Jenny up, and flew her to the Native Service hospital at Tanana. He said that the doctors thought that Jenny would be all right, and that she wouldn't lose the baby. So the following day, I harnessed the team and mushed back to Hog River, arriving before dark.

I waited a few days, but Jenny's condition worried me, so I drove the dogs to Cutoff and I called the hospital on the village radio. News was good; Jenny was doing well. Much relieved, I headed my dog team home.

Traveling in the cool of the evening on crusted snow, we came to the steep bank of the Koyukuk River and headed down. The surface was rough where mud had frozen. I stepped on the brake, the brake claw caught, the brake stick broke, and the sled rolled. I tried to stop the rolling, but the bank was very steep and the dogs were moving fast. I was tossed into the ice-filled river. The swift, frigid water constricted my chest so I could hardly breathe as I frantically splashed shoreward. The dogs continued on their way.

The weight and bulk of my wolfskin parka and heavy clothing dragged me down as I was swept downstream. Soon the current pushed me against the ice's edge along the river. Breakup was near, and the ice was candling and caving in. I couldn't touch bottom, and the rushing current kept pushing my legs downstream, as I clung to the rotten ice.

I had discarded my mittens when I hit the water, and my bare fingers soon became torn and raw from clinging to the ice. I struggled to pull my knife out of its sheath on my belt, then jammed the blade into a crack in the ice. Carefully, I started to pull myself up onto the weak ice by the knife handle. I was nearly out of the water when the knife broke.

I plunged back into the numbing water, exhausted. I thought I was going to die, for the cold had penetrated my body, and it was difficult for me to move. Even thinking was difficult. Realizing I had one chance left, I tried again. I lifted one leg onto the ice. My boot caught and I inched my way up. I lay on the ice for a moment, half in the water, half on the ice, too weak to pull myself any farther.

My hands were numb and bleeding and the blood made them slippery; gripping the ice was almost impossible. Finding some tiny holes, I jammed my hands into them and pulled myself closer to shore. I don't know how long I lay stretched on the creaking ice, trying to gain strength. Finally, drawing a deep breath, I pulled myself upward and forward a few more inches. Alternately resting and pulling, I worked my entire body out of the water and onto the ice.

I couldn't move for a time. Then, keenly aware of the instability of the spring ice, I began wriggling toward shore. Stubbornly I crawled across that rotten ice toward the riverbank. I don't know how long I struggled to reach the muddy beach, but by the time I got there my energy was spent. I passed out or slept, I'm not sure which, soaking wet, numb, chilled to the bone.

I recovered consciousness with Dakli and a few of my other dogs licking my face. They had returned for me! Amazed by behavior so unusual for a dog team, I lifted my head and discovered the sled was still intact, although battered from bouncing on its side. Infused with new hope, I stood up.

With my dogs clustered around me, I staggered to the sled. Happily, my gear was still lashed inside. With badly cut hands that were clumsy and numb, I opened the waterproof bag. This was one time when my habit of traveling with extra clothing on the sled paid off. Struggling to get out of my wet things, I discovered my legs were badly cut and bleeding from the sharp ice—I had been too numb to feel the cuts. I put on dry long johns, pants, and shirt, and I was grateful for the warmth of wool.

Not having enough strength to ride the runners, I sat in the sled's basket and headed the dogs home. I watched the trail, calling "gee" (right) and "haw" (left) to Dakli. She promptly responded to every command. If she hadn't I wasn't sure I could cope with climbing out of the sled to push if we bogged down in soft snow.

I saw tracks where the team had run upriver about five miles without me. This told me that I had spent about an hour in the water and lying wet in the mud afterward, for that team traveled at about ten miles an hour. Dakli had turned them around by leading them in a big half circle, and had followed the trail back. If she hadn't returned,

I would have died.

At the cabin I yanked harnesses off all the dogs and turned them loose. Then I collapsed on the bed. I developed pneumonia, and for weeks breathing was painful and labored, my chest hurt, and I was so weak I could barely move.

While I recovered, the dogs were free to come in and out of the cabin. They caused no trouble, and took care of themselves. I managed to rouse myself enough to toss them their food—dried fish—every day, and they got water from the river.

The dogs often lay close to me when I could scarcely leave the bed. Dakli seemed to understand that her closeness helped, for she spent long hours near me as I slowly gained strength. I remember that great gray dog with much fondness.

In the 1920s and 1930s, a five-dog team was considered large among the Koyukon people. Individual animals then were much larger than the racing sled dogs that became popular in later years. My dogs weighed sixty to seventy pounds, and each could pull 100 pounds for hours at a time when in good condition.

Before metal chains were available, Athapaskans had a clever way of keeping their dogs tied. Most dogs would chew through the rawhide ropes used to tie them, so the early people tied a thong of moosehide around the dog's neck and tied the thong through a hole at the flattened end of a light pole; the other end of the five-foot pole was tied loosely to a tree, so the dog could travel around the tree, but could not reach the leashing. When tied this way, the dog could not cut the thong at its neck, or at the tree, nor could it chew the pole itself.

Until arrival of dependable airplanes in the 1930s, dog teams provided most of the winter transportation in bush Alaska. The government marked dog team trails and built shelter cabins that were used by all travelers. On major routes, roadhouses, about a day's travel apart, provided food and lodging for man and dog.

Early in this century mail teams had perhaps five to eight dogs. By the 1920s and into the 1930s, mail teams of up to twenty-five dogs pulled one, sometimes two huge freight sleds with unbelievable loads. Mail team drivers often hauled passengers as well as mail and freight; there was no other form of winter transportation between the far-flung villages of interior and northern Alaska.

Each summer many Yukon River residents dried tons of chum

salmon to sell as food for sled dogs. Dog liveries or kennels along the Yukon River and at Fairbanks boarded sled dogs during snow-free months.

Many of the dogs used in the Koyukuk and Lower Yukon, including mine, came from stock bred by Ben Derrick, one of the early dog team mail carriers. Reportedly, Derrick saw a wolf frequenting a woodpile across the Yukon River from his place, and tied a fine female sled dog nearby for the wolf to breed.

He then crossed the half-wolf dogs of the resulting litter with a fine strain of sled dogs. During his breeding program he even included a large hunting hound. Eventually, he had fine sled dogs that were slightly less than one-quarter wolf. The females of the line were invariably good workers. Some of the males were lazy, but when the males were good, they were very good. The dogs were selectively bred for toughness, heavy coats, gentleness, a willingness to work, and feet that could withstand the rigors of snow and ice.

I valued my dogs and gave them good care, keeping them in tight, warm houses. I provided dry grass for winter bedding, cooked for them daily, and made friends with all of them. This sounds like common sense, but not all sled dog owners on the Koyukuk and the Lower Yukon treated their animals this well. Sled dogs are work animals, not pets, and some owners regarded them simply as a means of transport and didn't believe in treating them gently. I have seen teams of dogs so wild and vicious that I feared to be near them. Some dogs are left tied all summer, with barely enough food to survive. Even in winter some dogs receive little attention, except when in harness.

Unlike most pet, farm, or hunting breeds known to Americans, sled dogs tend to be aloof and independent. A few wags of the tail may be an emotional response to a master. Nevertheless, sled dogs do respond to good care and affection. My dogs responded to my kindness, and I was fond of them. I believe this is what saved my life when Dakli turned the team and returned to look for me.

I once had to take about half a cord of firewood piled on my twelve-foot-long basket sled up the Koyukuk River, and my eight dogs romped along pulling that heavy load as if it were nothing. At Cutoff I needed to take the load up a steep, fifty-foot bank, and Jack Sackett stood nearby, watching. I stopped the dogs at the riverbank for a rest. I pretended confidence, as I prepared to try that climb. I knew I would have to help too. I started cussing, making believe I was angry at the dogs.

"C'mon boys, let's go," I yelled.

They pulled. I yanked on the towline, which was stretched so tautly that the hard cotton rope felt like a steel cable. Every one of those wonderful, powerful dogs tensed their muscles and leaned into their harnesses with their bellies right against the snow. The sled started to move, and it continued to slide up and over the top of that steep bank, with me pushing and the dogs pulling for all they were worth.

If I had had to bet whether eight dogs could pull that much weight up such a bank, I'd have bet against them. It didn't seem possible. "I've never seen such strong dogs, Sidney," said Sackett, which was high praise from an old-timer who had lived with sled dogs for half a century or more.

For heavy loads, like my load of wood at Cutoff, my dogs wore padded work collars, which weigh only a few ounces. On long trips, padded collars are best for heavy loads because they do not cause a rash inside the front legs of the animals like web harness.

I have great admiration for a well-trained dog team. I once watched Johnny Oldman with his dog team reach a steep riverbank. He had a heavy load in the sled, and he didn't want to take the dogs and sled down the bank together, so he unsnapped the team and walked them down onto the snow-covered river ice.

"Whoa," he commanded Buster, his leader. Buster stopped and so did the entire team.

Johnny then climbed back up the bank and pushed the sled, which slid down in a rush. Then, rehooking the towline, he was again ready to travel. The well-trained dogs hadn't moved.

Another impressive demonstration of control I saw was by Koyukon George Jimmy. He pushed his tiny, fifteen-pound racing sled into position, and, without tying or snubbing it down and with no one at the brake, stretched his towline out.

George turned his team of twelve high-strung racing dogs loose and called them one at a time to their harnesses. When they were all harnessed and hooked to the towline, the dogs, eager to run, stood trembling, ready to leap ahead. But they remained steady.

As they stood poised, George fussed around, getting organized. He put dog chains in a bag on the sled, tied on his marten-skin cap, put on his mittens, and finally stepped onto the runners. Then, at a barely audible sound from his lips, those twelve dogs shot forward like a single bullet.

Many of Alaska's finest racing dog teams have come from the Koyukuk and Lower Yukon country. In 1939 my brother Jimmy, in his first try at that race, won fourth place in the annual North

American Championship Sled Dog Race at Fairbanks. Sadly, he didn't receive the promised prize money, for the organizers of the race went broke. After that experience, Jimmy lost interest in the big-time races.

Then in 1956, when he was thirty-nine, at the urging of a group of Huslia villagers, Jimmy entered sled dog races at Fairbanks and Anchorage. Sled dog racing was then a major sport in Alaska. With three of his own dogs and others loaned by me and various friends, Jimmy became the "Huslia Hustler," a nickname hung on him by the press. In that one season, he won both the North American Championship at Fairbanks and the All-Alaska Championship at Anchorage, beating about thirty of Alaska's top mushers.

He didn't make much money racing dogs, for travel to the big cities, plus living expenses, ate much of the money he made. But for the rest of his life he enjoyed the fame he rightly received for his extraordinary achievements in those two races.

Although I had a fast team, I was raising a family and needed sure money. I knew I could stay home and in a couple of months make $1,500 to $2,000 on my trapline. If I had gone to Fairbanks to race I might have made $1,000 if I won—but after costs, little profit was likely.

So I stayed home and trapped, but many of my dogs raced when I loaned them to Jimmy and other well-known mushers such as Raymond Paul and George Attla. My dogs were always returned with thanks and praise for their performance. And I sold one dog to George Attla, who raced him for a couple of seasons. Later, in the early 1970s, he sold the dog for $1,600, a small price compared with the $4,000 or $5,000 commonly paid today for a top racer.

Nowadays, dogs are commonly bred for speed. A team that cannot run twenty-five miles an hour in a sprint cannot compete in Alaska's sled dog races. Finishing times for twenty- and thirty-mile courses, such as the three-day North American Championship, keep getting shorter.

My wife Jenny had a way with dogs. I once bought a dog team from Dr. Braflet, a dentist who practiced his profession from village to village along the Yukon River, hauling his dental equipment in his sled. He had left his practice, and I bought his team for $15 a dog. Most of them weighed around eighty pounds, and they were beautiful animals, but some of them were as wild as wolves.

I was nervous about a big yellowish fellow. He growled and bared his teeth whenever I came near. I was intimidated and he knew it. One day I decided to harness him, so I wore heavy clothing and heavy mittens, fearing he would bite. I unsnapped his chain and pulled him against my knee, and he turned and started biting.

Jenny, watching through the cabin window, charged to my rescue. Although she was pregnant, wearing a dress, and was bare-legged and bare-handed, she grabbed that big dog's collar and jerked him to the towline and slapped a harness on him. The dog cooled right down.

Jenny, who weighed no more than 100 pounds, said, "You're scared of him and he knows it."

And she was right. After that I'd go to him boldly and do exactly what she had done, and he never gave me a problem again.

Training and working with a good dog team is a joy. Years later, one fine March day, I took my five-year-old son, Carl, with me when I left the Hog River cabin to run my trapline. Carl (who was to win the 1,100-mile Anchorage-to-Nome Iditarod Sled Dog Race in 1974) had begun learning to trap, run dogs, and understand the out-of-doors. I had a tent camp on the trapline, and not far from it we met a pack of wolves. With a lucky shot I managed to kill one. The others fled.

We drove the dog team on through a portage. I stopped to check a trap, tied the sled's snubbing line to a tree, and walked to the trap. While I was gone, the dogs scented a second pack of wolves and grew excited. They lunged and leaped until the snubbing line broke, and away they went with the sled bouncing and flying in their wake.

That left Carl and me afoot. I had intended to cover my entire thirty miles of trapline, but without the team, I'd never make it—I couldn't pack Carl that far. Our tent camp was about eight miles away, so I decided to head in that direction, hoping the dogs would end up there. It was more likely they would tangle the sled, harness, or towline in trees or brush, or if they happened to catch and fight the wolves, some of the dogs might get chewed up or killed.

As I snowshoed along with Carl on my shoulders, I worried about the dogs, and was angry and disgusted. After several miles, as I walked along a lakeshore, Carl piped up, "Looks like dogs or something coming."

Glory be, here came our team trotting around the edge of the lake, pulling the still-upright sled. They bounded to us, tails wagging, grinning, happy. They had finished their wolf chase and returned as if it were an everyday occurrence.

Immensely pleased with my dogs, I grinned widely as I tucked Carl into the basket of the sled and called, "Come gee, Dakli, come gee."

19

BEAVER

✿

The beaver is one of nature's great gifts. This old dam builder is a wonderful, fascinating animal who brings alive the wildlands. I've spent days watching beaver gnaw down trees, then tow them or gnawed-off sections to their dams, lodges, and food piles. Weighing up to fifty pounds, occasionally more, the beaver is unique among the wildife of the Koyukuk, for in his life's work of building dams, he may create ponds that provide him with a year-round, safe home. In the pond he builds a large house of branches and mud, with underwater entrances, and, inside the house, an above-water resting place. All beaver don't build dams and form ponds—some build houses along banks of rivers.

Underwater near their houses, beaver store tree limbs for winter food. They eat the bark from these limbs; cottonwood, poplar, and birch are favorites.

Because of his fine, durable, warm fur and tasty flesh, the people of the Koyukuk have always made use of the beaver. In prewhite times, the Koyukon people had their own specialized method of harvesting the animal, in winter. After that, for about half a century, from the late 1800s until the 1940s, the main method of taking beaver was to shoot them with a rifle. This was wasteful, for many beaver were lost by sinking. Since the 1940s shooting beaver has been illegal.

One spring in the mid-1930s, my brother Jimmy and I decided to hunt beaver on Hog River. This was when Jimmy lived at Cutoff and I lived at Hog River; we were both in our twenties.

We started from Cutoff with two teams of five dogs each. Our plan was to travel to a point upstream from the Pah River portage, a trip of eighty miles as the raven flies, probably 100 miles by dog team. The area is hilly, with mostly spruce and birch timber.

We reached Hog River with no difficulty. The snow was still frozen, but each day the temperature neared the thawing mark. After going through the Sun Mountain area and over the hills, travel became difficult: the snow was slushy, and the dogs and loaded sleds sank deeply into it.

We camped for the night and set out early the next day to climb a big ridge while the snow was still hard from the night's freeze. The dogs could hardly handle our heavily loaded sleds, and we had to push with all our strength.

When we reached the top, I was so hungry I stopped to eat while Jimmy went ahead. I had a couple of bottles of seal oil, traded from a coastal Eskimo, and some old dried salmon. I ignored the moldy tinge of green on the salmon and ate greedily. Along with the moldy fish, I swallowed plenty of seal oil, which tasted good.

Jimmy had found a live beaver house and was waiting at it when I caught up. We camped nearby, preparing to start our beaver hunt. As it turned out, I wasn't able to participate in the hunt for a while. Afflicted by diarrhea from my meal, I spent about a day and a half sitting on a big willow branch as the seal oil dripped through me.

In the meantime, Jimmy shot a couple of beaver, so we had something decent to eat. When I recovered I joined in the hunt. I carried a new .25–20, while Jimmy had a .30–30. We used hard-nosed bullets that did little damage to beaver skins. We searched for active beaver lodges where beaver had been leaving the water to feed. We would quietly wait until the animals left the water, and then shoot them in the eye or nose. We had to quickly retrieve the animals, for if we didn't move fast a beaver sometimes kicked itself back under the ice in a death flurry. If we killed three or four or more in an area distant from camp, we skinned them so we didn't have to carry the heavy carcasses.

As we worked our way downstream, the weather warmed. When the snow froze during the night or early morning, we moved as fast as we could before it thawed and turned to slush again.

One day we had to cross a deep creek. The ice covering it looked solid and, though breakup was near, we decided to take a chance. Jimmy had the guns and ammunition on his sled; my heavier sled held food, camping gear, and other items.

Jimmy whooped at his dogs, and they sped across the ice. Stopping, he watched while I crossed. "C'mon guys," I yelled at my dogs and they followed in Jimmy's tracks. All went well for the first few feet. Suddenly, the ice broke and my sled sank in the swift water. I clung to the submerging sled as pieces of ice flew all about, but I had to turn loose when it rolled in the current. My load spilled and washed away; the only items left were those lashed to the sled with rawhide.

Jimmy grabbed my towline and, with the help of my dogs, pulled me and the sled ashore. I was soaking wet from feet to shoulders. Jimmy started a fire and I changed into dry clothes from the pack on his sled.

The current had swept most of our food out of reach under the ice. We managed to retrieve coffee, but we had no bacon, flour, salt, or sugar. As a result, for a month we ate mostly beaver meat. Without salt, I didn't like the taste, and eventually I couldn't eat any more beaver. When there was nothing else to eat, I burned the beaver meat thoroughly; burned beaver tastes better to me than unsalted beaver. Joe Beatus, a Koyukon elder of Cutoff, later told me that I'd have been better off not cooking the meat, that I should have eaten it raw. Maybe he was right.

We boiled or burned many geese that we shot, and made goose soup. I practically lived on that soup.

We brought sixty beaver skins home, and each of us made about $300—not an especially good take. I lost a lot of weight on that trip: my normal weight is about 160 pounds, and when I got home I weighed about 135.

On that trip, Jimmy and I were walking to a lake to look for beaver when we saw a big black bear on a nearby hillside. The bear eyed us, but we ignored him. We had plenty of beaver meat, which we were eating and feeding to the dogs, so we had no need for the bear. Suddenly, without a sound, the bear charged, bounding directly at us.

My rifle was over my shoulder, and I started to pull the case off. Jimmy fired, hitting the bear in the heart so that it died instantly, collapsing in mid-stride. It rolled between us while I was still trying to slide the case off of my rifle. Disgusted, I threw the gun case away, and I have never since carried a cased rifle while afield.

Beaver, which become very fat, are an important food animal for the Koyukon people. In prewhite times—before traps, snares, rifles, and steel ice-chisels—no one trapped beaver beneath the ice, the primary method of taking them today.

When a Koyukon hunter of the old ways wanted a beaver in winter, he first located all the "extra houses," or "hideout houses," that the beaver may use for feeding once ice locks them into pond and lodge. He then cut open all the hideout houses so they froze and became unusable for the beaver. Next, with an axe, he cut a hole through the top of the main lodge, which can be difficult, for frozen mud and sticks of a beaver house are hard as rock and may be a foot or more thick.

If the hunter had previously found every hideout house and made them useless to the beaver, he would find all the beaver lying together in the water inside the main lodge. Sometimes their chins would be resting on the platform at waterline, the only place they could surface to breathe. Frequently, the beaver behaved almost as if they were waiting for the hunter to take them.

The rest is hard to believe, and I was skeptical before I witnessed it. In 1935 my Uncle Weaselheart and his wife, Josie, told me that I should be ready if I wanted to see them "take" (kill all the beaver in) a beaver house at a lake about ten miles below Hog River.

Earlier, I had seen where Weaselheart had searched out and cut open all the hideout houses and allowed them to freeze. On the day I figured they might be taking the house, I went to the lake. Sure enough, Weaselheart was near the beaver lodge and Josie was inside it. She had already taken out one big beaver, almost as big as herself. It was an honest super blanket size. (Beaver skins are stretched round and graded into sizes: small, 40- to 44-inch diameter; medium, 45 to 49 inches; large medium, 50 to 54 inches; large, 55 to 59 inches; extra large, 60 to 64 inches; blanket, 65 to 67 inches; and super blanket, 68 inches and up.)

After they had chopped into the top of the lodge, Josie had climbed in. The beaver, on the resting platform, dived into the water of one of their exit tunnels. Then they lay there, facing Josie, their chins on the edge of their resting platform. Josie kneeled, and with bare hands she seized the largest beaver by both front legs. Once she had her hands on the beaver's legs, she never let go. She lifted the heavy animal past her chest and face, over the edge of the hole, and passed it to Weaselheart, who killed it with a club.

The old Koyukon stories say that beaver lifted in this manner will not bite or struggle, provided the person doing the lifting has no fear. All beaver living in a lodge are taken in such an operation. Tradition says that if the young ones are lifted out first, the other, larger, beaver may fight and bite.

"You want to try?" Weaselheart asked me.

Reluctantly, I said, "Yes."

Josie, in the beaver lodge, exploded in the Koyukon tongue. I could not understand her long harangue.

"Are you sure?" Josie then asked me. "If you are even a little bit scared you may get bitten. I wouldn't try it if I were you. If animals smell fear, they bite."

I decided she was doing all right, and maybe I had better just watch. Beavers have powerful jaws, and their teeth are big and sharp.

As I watched, Aunt Josie went back to work. She lifted the next-largest beaver out of the water, eased it past her chest and face, clearly within biting distance, and put it where Weaselheart could club it.

I watched her boldly catch and lift out five beaver, making a total of six that came from that house—parents, yearlings, and young of the year.

"Uncle Peter, why did Josie give you hell when you invited me to go into the beaver house?" I later asked Weaselheart.

"She say, 'Don't you know our old stories? They say you don't change places in the house after you take some beaver out.' The beaver will get scared of the new person trying to catch them, and the new person usually gets hurt. The beaver don't trust anyone anymore. They are then lost, for they swim off and die," he explained.

How many hundreds, perhaps thousands, of years were needed for Koyukon people to learn this technique? And only with instructions passed from generation to generation did anyone of my mother's generation know how to take beaver in this manner.

Spring beaver hunting with rifles, an annual activity for half a century, nearly wiped out Alaska's beaver. Half the shot beaver sink and are lost. I remember shooting ten or fifteen beaver, and returning home with seven or eight. One night I returned with twenty-two; I don't know how many sank.

A careful and experienced hunter went prepared with a spear and a throwing weight with hooks attached to a light rope for retrieving the animals. This saved many beaver that would otherwise have been lost.

Beaver and sea otter were among the most important animals in the early Russian fur trade, when Russia claimed Alaska. By 1910 Alaska's beaver seemed bound for extinction, and between 1910 and 1923, killing of beaver was prohibited. The season reopened in 1923, and in 1926 a season limit of twenty per hunter was set, but beaver again became so scarce that in the late 1930s and '40s the federal government closed the season. Beaver are prolific, and within a few short years they returned in good numbers. After that, shooting was prohibited, and each trapper was limited to a specific number each season.

Today in the Koyukuk, the animals can legally be taken only with traps and snares. At first the limit was five, then it went to ten and twenty. Now, in many areas of Alaska there is no limit.

Warden Sam White taught us how to trap beaver under the ice

using a simple pole set. This required cutting a hole in the ice of a beaver pond and thrusting a pole through it with bait sticks of poplar nailed to it. A trap was fastened to the pole near the bait sticks. Once we learned this system, we improved on it.

George Attla, Sr., became an expert at trapping beaver under the ice. He perfected a system that we call "the crooked stick set." One spring Jimmy happened to hit George's trail during beaver trapping season. Jimmy wasn't catching many beaver, so he followed Attla's trail and studied his sets.

The following winter he tried Attla's method. Like Attla, he used an L-shaped pole or heavy stick. The bottom half of the L lies beneath the ice and parallel to it. The top half of the L projects almost a foot out of the ice. A No. 21 jump trap, or a No. 4 jump trap with teeth, with the leaf spring nearest the pole, is tied to the horizontal arm of the L, exactly one shovel's depth (metal part only) beneath the ice. Bait sticks, usually poplar twigs, are shoved straight down the hole in the ice so they are just above the trap. This set catches mostly big beaver.

A good beaver trap costs $25 to $30 nowadays instead of the $5 or $6 I used to pay. Because of the high cost of traps, most who seek beaver now use snares, which are much cheaper. There are many variations in snare sets for catching beaver under the ice.

One year I caught 178 beaver with help from my family. One night I brought home twenty, including fourteen super blanket size and half a dozen smaller ones. I skinned them in the tent where we lived during beaver season. I used to skin a super blanket beaver clean in twenty minutes or less, and I finished skinning all twenty of those beaver before I went to bed that night.

I've always followed the traditional Koyukon custom of removing the innards of beaver in a special way. The procedure is to skin the beaver, leaving the feet and tail on the carcass. I remove the castorum (two large glands under the base of the tail) carefully, without cutting any tubes. Then I cut off the head low on the neck and carefully remove all of the viscera by cutting loose the kidneys, liver, stomach, intestines, heart, lungs—leaving all attached to each other and the head. The important food part of the animal, a neatly cleaned carcass, remains.

Then I throw the head and attached viscera back into the river or pond from which the animal was caught while chanting the old Koyukon words that mean "make lots more beaver." This is a way of showing respect for the beaver and appreciation for the privilege of trapping it.

About this ceremony, an Indian friend once commented, "It doesn't bother a person who doesn't know about it, but I know the traditional beliefs, and it bothers me if I don't observe them."

I'm in the same boat.

20

SPEARING GRIZZLY BEARS

❂

When war came in December 1941, at the Japanese bombing of Pearl Harbor, Jenny and I had six children—Franklin, Marie, Electa, Arnold, John, and Leonard. Nevertheless, I went to Anchorage to enlist in the Army. I had never seen such turmoil. People crowded the streets; construction continued day and night, with trucks and tractors running continuously.

At the Army recruiting office, I completed a questionnaire. The recruiter left and returned shortly with a civilian, who said, "I understand you can work with metal."

"Yes, I've done a little sheet metal work," I replied. Charlie Swanson had taught me some of the basics at Batza River, and I had once worked for a short time helping on a sheet metal job at Galena.

"We need sheet metal workers at Fort Richardson," he said. "You don't have to go into the Army. We'll give you a draft classification that will keep you out of the service."

"But I want to do my share," I said. During World War II every able-bodied Alaskan wanted to help his country.

"You can help best by working for us as a sheet metal worker," he answered.

I went to work at Fort Richardson near Anchorage as a sheet metal roofer on January 1, 1942. One week later I was promoted to sheet metal roofing foreman. I worked all spring and all summer, night and day, for as many hours as I could stand. I bought a house in Anchorage, and Jenny and the kids joined me. I had never lived under such stress. People were everywhere, crowding and pushing. We stood in lines to buy clothing, food, and cigarettes. Everyone was in a hurry. Living was expensive, although I was making more money than I had ever dreamed of making.

That fall, as I put roofs on military buildings, hundreds of flocks of geese flew over. With every flock heading south I'd raise my eyes and remember the sweet silence of the Koyukuk, the smell of spruce forests, the yelp of sled dogs, and thousands of square miles of beautiful, unpeopled land. Those great Vs of birds and their wild calls seemed to be telling me, "Sidney, you weren't bred to live like this. You don't belong in this crowded place."

Finally, I went to the colonel in charge of the base. "I've got to leave, Colonel," I told him.

"Why? You're doing a good job."

"I've trained a man to do my job."

I was unable to express my strong feeling of homesickness, but somehow he understood. He called Galena, where a new Air Force base was under construction, and found me a job as foreman of an oiling truck and a crew of twenty men. With relief and gratitude, I agreed to take the job. Jenny and I sold our Anchorage house and moved to Galena.

At Galena I was only a ten-minute walk from the Alaskan wilds where I had lived most of my life. I renewed my ties with the forests and streams by hunting, trapping, picking berries, and fishing in my off-hours.

The Galena Air Force Base was originally a Civil Aeronautics Authority (today the Federal Aviation Administration) airfield. During World War II, it was the first stop for Russian pilots flying American lend-lease warplanes from Fairbanks to Russia. During the war, I saw as many as 132 Bell Airacobra (P-39) fighter planes parked there, awaiting improved weather so they could fly to Nome. Altogether, the Russians accepted 7,929 American warplanes at Fairbanks and flew them to Nome via Galena. From Nome, the planes flew across the Bering Straits to Siberia, then to the Eastern Front, where they flew in combat against the Germans.

The Air Force decision to build at Galena created a boomtown on the north bank of the Yukon River, 575 river miles from the Bering Sea. About thirty-five people lived in Galena in 1941 at the start of construction. With the influx of people, the quiet village became a noisy tent city. During wartime, Galena's population ballooned to at least 3,000.

The Air Force first arrived at Galena via the Yukon River with six barges full of tractors, trucks, and cranes. Twenty soldiers were dumped on the beach with that heavy equipment. They had no blankets and no housing. The Koyukon people of Galena took those GIs into their homes as if they were their own kids, including the commanding officer, a Lieutenant O'Neil. The men slept and ate at the homes of Native families, while they ran the tractors, cranes, and trucks to build the airfield.

The Galena Native homes were mostly small, simple log cabins, but they were warm and open to these hardworking young men. They became homes away from home for the soldiers, and many close relationships were forged.

That winter, soldiers built a huge domed airplane hangar. To bolt the girders in place, they worked 150 feet in the air from buckets lifted by draglines, never losing a day of work, no matter how cold or how windy. I saw them working at −58 degrees. Those rugged men became highly respected for their accomplishments during the time they lived at Galena. Some of them fell in love with Alaska and our way of life. Upon discharge from the service, many settled in Alaska and married Native girls.

Life changed for many local residents who found permanent jobs at the Galena Air Force Base. From seasonal trapping and commercial fishing, with a consequent seasonal income, they converted to a partial cash economy with year-round income. Most continued to largely depend upon game and fish for food.

In 1939, the last boat that Jimmy and I whipsawed lumber for and built at Hog River was the thirty-two-foot *Koyukuk*. She was long and skinny, with a five-foot beam and a reverse-curve bow. With the twenty-horsepower Kermath marine engine we installed, the *Koyukuk* could make about twenty miles an hour, fast for the time.

Jimmy's personal Pearl Harbor on December 7, 1941, was the death of his wife Celia that day, from tuberculosis. Jimmy and Celia had a daughter, Christine. Three years later Jimmy married Flora Charles. In time they had seven children, but Jimmy and Flora split up, and Jimmy kept all the kids and later married Marion, a girl from Koyukuk, who helped Jimmy raise all those kids plus an adopted daughter. When Jimmy and Marion split up, he never remarried.

In 1943, with the *Koyukuk*, Jimmy started towing rafts of floating gasoline barrels from Nenana to the Air Force base at Galena where the fuel was needed for Russia-bound warplanes. The barrels were held together with two-by-four frames, and some of the rafts held as many as 2,000 fifty-five-gallon drums. Jimmy towed these rafts down the Tanana River to the Yukon River, then down the Yukon to Galena.

At Galena, the army picked four drums at a time out of the water with a dragline. Thousands of those barrels, empty and full, were eventually scattered around Galena, along back trails and in the woods. Alaskans nicknamed gasoline drums "tundra daisies," for they seemed to sprout everywhere in the Territory.

In the spring of 1943, after sticking to my wartime jobs at Anchorage and Galena for seventeen months almost without a break, I applied for a month of leave and mushed a dog team from Galena to the headwaters of the Huslia River, a tributary to the Koyukuk. I wanted to make a lone hunt for beaver. After the stress of wartime work, the hunt and the solitude were more important to me than any money I would make. But on the way, at Cutoff, I encountered Louis Golchik, a Koyukon elder, who was dying of tuberculosis, and he asked me to take him with me.

"Sidney, it will be my last hunt, for I don't have long to live," he said. "I promise I won't be in your way."

"Sure, Louie," I agreed, for he was a wonderful old man. "If you'll take care of camp, I'll do the rest."

We traveled by dogsled, pulled by two of my poorest dogs and three dogs given to me by Steven Attla. Attla was leaving for military service, and he had to get rid of his dogs before he left. Upon reaching our destination we killed the dogs, and, after breakup, drifted back downriver in canoes we made with spruce frames carved with axe and knife, and covered with canvas I had hauled in the sled.

During our hunt we lingered over many evening campfires when I should have been hunting, because the failing Louis wanted to share his memories. During that time he told me of the last Koyukon winter spear hunt for grizzly bear. He had been one of the hunters.

I have hunted with several older Koyukon men who sometimes talked about the old ways and the old days, including Johnny Oldman, Little

Sammy, Edwin Simon, and Louis Golchik. Many aspects of old Athapaskan culture are almost unknown because of a taboo against talking about them. In modern times, many elders have been reluctant to talk because they don't want to be considered superstitious, for some of their beliefs would be so labeled today. Another compelling reason for silence was humility. Because he was dying, Louis Golchik was willing to talk about forbidden subjects.

For many years, out of respect for the elders, I have not discussed many of the old beliefs or repeated stories I heard. But most of the elders I once knew are gone, and many young Koyukon people are unaware of the old beliefs. I am in my last years and I would like to see preserved a few of the old beliefs and stories.

Early Koyukon hunters never talked about big game animals in the presence of a woman. This was a cultural taboo, and was particularly true for the brown or grizzly bear. Their respect for "the big animal," as the grizzly was always obliquely referred to, was close to fear. This is not surprising, considering that the early hunters had to face this, the largest and fiercest North American land carnivore, with nothing more than a spear or bow and arrow.

That some Koyukon people deliberately sought the grizzly bear with a spear has always amazed me. Hunting a grizzly with a spear required detailed planning and preparation. The spear handle, upon which the hunter's life depended, was the most critical part of the preparation. Before venturing after a bear, spear in hand, the hunter had to know if the spear could withstand the powerful blows of a grizzly bear's paws.

The handle, helve, or length of the spear, always cut in July, was made from a birch tree growing on level ground. The best birch for a handle grows near a river where large spruce trees provide shade from the hot summer sun. Slow-growing trees not more than two and a half inches in diameter were sought. The bark had to be pinkish brown, with no loose bark. Very small, clean, horizontal lines on the growing birch were a sign of its strength. A suitable birch tree was cut, leaving about a foot-long stump.

To test the grain and the quality of the wood, a piece was cut from above the section to be used as a handle. An axe was placed dead center across the end of the sample and hammered in a short way with a block of wood. If the birch didn't split, the axe was removed and wedges of hard dry spruce were driven into the cut. If the birch still didn't split, it was considered suitable.

The birch handle was then burned with the bark on. Heat was driven from the outside into the center of the wood, tempering it. After the bark was burned off, the pole was hung from the butt end to dry in the shade in an out-of-the-way spot where no woman could see it.

After many weeks of drying, it was again tempered by fire, with the shine being slowly burned off. The end on which the point was to be fastened was narrowed. The handgrip was left full size.

The handle was then tested by beating it on a large tree that had the bark peeled from it. After beating it in every way possible that might break it, the pole was placed over a fire to see if expansion of the wood revealed any cracks. Even a hairline crack was sufficient evidence of weakness to discard a handle. Only a handle that passed all of these tests was considered suitable for a spear.

Both the point, often made from a sharpened bone from a grizzly, and a crossbar were attached with wet rawhide. As rawhide dries, it shrinks. This tightened both the crosspiece and the point so that both were rigidly attached. The crosspiece, fastened about nine inches from the tip, acted as a stop, preventing the spear from entering the bear too far.

When the grizzly was hunted during summer or fall, the hunter most often went alone, for more than one hunter could distract a bear, making him more unpredictable. The hunt was ruined if a woman learned about it—for that put a curse on the hunt that could cost the hunter his life. Sometimes a woman, learning of a hunt, warned the man. "Don't go. We've heard of your plans." When that happened, the hunter canceled the hunt.

If, after many days of a summer hunt, a hunter failed to locate a bear, the bear was telling him that he (the bear) had the advantage. Perhaps, the hunter would believe, someone had talked or bragged about the hunt. If all went well and a lone hunter sought the big animal in summer or fall, he tried to find it on hard ground atop an open ridge. In spring or fall, frozen ground was acceptable, although it is sometimes slippery. The hunter had to select a place with ground on which the end of the pole would not slip after the spear had entered the bear's chest.

The grizzly bear fears no other animal. In encounters with man, he normally goes on his way in peace. But when challenged, surprised, or angered, he may attack. His great strength and size, his huge teeth, and his five- to seven-inch-long claws make the grizzly a formidable killer. A grizzly can break the neck of a moose with one swat, and a big grizzly can carry a 1,000-pound moose in his jaws.

In snow-free months, early Koyukon hunters seeking an encounter with a grizzly approached the bear and taunted it by shooting it with blunt arrows. This angered the animal, and usually it charged. The hunter held his ground. From a full charge the bear habitually reared on hind legs within reach of the spear tip. The hunter quickly plunged the point into the animal's chest. Instantly, the hunter jammed the end of the spear handle against the ground and held it there, literally for dear life. The bear pushed forward—it never retreated. Both front paws beat upon the spear handle. The bear sometimes pivoted on the cross bar, and circled as he tried to reach the hunter. The harder he tried, the more damage the spear point did to his lungs and/or heart, and soon the grizzly toppled to the ground, dead or dying.

Early in this century a photographer arranged to take movies of a Koyukon hunter killing a grizzly in this manner. All went well until the bear charged. The photographer lost his nerve and fled while the Indian killed the bear, so he failed to get pictures of the actual killing. He did return shortly to take still photographs of the bear and the small Indian with a spear. The spear, tipped with sharpened bone made from the forearm of a bear, was only five to five and a half feet long—shorter than the Koyukon hunter who used it. I once saw one of these pictures hanging on a wall in an old building at Tanana.

Austin Joe and Chief Paul, two Koyukon hunters from Koyukuk Station, decided to make a winter hunt for grizzly with a spear. Both had helped take bears from a den about ten years earlier. This was to be their last great test, the end of an era, for they realized that no Koyukuk Indian was likely to make such a hunt ever again. The knowledge of how to make such a hunt, and the tradition of making them, had nearly died out.

To the old Koyukon people, killing a grizzly with a spear was the supreme test of a man as an individual, and as a hunter. A winter hunt for a grizzly in its den was more complex than a summer hunt, for it required cooperation of at least three skilled, strong, and agile hunters. To kill one or more grizzlies at a den tested a hunter for speed, quickness, and character. His actions determined whether he could control fear, if he were a liar, whether he could keep his mouth shut, and whether he was a braggart.

The hunt the failing Louis Golchik described for me occurred about 1917, and I believe it was the last successful Koyukon winter spear hunt for grizzly. Here is his story:

That fall Chief Paul asked Tom Patsy and me to accompany him to 3,000-foot Heart Mountain (its base is in the shape of a heart), about forty miles up the Koyukuk River. His purpose was to hunt (with rifles) black bears for meat while they were feeding on blueberries, fattening themselves before winter.

After we had killed a black bear, Chief Paul told us that we had been chosen to prepare for the supreme test of a Koyukon hunter—to take a "big animal" from its den with a spear.

"You are the fastest and strongest young men on the Koyukuk and lower Yukon," Chief Paul said. "You will be the fast men on this last great spear hunt for the 'big animal.'" Both of us were relatively small, 5 feet 7 inches tall and weighing about 135 pounds, but strong.

I had never been so honored, but I couldn't discuss the honor—that would have been bragging. I knew stories of famous hunters who had speared the "big animal" both in the Koyukuk valley and in the Nulato and Kaltag areas, but no Koyukon hunter ever admitted that he had taken, or helped take, a "big animal" with a spear.

Chief Paul explained the rigid requirements: not one word of the hunt could be mentioned. Idle talk could cost us our lives. We were not to ask how the old-timers hunted "the big animal" because no real hunter who had killed a bear would talk. A braggart wasn't worth listening to.

"When the time comes, two of us will teach you," said Chief Paul. That surprised me. "Where is the other hunter?" I asked.

"He is finishing some secret work. You know him. You will meet him this winter about one month before we try to take a 'big animal,'" Chief Paul answered.

When the black bear hunt ended, Chief Paul told Tom and me to keep in shape by running to toughen our muscles. "I want you to secretly practice the pole vault, too," Chief Paul said. We were to constantly think about what we had to do to beat the "big animal" in order to be real men and proud Indians like our forefathers.

"Even when you defeat others in running or wrestling, never say you are faster, stronger, or better. That might hurt people's feelings. It might also give you problems during the hunt," Chief Paul warned.

Chief Paul told me that a message would reach me in early December telling me where to go, and I was to travel by foot to a place somewhere on the Kateel River to meet the other hunters. I left the Yukon River that fall and stayed with my sister, Martha Cleever, and her husband on the Koyukuk River below the Dulbi River. Tom Patsy spent the fall at Chips Island, in the Koyukuk River, below the Kateel River.

In December, word came that Chief Paul wanted me to travel to Chips Island, so I set out on snowshoes, camped one night, and arrived next day. I was in the best physical shape of my life.

At Chips Island, I met five people—Tom Patsy, Austin Joe, Chief Paul, and Andrew Paul, Chief Paul's son. I will not mention the name of the other man, because it could embarrass relatives who are still living. He had bragged about taking a "big animal" single-handed with a spear.

Chief Paul spoke to us. "Austin Joe has found the den of a female 'big animal' with two almost-grown cubs. Tomorrow we'll cross over to the Kateel [a river that flows into the Koyukuk from the west]. There we'll practice at an old bear den, and you will learn what must be done." Austin Joe had also carefully prepared the spear for the hunt, following all the old traditions.

After a walk of a day and a half to the old den, we rehearsed carefully. Each of us had a role, and each of our lives depended on the quickness, bravery, and ability of the others.

To test Tom's and my pole-vaulting ability, a big fire was built of spruce boughs. Each of us had to vault through the flames while wearing a fur parka. A scorched parka would have disqualified us for the spear hunt for "the big animal."

Both of us qualified.

When we were ready for the hunt, the wind was wrong, blowing from the east. Because of the location of the den, we needed a north wind, and the stronger the better. After waiting a day or two for the right wind, we camped within a mile of the den. The following day we studied the den from a distance, becoming familiar with the approach, and planning the route each of us had to follow to reach our positions at the den.

The last evening before the hunt we told traditional stories of long-ago hunts, tales handed down from generation to generation. Included were stories about hunters who had died when their spear hunt for the "big animal" went wrong.

Conditions were perfect at daylight next morning. A light wind blew from the north, and the temperature was mild, about o. We didn't eat breakfast because we feared conditions would change if we delayed. Chief Paul gave last-minute instructions, and the five of us swiftly moved to the occupied den.

Tom Patsy, the fastest, carried an eight-foot vaulting pole of tough, dried birch. He dashed to the den entrance, vaulted over it and drove his vaulting pole across the den mouth. I followed and quickly drove my pole into place so that the two poles formed an X across the den opening. "Big animal" dens usually have dry loose soil at the entrance, which permits poles to be driven into the ground so they won't slip easily.

The two vaulting poles Tom and I held functioned as a gate, keeping the "big animals" in the den until the man with the killing spear was ready. The commotion we caused by vaulting into position and closing the den with our vaulting poles brought the old female to the mouth of the den almost as soon as the poles were in place. In front of the den, Austin Joe quickly cut a hole in the ground into which the handle end of the killing spear could be planted. Meanwhile, Chief Paul talked to the "big animal" in a language unknown to me. I was later told it was bear talk.

Would the "big animal" accept the spear? Perhaps we would have to use one of the two .30-30 rifles we had brought. If the "big animal" didn't accept the spear, there could be many possible reasons: Did someone brag? Had word of our hunt somehow leaked? Had a woman seen the spear? Did any woman know about the hunt?

While Austin Joe dug the hole, Andrew Paul and the other man joined Tom and me in holding the gate poles to prevent the "big animals" from pulling the poles in or pushing them out. Austin Joe finished the hole and Chief Paul set the spear handle into it and braced himself. "Let the first one out," he called. We pulled our poles back, opening the den, and the big female rushed directly into the spear held by Chief Paul. The spear entered the "big animal's" chest. The crossbar held the animal off so that her powerful claws and teeth could not reach him.

Chief Paul held the handle firmly in the hole in the ground, and with a mighty heave, using the momentum of the charging "big animal," threw it right over himself. The big female flew about twenty-five feet downhill, with its chest organs ripped to shreds, and landed with a thud. It rolled a few feet and lay dying.

The instant the big female left the den, Tom and I jammed our poles back into the ground to re-form the gate. Two nearly grown cubs remained in the den.

Now the test: Chief Paul handed the spear to the man who had bragged about taking a bear single-handed with a spear. Chief Paul spoke, "I helped take a 'big animal' once with a spear. I never talked about it before. I know this is my last 'big animal'—the one you see lying there, dead. This could be your last one too. Now you try, because I don't believe you ever took a 'big animal' with a spear.

"We never told you that we were going to try to take the "big animals" with a spear because we were afraid you would talk. Maybe you wouldn't go with us. I want to demonstrate to these men how not to brag, and why no Koyukon should talk about taking 'big animals' with a spear, trying to make a big man of himself."

Obediently, the man accepted the spear. He tried to get the young "big animal" at the mouth of the den to accept it. To test the "big animal," he placed the point of the spear under its mouth, near the throat. The "big animal" slapped the spear aside. This meant he sensed fear in the man holding the spear. If the weapon had passed his face without the "big animal" slapping it aside, it would have meant that the man holding the spear was brave enough to handle that "big animal."

The "big animal" pushed the blade aside not once, but twice, indicating that the man was afraid. Then Austin Joe grabbed the spear, saying, "You lie. You never took a 'big animal' by yourself with a spear. This one tell us. I never took one either, but I never lie. Now watch this."

With that Austin Joe called, "Open the den." Tom and I pulled our poles clear. One of the "big animals" charged. Austin Joe set the spear and the charging "big animal" impaled himself upon it. Like the old female, the big cub was thrown through the air with lungs and heart shredded. The dying "big animal" landed far downhill, near the adult.

Austin Joe handed the bloody spear once more to the braggart, with the same results. The last "big animal" in the den pushed the blade aside.

Then the spear was handed to one of the younger people. The third "big animal" charged and impaled himself, and the spearman tossed it down the hill to join the first two dead animals.

"One of the younger people," was, of course, Louis. Old Louis Golchik refused to brag, even though he knew he was near death.

For many years the eighteen-inch-long metal blade from the spear used on that hunt was displayed in the home of trader Dominic Vernetti at Koyukuk Station. With lingering belief, Louis told me, "That spear point would not be good for another hunt. Too many women's hands have touched it. Too many people have seen it."

Louis Golchik died a few weeks after we canoed down the Huslia River at the end of our beaver hunt.

Jenny and I were divorced in 1944. We remained friends, and we both stayed close to our children. Later that year I married Angela Pitka, a Koyukon girl of eighteen. Tall and strikingly beautiful, she was a woman of great determination and ability. She lost both of her parents early in life, and was raised by an older sister and an aunt.

In 1945, at war's end, Angela and I moved from Galena to Hog River, where I took up my old life on the trapline. I took enough fur so we had some cash. I killed enough game and caught enough fish to permit us to eat and live well. Ours was a simple wilderness life, much as I had lived for years before the war.

In some ways, those years on the trapline with Angela were the best of my life. She helped me whipsaw lumber so I could build boats. She cut firewood, helped run the traplines, and caught, cut up, and dried fish. She often stayed alone while I was off running distant traplines or working at other jobs, which I was forced to do in order to make enough to take care of our growing family. Every year we had a new baby. First came Roger, then Elma, Carl, Annie, and Agnes. There were to be more.

21

KOYUKUK MOOSE

September in the Koyukuk valley has a special feel. Dark nights have returned, there is less heat to the sun, and at midday tree shadows have noticeably lengthened from those of summer. Nights, brilliant with Northern Lights, are crisp, and ice forms on the edges of ponds—a forecast of things to come. Yellow, gold, and red leaves splash the forest and hills. Great Vs of cranes and geese bound for a warmer land pass over, their musical cries drifting in their wake.

It is the time to dig potatoes and use the last of the broccoli and cabbage that still hangs on in the garden. Blueberries, which ripen in the muskegs by the end of August, must be picked and sugared down before the frosts soften them. Crimson cranberries are firm and ripe shortly afterward, ready to put up in baskets or kegs. Firewood must be cut and split. Cabin chinking should be checked for tightness. Dried fish and meat must be stored. Early September is also time to hunt moose, before the rut begins and while the meat is still sweet and mild, yet when it is cold enough so that it won't spoil. One fine mid-September day in the late 1940s, I left our cabin in late afternoon, and, alone, poled and paddled a small boat up Hog River. I had planned an evening hunt, hoping to find a bull moose near the river. Moose had moved into the Koyukuk, and were becoming a more common part of our diet.

Moose are best hunted at dawn and dusk, when they are active. I eased my boat ashore, tied it, and with .30–30 rifle in hand, followed a winding, well-used game trail through the spruce and birch forest beside the river. It was sprinkled with fresh moose tracks. I wore moccasins and soft-fabric pants and jacket that made no noise as I eased past trees and through brushy thickets. I ghosted along for half a mile, then climbed to a favorite lookout where I could see a few acres of treeless tundra flats, the edge of a pond, and a few hundred yards along tree-lined Hog River. There I sat on a downed tree, watching, listening, absorbing the sounds, sights, and feelings of the land. I was content and fulfilled, one with the land. I didn't feel as if I owned it—I was, simply, a part of it, and it was beautiful and wonderful.

I have always loved the evening hunt, especially when it is calm and clear. As the sun nears the horizon, a hush descends on the forest and there is an expectancy in the air. Jays, thrushes, chickadees, and other small birds scurry about with occasional calls as they seek their night's shelter. The cool evening air is like wine, and a wool mackinaw and cotton work gloves feel good.

Moose may occasionally call. Cows sometimes make a peculiar, high-pitched, birdlike *chirrup* that carries for miles; bulls may emit a deep, resonating grunt. Even the sound of water flowing down a steep creek may be heard for hundreds of yards in cool, still air.

The shadows deepened. Two ravens flew over, playing in flight. One folded his wings and rolled upside down, only to catch himself when he had dropped twenty or thirty feet. The other imitated his companion. Ravens are masters of flight, and often play in updrafts. This big, intelligent black bird eats anything—mice, carrion, birds' eggs, fish. They live in the Koyukuk country summer and winter.

A great horned owl, an old acquaintance who lived somewhere in a nearby stand of spruces, called a deep, hollow *who who* several times. It's a wonderful sound. In my mind's eye I could see him sitting high among the branches, blinking his big yellow eyes, his round, eared head turning this way and that, as he contemplated the coming evening.

I saw movement among the spruces by the riverbank. As I watched, a large bull moose quietly walked into full view, perhaps 100 yards away. Something about the forest that evening—the hush, the feel of the crisp air, the growing darkness, the occasional sounds of birds, the *chirring* of a red squirrel—gave the evening a magic feel that seemed more intense than any other time I could remember.

The bull's yellow-gold antlers were clean, with no velvet hanging from them, and they projected a ghostly luminosity in the twilight. He stopped and stood quietly, listening and looking. He was what I had come for, and he was in easy rifle range. Yet I waited. Perhaps he would move closer. A careful hunter always likes his prey close; if the first shot doesn't down the animal, it is easier to get a second shot into it with the animal near.

The moose walked toward me, following the trail. If he continued, he would walk so close I could not possibly miss him. Again he stopped. He wasn't alarmed. He had probably just left his daytime bed, and, like a man awakening in the morning, he was stretching his muscles and his mind, readying himself for the evening feed. He was in no hurry. First he wanted to know what was going on around him— he was watching, listening, and scenting the air to see who or what was near.

I remained motionless on my downed log, eyes glued to the bull. He was a fine, big, fat, mature animal. His antlers spread more than five feet, and he stood a full six feet at the shoulders. In the fading light, he looked almost black. As he moved toward me, his body was occasionally silhouetted against the bright and calm water of Hog River. I prefer to take a small bull for winter meat, for they are easier to handle than a huge, old bull. Also, sometimes the meat of an old bull is tough.

He continued his unhurried way toward me, and I mentally prepared myself for what was to come. A cartridge was in the chamber of the rifle and it was loaded with 170 grains of lead. The tubular magazine was filled with four more cartridges, giving me five shots. To fire the first—likely the only one I would need—as I raised the rifle to my shoulder, I would draw the hammer back into the cocked position with my right thumb. To prevent a click that would alarm the moose, I would hold the trigger back. Once the hammer was back, I would release the trigger, then the hammer, and the rifle would remain cocked, ready to fire. I would aim at the bull's chest, the deepest part of his body. The bullet would go through his lungs. Or, if I shot a little lower, I could hit his heart. A quick, merciful, and sure death for the hunted is the goal of every experienced hunter.

If my bullet flew true, my big bull would stagger momentarily, then he would stand, head down, provided I remained perfectly still and he didn't see or smell me. After another half a minute to a minute, he would collapse, dead, drowned in his own blood. This bull would drop within 100 feet of the river. It would be an easy job to carry the meat to my boat. In other years, when moose were scarcer, I had killed them so far from a river that I didn't even try to pack the meat. Instead I had wrapped it in canvas to protect it from ravens and jays, and hung it high in a tree, to retrieve it with a dog team after snow came. This moose would pose no such problem.

The bull was within twenty-five feet. It was time for me to shoot. But the magic of the moment, the beauty of the surroundings, and the sheer magnificence of that great, alert but relaxed bull, compelled me to hold my fire. Also, I wondered, did I want this big, old animal? Would his meat be tender?

As I sat, knowing he was mine—all I needed to do was to raise the rifle and pull the trigger—he stopped, swung his head about and, for long moments, seemed to look straight at me. I remained frozen. Calmly, he swung his head back, and silently and alertly moved on down the trail, into the trees, and out of sight.

I didn't even lift my rifle. I'm not sure whether I chose not to shoot because he and the magical evening had given me so much pleasure, or because he was a bigger animal than I wanted.

A few days later I killed another, smaller bull, which provided us with our winter's meat. My vivid memory of that big bull still lingers, and in my mind at least, he still roams that wild trail on Hog River.

———

The Alaska moose is the largest deer in the world. Bulls weigh from 1,000 to 1,600 pounds or more. Cows weigh 800 to 1,200 pounds. Colors range from pale yellow to pure black. They have a great drooping nose, and huge ears, giving them a vaguely mulelike appearance. A moose may appear awkward and ugly, but, like other deer, it is graceful in action, and it can stride across rough ground with a swift and smooth gait. A huge bull can disappear into a thicket or heavy timber with scarcely a sound.

Bulls grow new antlers every year, shedding them usually in January or February, and starting the new growth in the spring. The main foods of moose are willow, birch, aspen, and other twigs, although they may graze on sedges, grasses, pond weeds, and other shoots.

Moose were virtually nonexistent in the Koyukuk prior to the 1900s, according to the Koyukon elders I knew. William Dall, the explorer, reported that in 1866 there were no deer (meaning caribou) or moose at Nulato and that food (for the people) was often very scarce. At the time, he said, the Koyukon people in this Yukon River village depended mostly on fish and small game. None of the old Koyukon stories I have heard mention moose in the Koyukuk, although some stories of the Upper Yukon mention the animal. There were no resident Koyukuk moose when I was a boy; the few that wandered into the valley from elsewhere were invariably tracked down and killed. Moose meat and the moose's valuable hide were highly prized by Koyukon and white residents, and when a moose track was found, every effort was made to follow and shoot the animal.

After Charlie killed the moose I had located on Hog River in 1929, I didn't see another moose in the Koyukuk until 1935, when I killed one at Hog River. People who lived downriver from Hog River told me that fair numbers of moose had moved into the lower part of the Koyukuk valley that year. I believe they came from the Melozitna and Tozitna river valleys to the east, where good numbers of moose had long lived.

The deep-snow year of 1937 was a turning point for moose numbers in the Koyukuk. That winter I saw snow completely bury a cabin at Clear Creek built by Charlie Swanson and George Lighten, and the ridgepole of that cabin was fourteen feet above ground.

After that incredible snow pack settled, moose could travel easily anywhere in the Koyukuk, for they sank in only about eighteen inches, which their long legs handled easily. With the good traveling conditions, more of these big animals drifted into the Koyukuk from the Melozitna and the Tozitna river valleys, and perhaps from the Yukon River valley, scattering up and down the entire Koyukuk. Since then, moose have been a dependable source of food for the residents.

Koyukuk old-timers John Oldman and Edwin Simon often said that they didn't really know how to hunt moose because the animal was new to the Koyukuk. They told how, during their trapping years in the early 1900s, they sometimes ran into moose tracks in heavy winter snow, and always followed the trail until they killed the moose, even if it took days. That, they said, was all they knew about moose.

During that deep-snow winter of 1937, I killed a moose for my uncle Hog River Johnny and his family. I drove my dog team to their cabin to tell them about it.

"You want me to bring you the moose?" I offered. I could have hauled the meat in two loads.

"No. We'll go to the moose," Johnny said.

That was the old Koyukon way. When a hunter killed big game, his family moved to the animal. Using my dog team, I helped my uncle and his family travel to and set up camp where I had killed the moose.

Uncle Johnny and his family butchered the horse-sized cow moose on the site much as Chief John and Big Mary had done. They worked on that animal for days, and used every bit. They even put out a few marten traps and made themselves at home in the traditional way.

My uncle Weaselheart, trapping on the north side of Sun Mountain that winter, saw moose in numbers for the first time, and learned that a moose has a temper. One day he passed a moose walking in the deep snow, and in a casual way, he tossed a stick at it. Angered, the moose charged, but it broke through the snow crust with every lunge. Weaselheart, short-legged and heavy, wasn't very fast on snowshoes, but he quickly figured out how to escape the angry moose.

Where tops of willows projected from the snow, drifts were twelve or fourteen feet deep. Taking a chance, he ran across some of the willow tops where his snowshoes supported him nicely. The moose followed and floundered in the loose snow among the willows, so Weaselheart escaped.

Mistreatment of an animal brings bad luck, according to old Koyukon tales, and Weaselheart wryly admitted he had momentarily forgotten those stories. "Never again," he vowed. "Don't play with animals," he warned me.

I have experienced many thrilling moose hunts with my family. I have instructed my sons and daughters on how to hunt, and I have allowed them to shoot the moose we find, for success brightens the lives of young people. They liked to help to provide food for the entire family. The stories of our family moose hunts which my kids told their friends did them all good. I always enjoyed teaching them the old customs.

We hunted mostly in and around lakes on brush-covered flats where I could teach them the art of hunting. They learned to watch the wind direction, for a moose has an acute sense of smell that can detect a man for hundreds of yards. When we spotted a moose we wanted, we often removed our shoes to reduce walking noise. I warned the family not to wear jeans or other stiff fabric clothing that is noisy in the brush. They soon learned that a light rain makes hunting easier by reducing the noise they make.

My son Arnold once used the skills I had taught him to kill a three-year-old bull moose with a bow and arrow. After studying wind direction, he concealed himself behind a tree and shot that moose at a range of about four and a half feet.

While the kids were growing up, each fall my wife Angela and I took them on hunts for meat to carry us through the winter. We killed moose, black bears, ducks, and geese. We picked blueberries for syrup for hotcakes, and cranberries for preserves.

Most of my boys are men now, and each takes his family on hunts like those Angela and I used to make. We included the girls in our family hunts, too. Too many men want to hunt with just other men or sons. I've learned that women get more fun out of hunting than most men, and our girls probably worked harder at hunting than the boys. They were eager to learn how to cook over campfires, and how to clean and dress meat. They liked knowing all the little tricks too, like cutting a brush pile to lay the meat on to keep it clean and to cool it quickly by allowing air to circulate around it.

I've seen some tremendously big moose. One early afternoon while on a family hunt on the Koyukuk River above the old town of Cutoff, my family was traveling in a riverboat. Angela and I had five children then, all under ten. We spotted a moose about a mile away, as he bedded down not far from the riverbank. Angela took over the steering while I moved to the bow with my .30–30 Winchester lever-action rifle.

A seven-horsepower outboard motor pushed the long boat. Angela threw a piece of canvas over the motor to muffle the noise and then she carefully eased the boat upstream toward the moose. We all crouched, listening to the sound of the boat pushing water aside and the low mutter of the muffled outboard. The wind was blowing from the moose toward us, so it couldn't catch our scent. Every Huntington there knew that the moose would be alerted if he noticed our slow-moving boat or saw one of us make a sudden move. Not one extra sound came from the boat. All eyes were fastened on the moose. Ahead of us was our winter's meat supply; we were all thinking of steaks, chops, roasts, and stews.

From a mile away, the moose didn't look especially large. I'd have guessed that his antlers spread about fifty-five inches. He was about fifty feet back from the bank, lying in the goose grass among twelve- or fourteen-inch-high young willows.

As we neared the moose, the five-foot-high cutbank hid us from him and helped to muffle the motor noise. When we got into the shallows, Angela cut the motor, and we slowly paddled and poled the boat. As we came along under the bank he raised his head, as most wild animals do from time to time, while chewing his cud. He was facing the woods. As he lifted his head to look around, I stood up in the bow, aimed, and nailed him right behind the ear. His head dropped, and that was all. He didn't move a muscle. The bullet hit his brain. He never knew what hit him.

I stuck an oar into the soft mud bank, tied the boat to it, and we went to examine our prize. I couldn't believe the size of that moose. "Holy criminy, what am I going to do with this animal?" I asked Angela.

I probably wouldn't have taken him if I had realized how big he was. In relation to his body size, his sixty-two-inch-spread antlers were small. One hindquarter later weighed 284 pounds. Two hindquarters totaled 586 pounds. I estimated the front quarters at 300 pounds each (front quarters weigh more than hind). That's 600 pounds for the front, 586 for the rear, for a total of 1,168 pounds of meat. The meat from a moose usually weighs about fifty percent of the animal's live weight. Alive, that moose probably weighed a ton.

We let the carcass cool for a couple of hours while we set up camp and prepared to go to work. Angela wanted a good moose hide, and decided this one would do. Unfortunately, the finest moose skin comes from pregnant cows killed in late March. Such skins, stretched from a cow carrying her calf, are more uniform in thickness than other moose hides. But such hides aren't available legally.

We had to use ropes and spring lines to hold the legs up so I could cut up the animal. Although I was young and strong, I couldn't even lift one leg.

We managed to roll him on his right side, which I've found is best for dressing a moose because the blood flows out more freely. Removal of the viscera is also easier when the moose is on his right side.

We left the hindquarters intact, but cut the front quarters into smaller easy-to-carry pieces. We hung all the meat in nearby trees to drip and dry. Angela carved the meat from the head. We left behind nothing edible.

Edwin Simon and Bobby Vent, on a hunt, came along shortly after we had killed the big moose. They stared at the animal in disbelief.

"That's as big as they come," Edwin remarked.

"It'll probably be tougher than hell," I replied in disgust.

"Don't be sure," he said. "If you caught him when he was asleep that makes a difference."

Bobby and Edwin camped with us and helped me load the hindquarters into our boat.

We were in a good spot for moose, and had hopes another would appear while we were butchering. Sure enough, about daylight a fat young bull walked right into camp. Angela shot it. We stayed another day to clean and care for the meat of that animal.

Edwin was right about the meat of that big moose. I hung it twenty feet or more above ground where flies usually won't bother meat. At Christmas, when visitors came, we ran low on meat, so I knocked a hindquarter of the huge old moose down. Two of us had all we could do to haul the aged meat into the house. After Angela thawed and cooked it, I rated that old bull as the best moose meat I ever ate.

The greatest abundance of moose in the Koyukuk occurred between 1945 and 1955. By then, moose had become our "livestock," as important to the Koyukon people as cattle, sheep, and hogs are to residents of agricultural states. Traditions become established quickly, and within a decade and a half, it became traditional for many Koyukon families to make an early September moose hunt in the Koyukuk valley. It made a wonderful change in our lives to have fine moose meat to eat through the winter.

In the middle and late 1950s, wolves, which like the moose had been absent from the Koyukuk valley, followed the moose into the Koyukuk. Because moose was the wolves' main food, the wolves quickly increased, and as they did so, they killed more and more moose, and Koyukuk moose numbers began to dwindle.

22

KOYUKUK WOLVES

A few years ago my son Gilbert, trapping on the Big Portage just below Coffee Can Lake along the lower Koyukuk River, caught a wolf in a trap. Gilbert had never seen a wolf in a trap.

"It looked like a beautiful gray dog," he told me. And because he didn't want to kill a fine sled dog, he approached the animal to release it. He planned to put a rope around its neck, so he could handle it and examine the foot for injury. As Gilbert neared, the wolf lay down and made no attempt to bite, nor did it fight the trap. As Gilbert worked to open the trap, the wolf pulled as far from him as he could and turned his head away.

"I could have petted him," Gilbert said.

Once released, the wolf stood up, looked at Gilbert (probably in amazement), and swiftly ran off. Only then did Gilbert realize that the animal was a wolf.

Gilbert's mistake is common; wolves do look like and to a degree behave like dogs, and many people unfamiliar with wolves and their habits think of the wolf and man's best friend in the same terms.

The wolf is Alaska's most efficient predator. He lives by killing other animals. His senses of smell, hearing, and sight are acute. He is intelligent, and hunts cooperatively in small groups or occasionally in large packs. Koyukon hunters have great respect for the wolf, and consider only the bear and perhaps the wolverine to have greater spiritual power.

Mature wolves weigh from 75 to 150 pounds. Black wolves are common and other colors include gray, white, and a brownish shade.

Some wolves have a dark mask. Although wolves and dogs belong to the same family, wolves commonly kill and eat dogs that stray from camps or settlements; occasionally a dog chained near a cabin or at the edge of a village is killed by wolves. In the late 1970s, many Fairbanks residents became upset one winter when wolves killed many chained dogs at homes on the outskirts of that city. Once in a great while a female dog in heat may breed with a wild wolf.

One quiet evening in the fall of 1939, while hunting moose, I sat on a log at Hog River, looking over a little clearing. It was the time for moose to come out to feed. Then, for the first time in my life, I heard a wolf howl.

I turned toward the sound, listening. Again came the long, low, quavering howl. It had a nice tone. To some people, the howl of a wolf is spine-tingling or "chilling." But I enjoy hearing it, for it is a natural sound in the wildlands of Alaska.

When I was a boy, no wolves lived in the Koyukuk valley, or they were so few that we were unaware of them. We never heard one and we never saw a track. With none of their major prey—moose and caribou—living in the Koyukuk, they had no reason to be there. Throughout most of Alaska, besides moose and caribou, wolves also kill and eat Dall sheep and Sitka deer. Snowshoe hares are an important food in some years. In summer, moose and caribou calves are a common food.

When moose became established in the Koyukuk in the late 1930s and then wolves arrived, as trappers we were pleased to be able to catch the animals for their valuable fur, although we quickly learned that wolves are smart and difficult to trap. At first, most of the furs were kept and used by Koyukon women in making winter clothing. Wolves continued to increase, for moose were abundant. An adult wolf eats six to seven pounds of meat each day, and a pack of ten wolves eats sixty to seventy pounds of meat daily. This is about fifty adult moose a year, or about 120 caribou. By the mid-1950s, wolves had increased enough to be a threat to the Koyukuk moose population.

In 1972 Governor William A. Egan appointed me to the Alaska Board of Fish and Game. This board developed all hunting, fishing, and trapping regulations for the state, and established policies for fish and game. At our long meetings, we studied reams of scientific information on various populations of fish and game, heard reports from fisheries and game biologists, and held public hearings. When the board was split in 1975, Governor Jay Hammond appointed me to the Board of Game, where I served until early 1992. As a member of these boards, I learned much about wolves from scientists who provided us with basic biological information on Alaska's wildlife.

Millions of dollars have been spent on studies of Alaska's wolves and their way of life.

The availability of food—primarily moose, caribou, deer, sheep—is the primary determinant of wolf densities in Alaska. When these prey species are abundant and easily taken, wolves fare well and have larger litters, and more pups survive their first year.

When food is scarce smaller litters are produced, and mortality of pups increases because of starvation and cannibalism. Under these conditions, fifty to sixty percent of pups born each spring usually die within eight months.

A number of studies in Alaska have shown that when the ratios of wolves to moose drop below about one wolf per twenty moose, the moose population is unlikely to maintain itself, and it will probably decline. In some cases moose have been entirely killed off from an area by wolves, at which time the wolves had nothing to eat and they themselves either starved, or left that area, leaving the land with no moose or wolves.

Many people believe that wolves take only sick and misfit prey. Several Alaskan studies have shown that usually wolves take moose or caribou in almost exactly the same proportion as found in the prey population. A cow moose heavy with calf is the most valuable moose, from the standpoint of the moose population, yet such a cow is most vulnerable to wolves. Moose and caribou calves are especially vulnerable, and they too are valuable from the standpoint of the moose population.

The Koyukons respect the wolf as an intelligent animal and an efficient killer of big game. Elders say that early Koyukon people viewed the wolf as powerful and important, and in the days before rifles they feared the animal. Until rifles, steel traps, and steel snares were available, it was not possible for the Koyukon people to take wolves in numbers. Rarely, wolves were killed with bow and arrow.

Throughout Alaska, wolf skins are prized for making parkas,

boots, and mittens. Among the Koyukon people, only men were supposed to wear wolfskin garments, but this tradition is not strictly observed today. The most important use of wolf fur is for a parka ruff. It is used in conjunction with wolverine fur; the wolverine fur lies immediately next to the face where the bulk of frost forms from the breath on cold days. Long, stiff wolf fur protects the face from wind, and the coarse hairs shed frost easily. A good wolf parka ruff can extend a foot or more beyond the wearer's face.

Wolves don't attack humans, although I am aware of one wolf attack on a child. Many years ago in the Bettles-Wiseman area of the Upper Koyukuk, toddler David Tobuk was playing on a beach along the river. Suddenly a wolf ran out of the brush, grabbed him by the head with powerful jaws, and carried him off.

A nearby Koyukon Indian named Napoleon, who saw the wolf steal the child, ran after the wolf with a rifle and shot it. I knew Napoleon, who told me the story.

David Tobuk survived. He was captain of the *Teddy H.*, trader Sam Dubin's steamboat, which rescued us after our mother's death. David carried a large scar on his face from the wolf attack. Occasionally the scar became raw, and it bothered him all his life. Photos of David I've seen always show him with his head turned to conceal the scar.

———

Eskimos tell interesting stories about the wolf. A few years ago I hunted in the Kobuk Valley in Eskimo country and killed four caribou from a herd. While dressing them, I was careful to save the legs for the skin, which makes fine winter boots. Two Eskimos, both about my age, arrived while I was working on the caribou.

"Sidney, you're doing a good job, but you're doing one thing wrong," one said. I remained silent, knowing that these Eskimos were probably going to share a belief that they wanted me to observe.

"You aren't taking the hooves off. You should do that," one suggested.

"OK. I'll do that," I agreed.

They showed me how to cut all the hooves off—a simple job. Then they put all sixteen hooves on a string. As I continued to work on the caribou, one of the Eskimos said, "This practice comes from an old story. We know the story is true, so we always cut the hooves off like that."

Then the Eskimos told me their story:

A long time ago there were more caribou than now. Our people could kill caribou year-round. The animals never left. There were really too many caribou in the Kobuk valley. Soon wolves became thick, and they, like the caribou, were all over the place. Our people had no way of killing them except with bow and arrow. They managed this difficult feat once in a while. So many wolves roamed the area that the Eskimos' lives were in danger, for the wolves were fearless.

The wolves killed many caribou, and dead caribou lay everywhere. Day after day the wolves killed, and in about two years few caribou remained. Then the wolves started to kill and eat each other. Soon they were so hungry they started to attack the people. The Eskimos had no safe place to flee to, but old legends told them what to do.

The legends told the Eskimos to go into their underground igloos, where they could keep fires going to keep warm. Since they couldn't leave their igloos because of danger from wolves, they began to run low on food. They knew that if they stayed inside their igloos long enough, the wolves would kill each other off; then the people would be safe.

Soon the Eskimos had nothing to eat, so they began boiling caribou hooves, which keep for a long time hanging in a cache. The hooves, of course, have some dried tendons and meat attached. They supply some nutritional needs. The hooves must be boiled and boiled before the broth is ready to drink.

The Eskimos kept alive by boiling the caribou hooves and drinking the broth while they waited and watched. When the wolves no longer appeared, they ventured out of the igloos to resume life. They traveled to lakes and rivers to catch fish. By then the caribou were all gone, having been killed by wolves. The wolves were also all gone, for they had eaten one another or starved to death.

This story fascinates me for several reasons. It may be based on a time when wolves with rabies attacked Eskimos, or when healthy but very hungry wolves attacked these people. This traditional story also parallels the findings of Alaska's wildlife scientists—that wolves in Alaska can and do sometimes wipe out their prey and then starve or depart the area. This may be why there were no wolves or moose in the Koyukuk in the late 1800s and the first three decades of the 1900s. And the Eskimos' story of wolves eating wolves is supported by findings of modern scientists; wolf cannibalism is a trait well known to wildlife scientists, as well as to the Koyukon people.

In 1956, Donald Stickman, son of my Koyukon friend Joe Stickman of Koyukuk Station, operated a small air charter service on the Lower Yukon. While flying above the Koyukuk River one day, Don saw twelve dead moose lying on a gravel bar, and landed to investigate. Wolves had killed the moose but they had eaten little meat. On some of the moose, only the tongues had been eaten. The wolves had ripped open the moose stomachs to eat the fat, kidneys, and livers. Most of the red meat of the moose was untouched, leaving it to go to waste.

The moose had become the most important single source of meat for the Koyukon people. Don remembered the 1920s and early 1930s when moose were rare and people had to work hard for the fish and small game they needed for food. Moose in the Koyukuk made life easier.

Don flew up and down the Koyukuk valley, searching for wolves, and he discovered more wolves lived there than anyone had imagined. He obtained a permit from the U.S. Fish and Wildlife Service, and, with my brother Jimmy as gunner, started hunting them from the air. That winter they killed 149 wolves. At the same time, trappers from Huslia, Hughes, Allakaket, and Alatna made a special effort to catch more of the big predators.

In the winter of 1957–58, a U.S. Fish and Wildlife Service agent reported finding more than 200 dead moose that he identified as wolf kills in the Koyukuk valley. Again Don Stickman and Jimmy hunted wolves from the air, and that season they killed another 150.

That was enough to change the balance, and Don and Jimmy stopped hunting wolves. There were still wolves in the Koyukuk, and they are still present today. The wolves continue to kill moose, but wolf numbers had been reduced so that the moose herd was no longer threatened with decimation.

During the 1950s, the U.S. Fish and Wildlife Service, which managed Alaska's wildlife when Alaska was a territory, employed six or seven full-time predator control agents who ranged over Alaska killing wolves. To the federal government, wolves were undesirable vermin that threatened valuable moose, caribou, and other animals. These agents used strychnine baits, often dropping them from airplanes. This use of poison was repugnant to most Alaskans. The poison killed not just wolves, but bears, birds, and other furbearers that ate it. The predator control agents also hunted wolves with airplanes as another way of attempting to reduce their numbers.

When Alaska became a state in 1959 and management authority of fish and game was transferred from the federal government, Alaska halted statewide wolf control, banned the use of poison for any reason, dropped the bounty on wolves, and classified the wolf as both a furbearer and a big game animal. Aerial hunting for wolves as a sport was banned.

Wolf management in Alaska is controversial. A very few Alaskans would like to see all wolves destroyed, while others strongly oppose killing wolves, for any reason. Most Alaskans feel that management of wolves, as for Alaska's other wildlife, should be based on the sustained yield principle, allowing monitored harvest through trapping and hunting where wolf numbers justify it.

I doubt the issue will ever be resolved to everyone's satisfaction.

On a July day in the mid-1980s, Angela and I and several of our older kids were at our fish camp on the Yukon River. One morning we saw some objects moving across the mile-wide river. At first we thought they were ducks, but with binoculars I made out seven wolves. We jumped into a boat and sped to the animals, circling them at a respectful distance. It was a pair of adults with five pups.

Why they chose to swim across that wide river I'll never know— they had left hilly country, which is good wolf habitat, to swim to a brushy flatland area.

Enjoying the sight, we followed them from a distance. When they reached shore the pups were nearly exhausted. As they left the water, each animal shook itself, spraying water all directions. One had to lie down for a few moments to recover. All seven stood looking at us for a few moments, and then they turned and disappeared into the brush.

23

BOOZE

❂

I was splitting firewood. The temperature was –50 degrees. In deep cold, dry spruce is brittle, and when struck by a sharp axe it usually splits easily. It is a satisfying chore, splitting firewood. I have always enjoyed seeing the chunks pile up, ready for the stove. It was January 1955, and I was at the Koyukuk River village of Huslia.

On this day the enjoyment ceased abruptly. The axe struck a knot on a chunk of frozen spruce, and a sliver of the knot flew up and imbedded itself in my right eye. When I pulled at the sliver, some of my eye fluid flowed out. I ran to the schoolhouse, where Eunice Berglund, the itinerant nurse, happened to be. All she could do was put pontocaine, an anesthetic, into my eye.

I suffered a lot of pain that night. The next day it was too cold for a plane to fly me to medical help, and I went through hell. On the following day, although it was still terribly cold, James "Andy" Anderson, the Wien Airline bush pilot at Bettles, flew to Huslia and took me to the hospital at Tanana. A doctor took one look, gave me more pontocaine, and Andy flew me to Fairbanks to eye specialist Dr. Hugh Fate.

Dr. Fate worked on my eye all night, removing as much of the wood as possible. I had partial vision with the eye, but the damage caused a reaction to my other eye. By fall, I was using pontocaine daily. Despite the medication, the injured eye throbbed painfully all the time, and I had to go back to Dr. Fate.

"Sidney, your eye is deteriorating badly and it's affecting your good eye. That right eye has to be removed. You'll never see well with it again anyway. Removing the one will help the other."

The pain was so persistent and intense that I actually looked forward to having the eye removed. After half a year of steady pain, the relief was simply wonderful. In a short time I was fitted with a glass eye, and strangers seldom spot it. With one eye I could read, work, and manage daily life without difficulty. I lost depth perception, of course, and was unable to shoot flying geese for many years. But I learned the right formula, so now I do fairly well on wing shots. I've had no problems aiming with a rifle.

Prohibition, in effect from 1920 to 1933, didn't stop people in the Alaska bush from drinking. In fact, it fostered a pretty fair bootlegging industry in the Koyukuk and Lower Yukon country. Beer drinkers could legally make beer at home. A three-pound can of malt syrup and about a pound of sugar could produce about seven gallons of pretty good beer in five days.

Charlie Swanson liked beer, and Dad drank it occasionally. When we all lived on the trapline together, the job of making beer often fell to Jimmy and me. Dad regarded beer as a food, a beverage to accompany meals. Beer was not a big deal to us kids.

I got high on alcohol for the first time when I was twelve or thirteen years old. Jimmy and I were bottling beer for Dad and Charlie, pouring it into bottles. We had a capper that fit all sizes of bottles, and we had just made a batch in a twenty-five-gallon barrel. To get the beer out of the keg, we had to siphon it with a small rubber hose. Each time I started the siphon, I sucked a slug of beer into my mouth. Naturally, I swallowed it. By the time we had bottled twenty-five gallons of beer, I felt pretty high and had to go to sleep. When I awoke I was violently ill from all that raw beer.

Before I married at the age of eighteen, I drank some. Jimmy and I used to make our own whiskey, competing with some of the villagers to see who could make the best booze. At times it seemed as if almost everyone in the Koyukuk and Lower Yukon country owned a still. We bought a twenty-gallon copper clothes boiler with a lid that could be tightly sealed. The boiler held about ten gallons of brew. We made a neat coil from three-eighths-inch copper tubing, and we soldered all our connections. Bootleggers I knew believed that the tubing had to be at least fourteen feet long to make good booze.

Some Indians dismantled shotguns and rifles, such as a .30–30 Winchester, to use the gun barrel for the condenser to make booze. For some, booze was more important than guns. In the early 1930s, a Model 94 lever-action Winchester cost $23. I knew individuals who would lie down at the end of a gun barrel, waiting for the condensed booze to drip into their mouths. These were the drinkers who suffered. Blindness and even death sometimes resulted from the strong stuff.

My uncle Hog River Johnny went blind from drinking bad booze, as did many others in the Koyukuk. Some of the bad booze contained fusel oil, an acrid poison that accumulates in insufficiently distilled liquors. Home-distilled whiskey was especially bad if it weren't run through charcoal or distilled sufficiently.

In our bootleg business, Jimmy and I sold a ketchup bottle full (slightly more than a pint) of whiskey for $5. We each had our own barrel and we tried to outdo each other in quality. At the time, neither of us drank much.

In the 1930s, many Koyukon Indians commonly traveled to Cutoff for holidays, or after trapping season ended. Everyone wanted to try the other fellow's booze. We all feared the government revenuer, a fellow named Senif. He never did come to Cutoff, despite our fears. Nevertheless, we always cached our gallons of booze in snowdrifts and among the trees out of sight before entering the village. After everyone except the revenuer was in the village, we would retrieve the hidden booze and have a big party.

Some of that stuff was absolutely terrible. I often recall how my friend Little Sammy once reacted to another fellow's booze. When offered a bottle, Little Sammy gulped a big swallow. He made an awful face and he choked so he could hardly talk. Nevertheless, he croaked, "Boy, that's good stuff!"

Drinking was a phase I guess I had to go through. I used to have a good time drinking, or at least I thought I was having a good time. As the years passed, I drank more and more. After Prohibition ended in 1933, I would leave my trapline at the end of the season, go to Cutoff or Koyukuk to pay my bills, charter an airplane to fly to Ruby, and return with a planeload of booze. Everyone who wanted to drink with me would show up and I'd hand each a full bottle. I love the taste of Scotch whiskey, and over the years, I probably drank enough of it to float my house.

Once at Koyukuk, in the late 1940s, I started drinking with my buddy Haymon Henry, a fine old Koyukon. I don't know how many days our party lasted, but I forgot to eat. We danced and drank; I don't remember everything, but I thought we were having a great time. I finally realized it was time to return to my trapline. Haymon had a camp and trapline near mine, up the Yuki River on the south side of the Yukon, near Galena.

When we left Koyukuk, I didn't have any whiskey because Dominic Vernetti wouldn't sell me any, cash or otherwise. "You've been drinking long enough, Sidney," he told me.

Haymon and I chartered the plane of Hans Rutzebeck, who flew us to Haymon's camp. Haymon gave me one last drink of whiskey from his bottle, and then Hans flew me to a lake a few hundred yards from my tent camp, where he landed his ski plane in deep snow.

Hans unloaded me and my gear and took off. Snow blasted high as the little Call Air plane lifted into the air. I staggered around for a while, fell, and had difficulty getting up. That last slug of booze from Haymon's bottle hadn't helped my condition.

Although the temperature was about −50 degrees F., I threw a caribou hide on top of the snow beside the trail, unrolled my sleeping bag on it, and crawled in. I had a new Woods eiderdown sleeping bag for which I had paid $250—a lot of money then. Sometime during the night I awoke, feeling as if something were sitting on my legs. I couldn't move either leg. But I could move my hands. The Colt Woodsman .22 pistol I always carried was inside my sleeping bag. I found the gun and fired a couple of shots toward the end of my sleeping bag at whatever was sitting on my legs. If anything was there, it got off. It might have been my imagination or a nightmare, I don't know. I was in bad shape.

I got up at daylight. The weather seemed warmer, and I felt a little better. I put on snowshoes and walked the several hundred yards to my camp. Snow had collapsed my tent over the woodstove. I straightened up the mess. As I worked, I began to go through withdrawal—I couldn't eat and I had the shakes. Nonetheless, I thought I was in good enough shape to cover my ten-mile-long trapline, so I set out.

On snowshoes, I crossed the lake and started up the hill. Looking ahead, toward the mountain, I saw a huge pink elephant coming over the top of the ridge. I stared at this incredible sight, then closed my eyes. I looked again. The pink elephant was still there, walking toward me.

I couldn't handle that. I turned in my tracks and went back to my tent as fast as I could go. After building a fire, I warmed some water and took a sponge bath. Then I drank a little coffee and crawled into my sleeping bag. When I fell asleep, whatever it was again settled on my legs. I awoke, feeling my legs being pushed down. Again I fired my pistol at the unseen something, and the weight seemed to leave my legs.

The next time I awoke, I was in good enough shape to run my trapline. In a few days, I was all right and eating ravenously. Hans Rutzebeck returned and landed his ski-equipped Call Air on the nearby frozen lake.

"How you doing, Sidney?" he asked.

"OK now. I had to chase an elephant off the hill up there the other day, though," I told him, sheepishly.

"That bad, were you?" he commented.

"I guess I was," I admitted.

"I wasn't going to pick you up, but I landed at Haymon's camp and he was worried about you, so I thought I'd check."

I told him I'd run my trapline, had caught quite a bit of fur, and I was ready to fly back to Hog River to take care of my trapline there.

That winter I ran three traplines. Angela and the kids, with a dog team, lived at Hog River, near one line. I had another trapline on the Huslia River not far from there. My third line was the one at Yuki River where I had seen the pink elephant. Hans flew me between the three traplines all winter. My flying bill came to about $2,800 for the season, and I trapped about $11,000 worth of fur—one of my really big years.

We loaded my furs, sleeping bag, and other gear into Hans's plane. The lake, only 650 or 700 feet across, offered a short run for takeoff. The air was still. I had cut down tall trees at the edge of the lake, leaving an opening for a plane to fly through. Hans headed for that opening with the engine wide open, but he couldn't get airborne. He stopped, turned the plane, and tried to take off in the other direction, taking advantage of the ski tracks he had just made.

The dense −50 degree air gave the wings good lift, but the engine didn't run smoothly because of the extreme cold. Finally, Hans lifted the plane off the lake. We were at low altitude, still climbing, when the carburetor iced up, the engine coughed a few times, and died. The airplane staggered on the edge of a stall, one wing dropped, and down we went, nose first into the ground. We hit a stand of small spruce trees and skidded for a ways, splintering trees and ripping fabric from the plane. Then we slid between two large trees and stopped. The wings were half ripped away, and gas poured from the two wing tanks.

"Get out before it blows!" Hans yelled.

Neither of us was injured, and we got out quick.

No explosion occurred, and we hiked back to my camp. Hans was terribly upset about the loss of his $5,000 airplane and he wanted to walk to Galena immediately. In a straight line the distance was about fifty miles, but afoot he would have had to travel closer to 100 miles.

"Take it easy, Hans. Someone'll pick us up after while," I consoled. We waited eight days until a Pan American Airways plane (Pan Am was one of Alaska's early airlines) circled after the pilot spotted the wreck. He notified another pilot with a small plane who flew in to pick us up.

Through the thirties and forties I continued to drink. I sold the stuff, but often I was my own best customer. Eventually, in the 1950s I felt I needed booze all the time. I tried tapering off, but it didn't work. I suppose I would have been classified as an alcoholic.

I've heard people talk about how sick they have been from heavy drinking. Believe me, I've been there. One of my worst drunks lasted more than forty days. That binge was a by-product of the 1945 flood of the Yukon River. I was at Galena when the flood came. Everything floated off, including fifty-five gallons of medical alcohol from a warehouse at the Galena Air Force Base. I salvaged the full porcelain-lined barrel and, with friends, mixed the stuff with fruit juice or whatever else was available. It took a couple of us six weeks to drink it up.

After being on that stuff, I woke up one morning and looked across the Yukon River: everything appeared orange. My eyes were blood-shot, I guess. I was scared enough to quit drinking—for a time. I didn't stay dry long. When the village of Koyukuk seemed absolutely dead, I'd go to Dominic Vernetti's store and buy a few cases of booze and beer.

"C'mon boys, let's have a dance," I'd invite. And we'd have a heck of a party. I really enjoyed partying. I met friends that way; some of my best friends were my drinking buddies.

The Indians in the Koyukuk and along the Yukon have used booze since white men arrived. Many of the villages have liquor stores, although a few have voted themselves dry. I've noticed that people who come to Galena from villages where alcohol is not available drink heavily. Some drinkers sell their guns, their traps, their snow machines, any possession worth money, to buy booze. Today, drugs are available in Alaska's Native villages, and the combination of drugs and booze is frequently lethal.

Oceans of booze have been sold to Indians, Eskimos, and Aleuts in

Alaska's villages. Money spent on drinking could have paved many village sidewalks with gold. Alcoholism is a tragedy for which the people themselves must develop a solution.

Throughout my drinking days, I always paid my bills and managed to support my family. But the day arrived when I realized that I had to lay off the booze. Angela contracted tuberculosis and had to go to a hospital for six months, leaving me to care for our fourteen children.

———

Tuberculosis, known as "the scourge of Alaska" in the thirties and forties, is a terrible disease that was probably brought to Alaska by the early Russians. It was the most deadly of all the infectious diseases to which Alaska Natives had had no prior exposure and hence no immunity. Wherever explorers, traders, miners, settlers, and missionaries went, the incidence of tuberculosis increased among the Natives.

Tuberculosis is a bacterial disease that develops slowly compared to diseases like whooping cough, measles, smallpox, and typhoid. It is usually transmitted from one person to another through the air— spray droplets from a sneeze or a cough. Most often attacking the lungs, it leads to difficult breathing and eventually to death. Tuberculosis of the lungs was also known as "consumption."

Crowded living conditions, poor ventilation, and undernourishment assisted in the spread of tuberculosis among Athapaskans of Alaska's Interior. From the 1920s through the 1940s it affected in one way or another virtually every Indian in the Yukon and Koyukuk valleys. It came close to home for me.

About 1924, while she was at Anvik Mission, my sister Ada went for a long winter walk with a group of girls. One of the weaker girls was poorly dressed and became cold, and Ada removed her own coat and put it on the girl. By the time they returned to the mission Ada was thoroughly chilled and she contracted pneumonia, which broke her health. Her resistance low from pneumonia, she soon was infected with tuberculosis, which killed her several years later.

When I first started living at Hog River, I remember returning to the Yukon River in spring to discover that many of the pretty young girls I had known and danced with the previous fall were dead from tuberculosis.

My uncle Hog River Johnny and his wife Molly, living at Cutoff, had six healthy children when the disease struck their family. Within two years all six children, plus a newborn baby, had died. They built a new home and moved into it, also at Cutoff, and started another family. They had seven more children that ranged from three to eighteen. The oldest was married. Then all seven died of tuberculosis.

Some of those kids were older than I was, some were about my age. I frequently stayed with the family when I was in Cutoff. In the winter of 1933, I offered to take Walter, who was eighteen, and his twelve-year-old sister Mildred, to the Tanana hospital with my dog team, but they were too weak with tuberculosis to make the trip; they would be taken by boat after breakup, it was decided. They didn't live to make it. I happened to be there when Walter and Mildred died within an hour of each other. The poor frightened girl watched Walter gasping for breath as he died, and an hour later she was dead herself. She held my hand right to the last. I tried to comfort and encourage her, but it was hopeless. Being the same age, Walter and I had been close; we had hunted together. It was a sad time.

Molly contracted the disease and went to a sanitarium in Washington State for three years and returned, apparently cured. After her return, however, she recontracted the disease and died.

My uncle Weaselheart lost five of his six children to the disease. Why his daughter Liza survived I'll never know; she lived amidst all of those who died of that terrible disease.

I saw strong young men contract the disease and die within six months. We called it "galloping TB." Commonly eight or ten people from a village of forty or fifty died during a year. In the 1930s and '40s, for every six babies born on the Koyukuk only one survived—the other five died from tuberculosis. I saw it wipe out family after family.

In Alaska in 1945, tuberculosis caused more than 70 percent of the deaths caused by communicable diseases, and the highest death rate was among the Indians, Eskimos, and Aleuts. The disease reached its peak of destructiveness in Alaska within a year or two of the end of World War II.

Tuberculosis killed, maimed, or disabled thousands of Alaska Natives and not a few whites until it was gradually brought under control in the 1960s by a combination of intensive case-finding and the development of new antituberculosis drugs, notably isoniazid, which could be used not only as treatment but also as a preventative. Today several antibiotics are used together, taken continuously for several months, to cure the disease.

When my wife, Angela, contracted the disease, it had a sobering effect on me, literally. I went into the Galena bar where about twenty people were sitting around drinking and talking. At the time, drinks cost a dollar each.

"Set 'em up for everybody," I told the bartender. Then, for myself, I bought a bottle of beer, something I rarely drank.

"It'll be a long time before I have another drink," I told the crowd, as I set down the empty bottle.

That was in April 1963. Angela recovered, and I haven't had a drink since.

24

GALENA

I loved the life of a trapper, but as the family grew, the dollars I made on the trapline didn't stretch far enough. We had lived in Huslia for about ten years, and I had been trapping winters. Now, in the early 1960s, some of the kids were thinking about going to college, which called for a lot more money. I had friends who worked for the Air Force at Galena making good money year-round, and I decided to try to get a job there as a carpenter.

During two winters on the trapline I spent every night studying books on carpentering. I memorized the mathematics of the framing square. I learned how to frame a building, how to cut rafters, and how to build cement forms—all from those books. Then we moved to Galena in 1963.

I passed the union's written carpenter test and worked six weeks as a union carpenter. I went on to other carpentering jobs at Galena, working for $6 an hour. Next I took the carpenter's test for the Air Force, and got a high score, which landed me a job as a foreman—a job that lasted for twelve years.

In my spare time, I built and sold boats. In my life I've built 112 boats of various sizes, either for sale or for my own use. I once designed and built a sixty-foot-long scow for Dominic Vernetti to use on the Yukon River for hauling up to twenty tons of salmon. Building it upside down, I turned it over with human power, using double and triple blocks. Dominic also used that scow to haul freight for the U.S. Coast and Geodetic Survey.

At Galena, in addition to taking care of all the kids and running the house, Angela made fur slippers, parkas, mittens, and marten fur caps to order. After we were settled in, during the summers Angela and I put a gillnet in the Yukon to catch salmon for our own use. Runs of both chum and king salmon had greatly increased under state management. In fact, starting in the sixties, salmon, moose, caribou, black bear, and beaver were abundant; no one could remember when there had been such natural wealth in and around the Koyukuk.

After we had been fishing for several seasons, one day we caught far more fish than we could easily use. I called Frank Donaldson, in Anchorage, who owned a market and sold fish. "Send me twenty or thirty and let me see what they're like," he said.

After cleaning those fish until they were as shiny as a new dime, I made boxes for them, and we shipped thirty king salmon that averaged twenty-five pounds. Donaldson paid us thirty cents a pound for whole, uncleaned fish. Freight cost a dime a pound, leaving a profit, less labor, boxes and shipping, of about twenty cents a pound. Not bad.

At the time, Alaska had a Youth Corps program in which kids could earn a few dollars an hour and gain experience by working. My kids could not qualify for the program because I was employed, and so they had to try to find other jobs. Charlie and Henry, two of my boys, fruitlessly scoured Galena for jobs.

I remembered my own youth, when Dad, Jimmy, and I needed to make a stake to get back into the trapping business after the flood at Batza River. "We'll build a fish wheel," I told the boys. "That'll give you a way to earn a few dollars."

I wrote Whitney-Fidalgo Packing Company in Anchorage and asked if they could use some Yukon River chum salmon. It was fall, near the end of the annual salmon runs, so we had to hurry. The Whitney-Fidalgo buyer wasn't sure he could use water-marked salmon (salmon that have lost their bright silvery seagoing appearance and are changing color as they approach spawning). Hesitantly, he said he'd take a few.

I helped Charlie, Henry, and Terry Pitka, one of their friends, build the fish wheel and place it at our fishing site. They caught many chums and cleaned them carefully, and we built boxes and shipped them to Anchorage. "Send more" was the response. With this good news the company sent a supply of wetlock boxes designed for shipping salmon. By the time school opened, each of the three boys had earned about $1,000.

The following two or three seasons we continued to ship salmon to Whitney-Fidalgo, and each year our catch increased. Then a company executive came to Galena to talk with me about getting more salmon. To handle them, a holding facility, complete with a $50,000 ice machine, was necessary.

"Fine," I said. "If you want to install a plant, we'll do the work, but you'll have to finance it, without interest." The company agreed.

We built the plant at Galena for $139,000 in 1971. We then agreed to buy fish for Whitney-Fidalgo for two cents a pound. Local fishermen caught the salmon with gillnets and fish wheels and received the local going price.

The business grew. At one time, we had eleven boats picking up salmon from fishermen up and down the river from Galena and delivering them to our plant. Powered with big outboard motors, those boats traveled the fifty-five miles between Nulato and Galena in one hour and twenty minutes. Going downriver at sixty miles an hour, they could reach Nulato from Galena in forty-five minutes. On the return, they traveled at forty-five or fifty miles an hour with loads of from 2,000 to 3,000 pounds of salmon.

Within two years we paid off the construction loan on the fish plant. Once we sent seven full 737 Boeing jets out of Galena in one day. In one summer we handled two million pounds of salmon.

We operated four years, and in that time we lost to spoilage only one 1,800-pound tote of salmon. Whitney-Fidalgo, and others who received our fish, knew they could depend on receiving a fresh, well-cared-for product. During the last year we operated we had ninety-two employees, all Yukon River residents. Each day we airshipped 50,000 pounds of cleaned fish from Galena to Seattle; from there the fish was transshipped to Norway.

The air freight bills were frightening. Once I was in debt to Wien Airlines for $130,000. "That's absurd," I told a Wien accountant. "Every time a plane lands in Anchorage with our fish in it, send me a bill. Don't let my account build like that."

"We have to wait until the end of the month," he told me.

"No. That won't do," I insisted.

Once, for two consecutive months, I wrote checks for air freight bills of $180,000. Every time one of those jets came to Galena it cost $9,000. Sometimes we used Hercules aircraft at a rate of $10,000 per trip. Two trips were required some days. I once watched a Hercules take off from Galena with her belly loaded with our salmon. It was so heavy the tires looked flat, yet that powerful plane used only half of the 6,000-foot runway as it roared off toward Anchorage, 340 miles distant.

Shipping costs went up and the price we received for handling salmon went down. Our profits dwindled and the margin was close.

Finally our only profit was from the salmon eggs we sold to Japanese buyers—the eggs are a delicacy in Japan. I nearly killed myself on that salmon business, with round-the-clock operation for two months each summer and almost full time the rest of the year. When a Japanese firm made an offer to buy the plant in 1984, I was happy to sell it.

But many local Alaskans lost their summer jobs when I sold, and that worried me, so I looked for other possible business opportunities that could benefit local residents. It suddenly struck me that many people along the Yukon were experts at making fine smoked salmon, and most had sold smoked salmon for years. Even Angela and I had occasionally sold dried king salmon strips, often called "squaw candy."

Then one day, the state confiscated some of our salmon strips that had been bought and displayed by a Kotzebue merchant. "The strips don't meet state standards," a state official explained. Suddenly, after years of a profitable sideline for many locals, we were all out of business. "Before you can sell this product, you must have approval from state and federal agencies," an official warned me.

That sounded simple, so I started to follow through. Angela and I had a fine big smokehouse and good indoor working space near it. We decided to upgrade these into a government-approved facility, and to get government approval I started through the bureaucratic maze. I applied for permits, special numbers, and licenses from state and federal agencies. I even had to get a permit to drill for water for my plant. I drove a well twenty-eight feet and got good, pure water; then a different agency insisted I had to drive my well six feet deeper. I followed their instructions; water quality was no better at thirty-four feet than it had been at twenty-eight feet, but the requirement had been met so I was legal.

My smokehouse floor was washed gravel. The state required cement. The sheet metal walls of my smokehouse were too loose; supposedly they might let in blowflies that could walk on or lay eggs on curing fish. Anyone but a bureaucrat knows flies avoid smoke.

I drew plans for a new smokehouse and processing building, and submitted them to various agencies. My drawings brought lengthy discussions and new rulings. Patiently, I made the changes they asked for. In addition to buying a business license, I had to post a $10,000 bond to hire help to build it. To buy fish, I had to pay a three percent fish tax in advance, or provide a bond to that effect.

The plant had to have stainless steel tables with plastic tops on which to cut fish. Sinks had to be stainless steel, with hot and cold running water for washing fish. The entire plant had to be insect-proof, including the smokehouse.

It required more than a year to get a permit to discharge not more than 500 gallons of water into the Yukon River, and I almost didn't get that permit. I was told that I had to have a twelve-foot-deep seepage pit to meet the drainage requirements.

Frustrated by these standards, I traveled from the Lower Yukon River at Marshall to Dawson on the Upper Yukon and found that not one of the dozen or so companies along the river had a seepage pit; I was the only one expected to meet that requirement. All these plants, which were Japanese-owned, were discharging directly into the Yukon River. As an American citizen, I was not permitted to do what aliens were doing. When I pointed this out to some key people in government, I was told I could operate in the same way as the Japanese.

After two long years of dealing with the bureaucracy, my plans met every requirement of the state and federal agencies. We completed the plant in 1988 for about $70,000 with help from a state grant, and started operating it the following year.

Most commercial fishermen on the Lower Yukon, from Anvik to Ruby, catch chum salmon mainly for their roe, which they sell to Japanese buyers. Many of the fish themselves go to waste. My smoking operation makes use of these waste fish, and our smoked salmon is a fine product that can now be found in grocery stores competing with similar products from Washington State and Canada.

It is my hope that other locally owned salmon operations will spring up along the Yukon, using even more parts of each fish by smoking the meat and grinding the livers, hearts, and other organs into a paté for European markets. I hope to be able to share everything I learned about getting permits and the complex physical requirements for constructing a plant. I would like my plant to be a model for others, serving as a training center for anyone who wants to enter this business.

When I moved my family from Hog River to Huslia in the early 1950s, the village had no school. The Territory refused to grant money to build a village school, but Bishop William J. Gordon of the Episcopal Church promised $2,000 to pay for the roof, floor, doors, and windows, if the villagers would build a log schoolhouse.

The men of Huslia built a thirty-by-sixty log schoolhouse, and that fall the Territory furnished a teacher and books. Some of the twenty-four pupils were sixteen or seventeen—too old, they thought, to be going to school. Edwin Simon and my brother Jimmy persuaded them otherwise. Some families had already moved to their winter traplines, but Edwin and Jimmy rounded them up and convinced them to return to the village to attend school. At the time, they were not required by law to go to school.

John Sackett, the half Koyukon son of trader Jack Sackett, was the first graduate of the new school when he was nineteen. Later, he was to become an Alaska state senator. When he started school at Huslia, his desk was a wooden gasoline box from Standard Oil Company, and his seat was a round chunk of wood cut from a tree.

In the 1950s and after, many Native students left their homes to attend BIA schools at Mount Edgecumbe, at Sitka, in southeastern Alaska. Others went to Eklutna where I had gone, or even to Chimawa, a BIA school in Oregon. Whichever school they chose, students lost the guidance and teaching of their parents while they were so far from home.

After statehood came in 1959, Alaska's Department of Education gradually assumed the schooling of rural Alaskan children, taking over from the BIA. It was costly to maintain many small schools in villages scattered across Alaska, and state officials decided to centralize education for Alaska's Natives by closing many of the rural schools and building dormitories for rural students at Bethel, in western Alaska, and in Fairbanks and Anchorage. The children were to live in these dormitories while attending city schools.

I served on the Huslia school board until I moved to Galena in 1963, and there I was a member of the Galena school board for twenty-five years. I became a strong advocate of local education for young villagers at least through high school, and I encouraged all youngsters to get as much education as possible beyond that level.

I was convinced the dormitories were a bad idea. I wanted to give my own children direct guidance and support from home while they were in high school, which they wouldn't get if they were sent to some distant place for schooling.

"If you don't like it, why don't you tell the Board of Education in Anchorage?" one of the Galena school board members suggested.
"I will," I declared, in the heat of the moment.

In Anchorage, for three days, I listened to the State Board of Education. Although representatives from other villages were there, none were speaking out against the plan. The board continued to speak in terms of housing village high school students in Bethel, Anchorage, and Fairbanks.

During a recess I told an elderly woman who was a member of the seven-person board that I opposed their plan.

"Why don't you get up and say so?" she encouraged.

"I'm not used to interrupting people," I said.

"You raise your hand and ask for the floor," she said. "If the chairman doesn't recognize you, I'll object. I'll back you up. That's what this meeting is about."

When the session reconvened, I raised my hand. I was ignored and became embarrassed.

"This man wants to be heard," said the woman board member in a loud voice.

Finally, the chairman of the Board of Education gave me the floor. I walked up front and made my pitch:

"Schools with dormitories, as you are planning, would be institutions. They would resemble reform schools. The kids living there would have to be under strict discipline—something they have never experienced. Such conditions would create havoc with Indian and Eskimo kids.

"Kids, even at the high school level, need parental guidance; they need to be close to home." Then I returned to my seat.

There was a stunned silence. Suddenly, as if a dam had broken, other voices joined in supporting my view. Many of the Eskimo and Indian people there had been aching to speak, but they were too polite to interrupt the board. In the end, the Commissioner of Education said that this was the kind of response he had wanted.

That ended the dormitory proposal. Instead of dormitories, the state built high schools in every village. Some were too small to offer a full range of subjects. This brought on the Molly Hootch court case about 1964, which resulted in a ruling that required the state of Alaska to provide village schools comparable in every way to those in urban Alaska. Admittedly, some white elephants resulted, but we had moved in the direction of better education for rural Alaskans.

———————

In most interior Alaska villages, books have been learning sources for a relatively short time. Some schools, like the one at Huslia, opened their doors in the mid-1950s or later. The "white man's education" was new to most Native parents. Gradually they realized the need, and demanded formal education for their children, though sometimes they were uncertain of the reasons.

Most Native parents were dollar poor, but rich in their knowledge of Native ways of life and how to survive in the harsh wilderness of the North. Traditionally, parents were the teachers; their lifelong task was to educate their children in the old ways. Now their children left home daily to learn another way of life, in another world, and a vital link was often omitted because the parents were not included in the education process. While busy with their school studies, the children failed to acquire a "bush education."

But for rural Alaskans, education isn't just book-learning. It is also knowing how to built a boat, a fish wheel, a log cabin, or how to set a trap or a snare. It is knowing how to build a fire, how to dress for the cold, how to find your way in the woods. Bush education is my Aunt Josie's skill in removing beaver from a lodge. It is knowing how to be frugal with supplies, and how to care for equipment. It is knowing how to dress a moose or a salmon, how to repair a snow machine or an outboard motor, how to shoot a gun.

In the past, a bush education was enough. Today, to survive and prosper in rural Alaska, young people need both a bush education, and a white man's education.

25

REFLECTION

✦

I recently received a fine pocketknife as a gift from a Kobuk Eskimo who is a descendent of the Eskimo trader Schilikuk. I then sent him a present to honor his gift. These gifts are a way of demonstrating that the friendship between the families of my grandfather and the Eskimo trader Schilikuk continues. It is difficult to convey the satisfaction and pleasure that I feel at this continuing, more-than-a-century-old, close relationship.

Many Americans think of Alaska as an unpeopled, untouched wilderness. Indian, Eskimo, and Aleut people lived in these "wilderness" lands for centuries before the first whites arrived, and these original people had complex cultures, with ongoing relationships between different groups. These first inhabitants of the region established intelligent relationships with Alaska's wildlands before the dawn of written history.

A few paragraphs from a 1982 National Park Service publication, *Tracks in the Wildland, A Portrayal of Koyukon-Nunamiut Subsistence*, by Richard Nelson, Kathleen Mautner, and Ray Bane, speak of Alaska as home to these peoples:

> To most of us, the vast stretches of forest, tundra and
> mountain lands in Alaska constitute a wilderness in the
> most absolute sense of the word. In our minds, this land
> is wilderness because it is undisturbed, pristine, lacking in
> obvious signs of human activity. To us undisturbed land
> is unoccupied or unused land. But in fact, most of Alaska is

not wilderness, nor has it been for thousands of years.

Much of Alaska's apparently untrodden forest and tundra land is thoroughly known by people whose entire lives and cultural ancestry is intimately associated with it. Indeed, to the Native inhabitants, these lands are no more an unknown wilderness than are the streets of a city to its residents.

The fact that we identify Alaska's remote country as wilderness derives from our inability to conceive of occupying and utilizing land without altering or completely eliminating its natural state. But the Indians and Eskimos have been living this way for thousands of years. Certainly, then, theirs has been a successful participation as members of an ecosystem. In a world of environmental degradation this represents an exemplary form of human adaptation, fostering a healthy coexistence of man and ecosystem. Certainly, we have been incapable of utilizing our lands so well.

The country is anything but wilderness; at best it can be called a wildland.

———

In the early 1980s, I decided to try my hand at trapping again after being away from it for twenty-four years. Lynx furs were bringing from $300 to $700 each—wonderful prices.

Phantomlike, the lynx, Alaska's only wild cat, stands as tall as a Great Dane dog. Gray in color, weighing up to thirty pounds, with long legs, they are rarely seen. Their big feet function like snowshoes and carry them lightly over loose snow. Lynx numbers increase with snowshoe hare abundance, for hares are their primary food. Snowshoe hare abundance is cyclic, with peaks occurring at roughly ten years. From great abundance, hare numbers may decline to virtually no animals—and lynx numbers follow.

Although the lynx is big and strong, even a small trap will usually hold one of these animals, for they don't struggle much when caught. Lynx meat is veal-like, light in color, and mild-flavored, a favorite with many Alaska bush residents.

In the spring of 1982 I made a wide sweep, looking for lynx sign in the country across from my salmon fishing camp on the Yukon River, and sign appeared promising. At the time I thought back to a catch of lynx made before I was born, in the early 1900s, by old Chief Henry in the Red Mountain country of the Upper Koyukuk. It was the largest catch of lynx that I've ever heard about.

"How many you catch?" I once asked Henry.

"Two fourteen-foot basket sleds full," he replied without hesitation, for such success is unforgettable.

Lynx skins then sold for $1 each at Arctic City. The two basket sleds of lynx skins that he delivered to a fur buyer brought him "pretty near $300," he told me. It was, he said, the only time he had ever owned a sack of $20 gold coins. At 1980's prices (not considering inflation), Chief Henry's sackful of gold coins would represent less than half the price for one good lynx skin!

As I built and outfitted a trapping cabin and bought traps, I was disappointed at how few lynx traps $1,000 bought, and surprised at the changes in equipment and clothing over the decades. Instead of a dog team, I used a snow machine that could easily travel sixty miles per hour if I dared run it that fast. Synthetic fabrics replaced my old Metlicot pure wool underwear. I had an eiderdown sleeping bag rather than the black bearskin sleeping bag I had used as a boy. Despite the advantages of modern equipment, I was reminded that trapping itself is still risky, even for a sixty-seven-year-old with a lifetime of experience in the Subarctic.

I spent early fall at my new camp, cutting wide trails for my snow machine; a narrow trail is plenty for a dog team. I even had to cut out all the fallen logs that lay across the trail; a dog team and sled easily cross such logs, but a snow machine won't.

I finished cutting most of the trails a few days before trapping season. On October 28, the weather turned cold, with a temperature of −30 degrees. I loaded my gear in a plastic sled which I towed with my snow machine. The sled could double as a boat for crossing a creek, for it floated fairly high and dry.

I headed toward Eight-mile Creek, looking at side lakes, watching for a bear den. Throughout the day, before each crossing, I checked ice cautiously at every creek and slough and found no ice less than an inch and a half thick, even close to a beaver dam. I could zip right across.

As dusk fell, I was eager to reach home. I grew careless and sped the snow machine to about thirty miles per hour to cross a pond by a beaver dam. I ran about thirty feet onto the pond and broke through the ice. With me on it, the snow machine sank to the bottom through splintered ice and floating grass, and the frigid water came to just under my arms. I was soaking wet, alone, and far from shelter. I was in real trouble.

My survival hinged on obtaining gear from the sled, reaching shore with it, and quickly lighting a fire. Stepping off the snow machine, I waded back to unhitch the buoyant sled. It floated, holding the back end of the snow machine off the bottom of the pond. I had to plunge my hands more than two feet underwater to reach the hitch. The cold metal of the hitch at the air temperature of thirty below had instantly turned the water around it to ice. Fumbling, I got my belt knife out of its case and tapped the ice-encrusted hitch until it came free. It was a battle all the way. My arms got soaked to the shoulders, and I soon lost my gloves.

Turning toward shore, I knew I must quickly climb out of the water and cross the sixty feet of ice that appeared fairly solid. Pulling the sled, I tried climbing up on the ice and almost succeeded. My soaked clothing seemed to weigh a ton. Just when I was almost on top, the ice broke off, and I submerged. With my hair dripping, I came up cussing. I should have tested the ice with my axe before putting my weight on it.

The pond was only about five feet deep. I dug out my axe and inched my way along the ice's edge, tapping until I found a stretch that was firm enough to support me, and then I climbed onto the ice. I was growing weak, and the icy water plus the chilly air temperature were bringing me close to hypothermia. I'm lean, without much fat for insulation, so the cold penetrated quickly.

Everything I touched—the ice, the sled, the axe—froze to my wet hands, and they started to go numb. I had to cover them, so with my axe I cut the string on my bag from the sled and found gloves. Desperately, I managed to work my stiff, wet fingers into the fur-lined gloves, which sure felt good.

Dragging the sled, I trotted across the solid ice to shore, searching for a place suitable for building a fire. I had to have heat, and quickly. I spotted many dry bushes from old beaver cuts and a small dead dry spruce tree about four inches in diameter.

I chopped the tree down and piled it on some dry brush. My oil-soaked fire-starter rags were submerged with the snow machine, but there was a five-gallon plastic container of gasoline on the sled. Having lost my knife while struggling with the sled hitch, I used my axe to cut the rope across the gas can.

My hands were too numb to open the screw top, and after a few tries I quit wasting time and hacked a hole in the jug with the axe. I couldn't open the Marble steel match safe I always carry in my pocket with my stiff fingers, nor could my freezing hands operate the cigarette lighter I carry for starting fires.

For emergencies, I carried extra strike-anywhere matches inside a Ziplock bag in my shirt pocket. I also had a bag of matches in my toolbox, and another in a handy bag with my clothes. I pulled the matches out of my shirt pocket, but I couldn't grasp them with my numbed fingers. As the first match dropped in the snow, my tired mind asked, "What the hell now?"

I worked two matchsticks between my lips, with sulphur tips out, ready for striking. I poured gasoline over the pile of firewood, and moving my head, I swiped a match against the rough-sided Marble match safe. The match stick broke.

Would I die because I couldn't even light a match? How long would it be before searchers found my frozen body? After years as a woodsman, would people say that Sidney got careless in his old age and let the country kill him? Memories of men I had known who had frozen to death flashed through my mind.

I did not dare break the other match. I was growing light-headed and clumsy, but I simply had to succeed this time. With clenched teeth, I turned my head carefully, wiping the match against the match safe. It didn't light. Again I turned my head, slightly faster this time, and the match lit! I spit the flaring match onto the gasoline-soaked wood.

Whoosh! The gasoline ignited and the dry wood blazed.

I stuck my numb hands out gratefully above the flames, then pulled them back, remembering that I could burn them because they had no feeling. When sensation returned to my hands, I pulled out the waterproof bag holding my sleeping bag and cut the tie string with my axe.

Draping the bag over my shoulders, I allowed heat from the leaping flames to reflect from it while I removed my wet, partially frozen clothes. My Thinsulite underwear was wet but not frozen. I had a tough time removing my boots, and in the end had to use the axe to cut the laces. Both feet were beyond being cold; they were numb. I wrapped them in the warm wool sleeping bag liner.

As my hands began to come to life, the pain began, but I was able to pull off my Thinsulite drawers and hold them to the fire. They dried in minutes and when I slipped them back on they felt wonderful. My Thinsulite undershirt also dried quickly when I held it near the flames. I was pleased to discover this fast-drying trait of synthetic underwear; my old-style wool underwear would have taken hours to dry.

My feet began to sting and then to hurt, almost as if I were holding them in the fire. Even the bones seemed to burn. The pain in my feet was much worse than in my hands. The urgency of warming my freezing body made time move slowly, but actually all of this occurred within about twenty minutes.

I warmed some dry Duofold wool and silk underwear from my clothing bag, and pulled it on over the Thinsulite, and the warmth against my skin was most welcome. Out of my clothing bag I dug dry socks and pants. Drying my water-soaked parka would have taken hours, so I didn't even try, but put on my extra jacket, which had a hood, and I snuggled into it. My fingers were now warm enough to work a zipper. Gratefully, I put on my extra moon boots. These insulated rubber-soled boots aren't the easiest to walk in, but they are warm. With dry clothing from head to foot, I felt 100 years younger.

Darkness had fallen and I didn't know how far I was from where the trail crossed the creek, although I figured the distance wasn't more than two miles. I didn't want to camp by my fire, although I dreaded walking away from the comforting flames.

I drew wolf-skin mittens on over my gloves, picked up my axe, and set off, following the creek but staying on high ground. I had had all I wanted of freezing water. I wasn't about to walk on the creek ice. Cutting across the bends of the creek, I trudged through the rough terrain for about two hours before hitting my trail. From there I had to walk about ten more miles through the portage, across lakes, to my camp on the bank of the Yukon River. I kept moving, never pausing, knowing that a stop could have been my last one.

I was dog-tired when I staggered into camp at five o'clock the next morning. I built a fire in the stove and crawled into bed. For a few hours I was dead to the world. When I awoke about midday I was stiff and sore all over. My neck felt swollen and I could hardly move my head.

I rested all day. The next day, I took a spare snow machine I kept at camp for just such an emergency and went to retrieve the sunken machine. I managed to attach a line to it, and with a come-along fastened to the spare snow machine, I dragged it from its watery resting place. The poor machine was a big ball of ice when I finally pulled it onto the bank. After many hours I managed to deice it and get it running again.

I caught $16,000 worth of furs that winter, the most I ever earned in a year of trapping: 63 lynx, 150 marten, 100 foxes, and 8 wolverine. The least I ever made during a trapping season was $380 during the winter of 1933–34—a season I prefer to forget.

Although trapping is still a passion for many Koyukon people, unfortunately it is no longer economical to make a living from a trapline. Fur prices haven't risen like prices for other items—in fact, amounts paid for many furs today are not much higher than they were in 1928, and some fur prices are actually much lower. But today a trap costs eight times what it did when I was a boy. A $3 boy's axe—handy on a trapline—now costs $28. Gasoline used to cost 42 cents a gallon; today we pay $2.50 plus tax.

Feeding a dog team with purchased food is prohibitively expensive; those who own dog teams must catch fish to feed their dogs. Snow machines are more commonly used by trappers now (the average machine sells for around $4,000), and a full season can wear a machine out. Most who trap now do so as a sideline, and some regard trapping as recreation.

My early years on the trapline were my poorest times financially but the richest in satisfaction. Sadly, that old way of life is gone.

I love to start my summer day at five in the morning. The air is cool and fresh, and usually calm. Birds call, and the world seems to have renewed itself overnight.

One such morning I went to my fish wheel on the Yukon River and worked hard to remove a heavy drift log jammed in the wheel. Working alone, I finally yanked it out. I was balanced on the spar log, which anchored the fish wheel to shore, when suddenly, I had a terrible pain in my chest. I moved quickly to the beach on the narrow spar. Near shore, I fell. My legs were in the water, but I just lay there, in bad shape. I thought that my problem was lack of breakfast. I was growing numb from the cold water when I crawled out on the bank.

The pain slowly diminished. The sun climbed higher and my clothes dried as I sat enjoying the warmth. Then I finished tending to the fish wheel.

Several times that summer, I had dizzy spells but thought little of them. When nearing the seventy-year mark, a person must expect a few creaks.

The following winter while trapping I got my snow machine stuck, and while lifting and digging it out, I found myself lying in the snow, recovering consciousness with a hurting chest.

Gradually, my heart pains came more often. Over one summer I built a new home for Angela, figuring that if I died she would have a decent place to live. Our old house, where we raised so many kids, was too big for her if she was to be alone. As I worked to finish the new house, I had to rest often, allowing my heart to settle down.

In 1982, I found myself at Mary's Help hospital in San Francisco. Three arteries to my heart were blocked and I needed a triple bypass operation. With a concerned look, my doctor said, "Sidney, you have about a fifty-fifty chance of pulling through the surgery." The operation was scheduled for the next morning, but a crisis arose at three o'clock in the morning, and the surgical team decided to operate immediately.

Before operating, one of the doctors told me that he wanted to consult with Angela and our daughter Agnes, who had accompanied me from Alaska.

I asked, "I'm the one you're going to work on, right?"

"Yes."

"You guys are the engineers. Let's get to work on this thing," I said. "You say I have a fifty-fifty chance. I've played many a hand of cards, with big stakes, when the odds weren't that good."

Afterward the doctors told me they had a tough time persuading my heart to start up again after the surgery, and then I sailed through the first critical hour and a half after surgery. One patient I saw in intensive care couldn't handle the stress. He had plugs and drains all over him like I did, and he yanked them all out. Before the doctors and nurses could replace them, he was dead.

Rebuilding my strength took a long time. But that summer I was able to build a new house at my fish camp, and I did my usual commercial salmon fishing.

So, life goes on. I have a plastic eye, false teeth, two hearing aids, and three bypasses to my heart. I call myself the modern plastic man. But, modern or not, about seventy-five percent of the food we live on still comes from the wildlands along the Yukon and Koyukuk rivers.

In these later years, I often think how pleasurable my life with Angela has been. Angela is skilled in many of the old ways. She is always helping people make potlatches—some of which cost thousands of dollars and weeks or months of effort. Both the elders and young Koyukon people also come to her for help in making decisions in their lives. They ask her how to make various garments and how to prepare Indian foods. They use her patterns for fur boots, parkas, mittens. Every year to make preserves, jams, and jellies, she picks gallons of berries, including wild berries and domestic strawberries and raspberries which we grow.

When we got married, Angela said she wanted twelve babies. She had her twelve, and two more besides, before doctors convinced her she shouldn't have more. When Andrew, our youngest, was a teenager, the house seemed empty with just one youngster around.

So Angela suggested that we should adopt a baby.

Not long after, a young woman called to ask if Angela would care for her baby boy while she went to school for a few months. Angela was on the next airplane to pick up the baby. Mark was fun to have around, and we became very attached to him. Eventually his young unmarried mother allowed us to adopt him. He became our fifteenth child.

Angela is also an expert at making birchbark baskets, and has taught the art to all of our youngsters. Now she teaches this traditional skill to our grandchildren, and she spends time at Galena schools as a volunteer, teaching basketmaking.

Give some kids an opportunity and they grab it. For some years at Galena I had a dealership selling Polaris and Yamaha snow machines and Mariner outboard motors. My son Roger now owns that business. One spring a woebegone little Indian boy around thirteen years old came to me. I knew that his parents neglected him because they were often drunk. He barely had enough to eat or clothes to wear, but his greatest desire was to own a snow machine, and he told me he wanted to work for me so he could earn one.

"Fine," I said. "You come to me every day and I'll give you a job to do. You keep track of your time. When you have earned enough for a snow machine, I'll see that you get one."

That little guy arrived faithfully every day, and each day I assigned him a job, usually pure drudgery. He cleaned boats, shoveled refuse, straightened up a workshop, retrieved parts, and ran errands, helping with our salmon business.

He asked me to keep track of his time, but I insisted that he write down his own time. I wanted to show my confidence in his honesty, and I hoped he would see the practical value of arithmetic.

By Christmas he had earned a snow machine. Through this process he learned the value of work, and so was proud of his new machine and was determined to care for it properly. Today that young man is married, and a sober, hardworking citizen. He made himself what he is; my contribution was small but, I like to think, significant.

———

In 1966, a book, *On The Edge of Nowhere,* by James Huntington (my brother Jimmy) as told to Lawrence Elliott, recounted Jimmy's adventurous life to that date. In that account, the ages of Marion, Jimmy, and me, when our mother died in June 1920, were incorrectly given as "seven, five, and not quite two." The editors chose not to print our real ages, claiming that readers wouldn't believe the story. To set the record straight, I was born on May 10, 1915, and was five; Jimmy, born August 14, 1916, was three; and Marion, born December 2, 1918, was a year and a half.

In the late 1970s, Jimmy was elected to a two-year term in the Alaska House of Representatives. After that, Governor Jay Hammond appointed him to the Board of Fisheries, where he served two three-year terms. We didn't agree on many issues, for he was inclined to be liberal while I'm generally conservative. But that didn't keep us apart: we sometimes argued, but we respected each other's views.

When he was fifty-nine, Jimmy had a heart attack while trapping marten in the Hog River country. He lay under a tree for seven hours before he recuperated enough to get back to his cabin. After resting a few days, with the help of one of his sons, he pulled his traps and drove his snow machine all the way to Galena in one day—a hard day's work even for a man in good health. He boarded a plane that evening and flew to Anchorage and the next morning surgeons performed an emergency heart bypass operation on him.

That spring he had his Yukon River fish wheel running. His camp was six miles below my fish camp. Every morning during salmon season, at five o'clock, sometimes earlier, I went to check my fish wheel, three miles below Jimmy's place. I'd stop and we'd visit for a moment, or sometimes I'd just wave as I passed, happy to see him out and about.

That fall, amazingly, he hunted moose. Annually he made several trips by boat from Galena to Hog River, hauling fuel for his snow machine, planning to be back trapping in winter. He loved the Hog River country.

In March 1987, he fell ill and tried to drive his snow machine to the Galena Medical Clinic. He almost made it, but in great pain he stopped at a friend's house, and his friend got him to the clinic and called me. Jimmy and I talked while waiting for a medevac airplane to arrive from Anchorage.

"It's been kind of a bad year for me, Sidney," he said, not complaining, just stating a fact.

I told him we had both lived good clean lives that we could look back on with pride, that I felt we did what God intended for us to do—help make the world better for others.

"Sidney, I know. I don't think I'll see you again," he said.

The attendant closed the airplane door, and I watched the plane lift into the darkening sky. Jimmy died five minutes after takeoff.

In the summer of 1987 a reunion was held at Anvik Mission to celebrate the 100th anniversary of its founding. I attended that reunion and treasured meeting again with ninety-two-year-old Henry Chapman. It was my pleasure to thank him for making a home for me as a sad five-year-old in 1920. At the reunion I found the grave of Homer Collins, my childhood friend. Tears came as I stood by the grave and remembered my dear friend, gone for all of those sixty-seven years.

My grandfather, the trader, was probably born about 1850, perhaps earlier. That's about a decade after the first Russians arrived at Nulato. I was born ten years after my grandfather's death. Thus only two lifetimes (although mine hasn't ended yet) plus twenty years span the period since first contact with whites in Koyukon Indian country. At Galena I live in a modern house with electricity and all that goes with it, including television, telephone, automatic heat, and hot and cold running water. My grandfather saw many changes in his life, but I'm sure he never dreamed of anything quite like my comforts.

The Koyukon people no longer must roam, searching for better hunting and fishing. They live in permanent homes, with conveniences, and have good medical care. Few babies die, and starvation is no longer a danger. Medicine men no longer dominate their lives. The people still depend upon the land for most of their food, but that food—the fish and game—is abundant.

But the number of Koyukon people along the Koyukuk and Lower Yukon is about the same as when my grandfather was alive. And he would recognize the Koyukuk valley if he could see it today, for it hasn't changed much. The summer sun circles endlessly, and clean white snow blankets the land every winter. Spire-topped spruces still dominate the forests, and the white birch trees still shine in the winter moonlight. And through it all, the Koyukuk River still flows clear above Hughes, and slightly murky below.

EPILOGUE

❂

Sidney Huntington has been accorded many honors for his civic services to Alaska and Alaskans. A few include:

➤ 1980, named the founding father of the Galena, Alaska, city school system, and presented with an engraved silver plaque.
➤ 1986, Conservationist of the Year (Alaska Outdoor Council).
➤ 1987, Trapper of the Year (Fairbanks Trappers' Association).
➤ 1988, Trapper and Conservationist of the Year (Alaska State Legislature).

In 1989, the University of Alaska at Fairbanks conferred upon Sidney Huntington the honorary degree of Doctor of Public Service. The citation accompanying this degree read:

> Community leader, cultural link, and supporter of education, Sidney Huntington: During his lifetime, Sidney Huntington has successfully spanned two cultures—one dependent on hunting, fishing and trapping for food and money, and one which has led him to the highest levels of official service to his community and the State of Alaska.
> Born in Hughes, Sidney Huntington received only a third-grade education, but through his own efforts and self education, he was able to compete politically and professionally in a changing world.
> By reading carpentry books while working on a trapline, he taught himself the skills needed to land a job at the Galena Air Force Station. Once in Galena, he convinced the

community to become a first-class city, which allowed it to raise the revenue necessary to save its school.

Despite his own lack of formal education, Sidney Huntington spent 25 years on the Galena School Board, and has personally supported many students who would have otherwise been unable to receive a higher education. He and his wife Angela have raised 15 children, several of whom have been awarded degrees at the University of Alaska, Fairbanks.

Sidney Huntington's fairness, integrity and ability are attested to by his 17 years on the Alaska Board of Game, and the willingness of governors from every political background to put their trust in his decisions. Not only a community and state political leader, Huntington has established two salmon processing businesses in Galena in order to bring economic opportunity to the people of his region.

The University of Alaska, Fairbanks, salutes this distinguished leader who has clearly demonstrated his dedication to his family, his community, his region and his state, and proudly confers upon Sidney Huntington the honorary degree of Doctor of Public Service. This citation presented at the University of Alaska Fairbanks Commencement Exercises, May 7, 1989.

RELATED READING

✦

Alaska Department of Health and Social Services, Division of Public Health, Section of Epidemiology. *State of Alaska Tuberculosis Report*. Anchorage, 1986.

Alaska Geographic. *Alaska's Great Interior*, Vol. 7, No. 1. Anchorage: Alaska Geographic Society, 1980.

Alaska Geographic. *Aurora Borealis. The Amazing Northern Lights*, Vol. 6, No. 2. Anchorage: Alaska Geographic Society, 1979.

Alaska Geographic. *Up the Koyukuk*, Vol. 10, No. 4. Anchorage: Alaska Geographic Society, 1983.

Brooks, Alfred Hulse. *Blazing Alaska's Trails*. Fairbanks: University of Alaska and the Arctic Institute of North America, 1953.

Dall, William H. *Alaska and Its Resources*. Boston: Lee and Shepard, 1870.

Fortuine, Robert. *Chills and Fever; Health and Disease in the Early History of Alaska*. Fairbanks: University of Alaska Press, 1989.

Gruening, Ernest. *The State of Alaska*. New York: Random House, 1954.

Hulley, Clarence C. *Alaska, Past and Present*. Portland, Oregon: Binfords & Mort, 1953.

Huntington, James, as told to Lawrence Elliot. *On the Edge of Nowhere*. New York: Crown Publishers, 1966.

Madison, Curt, and Yarber, Yvonne. *Edwin Simon, Huslia, a Biography*. Blaine, Wash.: Hancock House Publishers, 1981.

Madison, Curt, and Yarber, Yvonne. *Martha Joe: Nulato*. Fairbanks: Spirit Mountain Press, 1987.

Marshall, Robert. *Artic Village, a Portrait of Wiseman, Alaska*. Fairbanks: University of Alaska Press, 1991.

Murray, Alexander Hunter. *Journal of the Yukon 1847–48.*
Haven, Connecticut: Yale University Press, 1965.

Stuck, Hudson. *Ten Thousand Miles with a Dog Sled.* New York:
Charles Scribner's Sons, 1914.

Thomas, Tay. *Cry in the Wilderness.* Anchorage: Color Art Printing,
1967.

Wickersham, James. *Old Yukon Tales—Trails—and Trials.*
Washington, D.C.: Washington Law Book Co., 1938.

INDEX

ABOUT SIDNEY HUNTINGTON

Half-Athapaskan Sidney Huntington, born in 1915, grew up in the Koyukuk River country of Northern Alaska, a region that most Americans consider frontier wilderness. In his early years, birchbark canoes, dog teams, and paddlewheel steamers were the primary modes of transportation. His Koyukon Athapaskan mother died when he was five, after which he lived at a Yukon River mission. Later, he attended the Bureau of Indian Affairs School at Eklutna, Alaska.

When he was twelve, he joined his father on a trapline. Home was a log cabin, and the Huntingtons lived mostly off the land. He was on his own at sixteen, trapping and selling furs, hunting and fishing for food, and annually growing a vegetable garden.

During his adventurous life, Huntington has learned the habits of wolves, moose, caribou, and other Koyukuk wildlife. Living in the wilds, he has had many narrow escapes, including a close call from a charging bear. He used his knowledge of wildlife when he served for twenty years as a member of the Alaska Board of Fish and Game and the Alaska Board of Game.

Wild game and Yukon River salmon still make up most of his food. He observes many of the old Athapaskan customs, and enjoys traditional stories that reveal the history and character of the Koyukon people.

Huntington lives with his wife, Angela, in the Yukon River village of Galena, Alaska.

ABOUT JIM REARDEN

A forty-three-year resident of Alaska, Jim Rearden has written four-teen books and more than 500 magazine articles, mostly about Alaska. In addition to *Shadows on the Koyukuk*, recent books include *In the Shadow of Eagles*, the life story of barnstormer-bush pilot Rudy Billberg, *Cracking the Zero Mystery*, the story of the first Japanese Zero airplane captured (in Alaska) and flown by the United States during World War II, and a novel, *Castner's Cutthroats, Saga of the Alaska Scouts*.

Rearden studied wildlife management at Oregon State College and the University of Maine. During his years in Alaska he has served as a federal fisheries patrol agent, taught wildlife management at the University of Alaska, Fairbanks, was the biologist in charge of the Cook Inlet commercial fisheries area, operated his own commercial fishing boat, was a registered big game guide, worked as a carpenter, and served for twelve years on the Alaska Board of Game. He is a private pilot with his own airplane.

Jim Rearden was Outdoors Editor for *Alaska* magazine for twenty years, and for sixteen years he has been a field editor for *Outdoor Life* magazine. He lives at Homer, with his wife, Audrey, in a log house he built himself.